THE WORKS OF
LUCIAN OF SAMOSATA

Complete with exceptions specified in the preface

TRANSLATED BY

H. W. FOWLER AND F. G. FOWLER

IN FOUR VOLUMES

What work nobler than transplanting foreign thought into the barren domestic soil? except indeed planting thought of your own, which the fewest are privileged to do.—*Sartor Resartus.*

At each flaw, be this your first thought: the author doubtless said something quite different, and much more to the point. And then you may hiss *me* off, if you will.—LUCIAN, *Nigrinus,* 9.

(LUCIAN) The last great master of Attic eloquence and Attic wit.—*Lord Macaulay.*

VOLUME II

OXFORD
AT THE CLARENDON PRESS
1905

HENRY FROWDE, M.A.
PUBLISHER TO THE UNIVERSITY OF OXFORD
LONDON, EDINBURGH
NEW YORK AND TORONTO

CONTENTS OF VOL. II

THE DEPENDENT SCHOLAR

THE dependent scholar! The great man's licensed friend!—
if friend, not slave, is to be the word. Believe me, Timocles,
amid the humiliation and drudgery of his lot, I know not where
to turn for a beginning. Many, if not most, of his hardships
are familiar to me; not, heaven knows, from personal experience,
for I have never been reduced to such extremity, and pray that
I never may be; but from the lips of numerous victims; from
the bitter outcries of those who were yet in the snare, and the
complacent recollections of others who, like escaped prisoners,
found a pleasure in detailing all that they had been through.
The evidence of the latter was particularly valuable. Mystics,
as it were, of the highest grade, Dependency had no secrets for
them. Accordingly, it was with keen interest that I listened
to their stories of miraculous deliverance from moral shipwreck.
They reminded me of the mariners who, duly cropped, gather
at the doors of a temple, with their tale of stormy seas and
monster waves and promontories, castings out of cargoes,
snappings of masts, shatterings of rudders; ending with the
appearance of those twin brethren [1] so indispensable to nautical
story, or of some other *deus ex machina*, who, seated at the
masthead or standing at the helm, guides the vessel to some
sandy shore, there to break up at her leisure—not before her
crew (so benevolent is the God!) have effected a safe landing.
The mariner, however, is liberal in embellishment, being
prompted thereto by the exigencies of his situation; for by
his appearance as a favourite of heaven, not merely a victim of

---

[1] The Dioscuri, Castor and Pollux, who were supposed to appear to
sailors in distress.

fortune, the number of the charitable is increased.   It is other- 2
wise with those whose narrative is of domestic storms, of billows
rising mountain high (if so I may phrase it) within four walls.
They tell us of the seductive calm that first lured them on to
those waters, of the sufferings they endured throughout the
voyage, the thirst, the sea-sickness, the briny drenchings ; and
how at last their luckless craft went to pieces upon some hidden
reef or at the foot of some steep crag, leaving them to swim for
it, and to land naked and utterly destitute.   All this they tell
us : but I have ever suspected them of having convenient
lapses of memory, and omitting the worst part for very shame.
For myself, I shall have no such scruple.   All that I have heard,
or can reasonably infer, of the evils of dependence, I shall place
before you.   For either, friend, my penetration is at fault, or
you have long had a hankering for this profession.

Yes, I have seen it from the first, whenever the conversation 3
has fallen on this subject of salaried intellects.   ' Happy men ! '
some enthusiast has cried.   ' The *élite* of Rome are their friends.
They dine sumptuously, and call for no reckoning.   They are
lodged splendidly, and travel comfortably—nay, luxuriously—
with cushions at their backs, and as often as not a fine pair of
creams in front of them.   And, as if this were not enough, the
friendship they enjoy and the handsome treatment they receive
is made good to them with a substantial salary.   They sow not,
they plough not ; yet all things grow for their use.'   How I have
seen you prick up your ears at such words as these !   How wide
your mouth has opened to the bait !

Now I will have a clear conscience in this matter.   I will not
be told hereafter that I saw you swallowing this palpable bait,
and never stirred a finger to snatch it from you, and show you
the hook while there was yet time ; that I watched you nibbling,
saw the hook well in and the fish hauled up, and then stood by
shedding useless tears.   A grave charge, indeed, were I to leave

it in your power to bring it; such neglect would admit of no palliation. You shall therefore hear the whole truth. Now, in leisurely fashion, from without, not hereafter from within, shall you examine this weel from which no fish escapes. You shall take in hand this hook of subtle barb. You shall try the prongs of this eel-spear against your inflated cheek; and if you decide that they are not sharp, that they would be easily evaded, that a wound from them would be no great matter, that they are deficient in power and grasp—then write me among those who have cowardice to thank for their empty bellies; and for yourself, take heart of grace, and swoop upon your prey, and cormorant-wise, if you will, swallow all at a gulp.

4   But however much the present treatise is indebted to you for its existence, its application is not confined to you who are philosophers, whose ambition it is to form your conduct upon serious principles; it extends to the teachers of literature, of rhetoric, of music,—to all, in short, whose intellectual attainments can command a maintenance and a wage. And where the life, from beginning to end, is one and the same for all, the philosopher (I need not say), so far from being a privileged person, has but the additional ignominy of being levelled with the rest, and treated by his paymaster with as scant ceremony as the rest. In conclusion, whatever disclosures I may be led to make, the blame must fall in the first instance on the aggressors, and in the second instance on those who suffer the aggression. For me, unless truth and candour be crimes, I am blameless.

As to the vulgar rabble of trainers and toadies, illiterate, mean-souled creatures, born to obscurity, should we attempt to dissuade *them* from such pursuits, our labour would be wasted. Nor can we fairly blame them, for putting up any affront, rather than part with their employers. The life suits them; they are in their element. And what other channel is there, into which their energies could be directed ? Take away this, their sole vocation, and they are idle cumberers of the earth. They have nothing, then, to complain of; nor are their employers unreasonable in turning these humble vessels to the use for which they were designed. They come into a house prepared for such treatment from the first; it is their profession to endure and suffer wrong.

But the case of educated men, such as I have mentioned above, 5 is another matter; it calls for our indignation, and for our utmost endeavours to restore them to liberty. I think it will not be amiss, if I first examine into the provocations under which they turn to a life of dependence. By showing how trivial, how inadequate these provocations are, I shall forestall the main argument used by the defenders of voluntary servitude. Most of them are content to cloak their desertion under the names of Poverty and Necessity. It is enough, they think, to plead in extenuation, that they sought to flee from this greatest of human ills, Poverty. Theognis comes pat to their purpose. His

Poverty, soul-subduing Poverty,

is in continual requisition, together with other fearful utterances of our most degenerate poets to the same effect. Now if I could see that they really found an escape from poverty in the lives they lead, I would not be too nice on the point of absolute freedom. But when we find them (to use the expression of a famous orator) 'faring like men that are sick,' what conclusion is then left to us to draw ? What but this, that here again they have been misled, the very evil which they sold their liberty to escape remaining as it was ? Poverty unending is their lot. From the bare pittance they receive nothing can be set apart. Suppose it paid, and paid in full : the whole sum is swallowed up to the last farthing, before their necessities are supplied. I would advise them to think upon better expedients ;

not such as are merely the protectors and accomplices of Poverty, but such as will make an end of her altogether. What say you, Theognis ? Might this be a case for,

> Steep plunge from crags into the teeming deep ?

For when a pauper, a needy hireling, persuades himself that by being what he is he has escaped poverty, one cannot avoid the conclusion that he labours under some mistake.

6 Others tell a different tale. For them, mere poverty would have had no terrors, had they been able, like other men, to earn their bread by their labours. But, stricken as they were by age or infirmity, they turned to this as the easiest way of making a living. Now let us consider whether they are right. This ' easy ' way may be found to involve much labour before it yields any return ; more labour perhaps than any other. To find money ready to one's hand, without toil or trouble on one's own part, would indeed be a dream of happiness. But the facts are otherwise. The toils and troubles of their situation are such as no words can adequately describe. Health, as it turns out, is nowhere more essential than in this vocation, in which a thousand daily labours combine to grind the victim down, and reduce him to utter exhaustion. These I shall describe in due course, when I come to speak of their other grievances. For the present let it suffice to have shown that this excuse for the sale of one's liberty is as untenable as the former.

7 And now for the true reason, which you will never hear from their lips. Voluptuousness and a whole pack of desires are what induce them to force their way into great houses. The dazzling spectacle of abundant gold and silver, the joys of high feeding and luxurious living, the immediate prospect of wallowing in riches, with no man to say them nay,—these are the temptations that lure them on, and make slaves of free men ; not lack of the necessaries of life, as they pretend, but lust of its super-

fluities, greed of its costly refinements. And their employers, like finished coquettes, exercise their rigours upon these hapless slaves of love, and keep them for ever dangling in amorous attendance; but for fruition, no! never so much as a kiss may they snatch. To grant that would be to give the lover his release, a conclusion against which they are jealously on their guard. But upon hopes he is abundantly fed. Despair might else cure his ardent passion, and the lover be lover no more. So there are smiles for him, and promises; always something shall be done, some favour shall be granted, a handsome provision shall be made for him,—some day. Meanwhile, old age steals upon the pair; the superannuated lover ceases from desire, and his mistress has nothing left to give. Life has gone by, and all they have to show for it is *hope*.

Well now, that a man for the sake of pleasure should put up 8 with every hardship is perhaps no great matter. Devoted to this one object, he can think of nothing, but how to procure it. Let that pass. Though it seems but a scurvy bargain, a bargain for a slave; to sell one's liberty for pleasures far less pleasant than liberty itself. Still, as I say, let that pass, provided the price is paid. But to endure unlimited pain, merely in the hope that pleasure may come of it, this surely is carrying folly to the height of absurdity. And men do it with their eyes open. The hardships, they know, are certain, unmistakable, inevitable. As to the pleasure, that vague, hypothetic pleasure, they have never had it in all these years, and in all reasonable probability they never will. The comrades of Odysseus forgot all else in the Lotus: but it was while they were tasting its sweets. They esteemed lightly of Honour: but it was in the immediate presence of Pleasure. In men so occupied, such forgetfulness was not wholly unnatural. But to dwell a prisoner, with Famine for company, to watch one's neighbour fattening on the Lotus, and keeping it all to himself, and to forget Honour and Virtue in the bare prospect of a possible mouthful,—by Heaven, it is too absurd, and calls in good truth for Homeric scourgings.

9   Such, as nearly as I can describe them, are men's motives for taking service with the rich, for handing themselves over bodily, to be used as their employers think fit. There is one class, however, of which I ought perhaps to make mention—those whose vanity is gratified by the mere fact of being seen in the company of well-born and well-dressed men. For there are those who consider this a distinguished privilege; though for my own part I would not give a fig to enjoy and to be seen enjoying the company of the King of Persia, if I was to get nothing by it.

10   And now, since we understand what it is that these men would be at, let us mentally review their whole career;—the difficulties that beset the applicant before he gains acceptance; his condition when he is duly installed in his office; and the closing scene of his life's drama. You may perhaps suppose that his situation, whatever its drawbacks, is at least attainable without much trouble; that you have but to will it, and the thing is done in a trice. Far from it. Much tramping about is in store for you, much kicking of heels. You will rise early, and stand long before your patron's closed door; you will be jostled; you will hear occasional comments on your impudence. You will be exposed to the vile gabble of a Syrian porter, and to the extortions of a Libyan nomenclator, whose memory must be fee'd, if he is not to forget your name. You must dress beyond your means, or you will be a discredit to your patron; and select his favourite colours, or you will be out of harmony with your surroundings. Finally, you will be indefatigable in following his steps, or rather in preceding them, for you will be thrust forward by his slaves, to swell his triumphal progress. And for days together you will not be favoured with a glance.

11   But one day the best befalls you. You catch his eye; he

beckons you to him, and puts a random question. In that supreme moment what cold sweats, what palpitations, what untimely tremors are yours! and what mirth is theirs who witness your confusion! 'Who was the king of the Achaeans?' is the question: and your answer, as likely as not, 'A thousand sail.' With the charitable this passes for bashfulness; but to the impudent you are a craven, and to the ill-natured a yokel. This first experience teaches you that the condescensions of the great are not unattended with danger; and as you depart you pronounce upon yourself a sentence of utter despair. Thereafter,

> many a sleepless night,
> Many a day of strife shall be thy lot—

not for the sake of Helen, not for the towers of Troy, but for the sevenpence halfpenny of your desire. At length some heaven-sent protector gives you an introduction: the scholar is brought up for examination. For the great man, who has but to receive your flatteries and compliments, this is an agreeable pastime: for you, it is a life-and-death struggle; all is hazarded on the one throw. For it will of course occur to you, that if you are rejected at the first trial, you will never pass current with any one else. A thousand different feelings now distract you. You are jealous of your rivals (for we will assume that there is competition for the post); you are dissatisfied with your own replies; you hope; you fear; you cannot remove your eye from the countenance of your judge. Does he pooh-pooh your efforts? You are a lost man. Was that a smile? 12 You rejoice, and hope rises high. It is only to be expected, that many of the company are your enemies, and others your rivals, and each has his secret shaft to let fly at you from his lurking-place. What a picture! The venerable grey-beard being put through his paces. Is he any use? Some say yes, others no. Time is taken for consideration. Your antecedents are industriously overhauled. Some envious compatriot, some neighbour with a trivial grievance, is asked his opinion; he has but to drop a word of 'loose morality,' and your business is done; 'the man speaks God's truth!' Every one else may testify to your character: their evidence proves nothing; they are suspected; they are venal. The fact is, you must gain every point; there must be no hitch anywhere. That is your only chance of success.

And now, take it that you *have* succeeded—beyond all expectation. Your words have found favour with the great man. Those friends, by whose judgement in such matters he sets most store, have made no attempt to alter his decision. His wife approves his choice; the steward and the major-domo have neither of them anything against you. No aspersions have been cast on your character; all is propitious, every omen is in your favour. Hail, mighty conqueror, wreathed in the Olympian garland! Babylon is yours, Sardis falls before you. The horn of plenty is within your grasp; pigeons shall yield you milk.

Now, if your crown is to be of anything better than leaves, there must be some solid benefits to compensate you for the labours you have undergone. A considerable salary will be placed at your disposal, and you will draw upon it without ceremony, whenever you have occasion. You will be a privileged person in every respect. As for toils, and muddy tramps, and wakeful nights, the time for those have gone by. Your prayers have been heard: you will take your ease, and sleep your fill. You will do the work you were engaged to do, and not a stroke besides. This, indeed, is what you have a right to expect. There would be no great hardship in bowing one's neck to a yoke so light, so easy—and so superbly gilded. But alas, Timocles, many, nay all of these requirements are unsatisfied. Your office, now that you have got it, is attended with a thousand details insufferable to all but slaves. Let me rehearse them to you; you shall judge for yourself whether any man with the slightest pretence to culture would endure such treatment.

Let me begin with your first invitation to dinner, which may 14 reasonably be expected to follow, as an earnest of the patronage to come. It is brought to you by a most communicative slave, whose goodwill it must be your first care to secure. Five shillings is the least you can slip into his palm, if you would do the thing properly. He has scruples. 'Really, sir—couldn't think of it; no, indeed, sir.' But he is prevailed upon at last, and goes off, grinning from ear to ear. You then look out your best clothes, have your bath, make yourself as presentable as possible, and arrive—in fear and trembling lest you should be the first, which would wear an awkward air, just as it savours of ostentation to arrive last. Accordingly you contrive to hit on the right moment, are received with every attention, and shown to your place, a little above the host, separated from him only by a couple of his intimates. And now you feel as if 15 you were in heaven. You are all admiration; everything you see done throws you into ecstasies. It is all so new and strange! The waiters stare at you, the company watch your movements. Nor is the host without curiosity. Some of his servants have instructions to observe you narrowly, lest your glance should fall too often on his wife or children. The other guests' men perceive your amazement at the novel scene, and exchange jesting asides. From the fact that you do not know what to make of your napkin, they conclude that this is your first experience of dining-out. You perspire with embarrassment; not unnaturally. You are thirsty, but you dare not ask for wine, lest you should be thought a tippler. The due connexion between the various dishes which make their appearance is beyond you: which ought you to take first? which next? There is nothing for it but to snatch a side glance at your neighbour, do as he does, and learn to dine in sequence.

16   On the whole, your feelings are mingled, your spirit per-turbed, and stricken with awe. One moment you are envying your host his gold, his ivory, and all his magnificence; the next, you are pitying yourself,—that miserable nonentity which calls its existence life; and then at intervals comes the thought, 'how happy shall I be, sharing in these splendours, enjoying them as if they were my own!' For you conceive of your future life as one continual feast; and the smiling attendance of gracious Ganymedes gives a charming finish to the picture. That line of Homer keeps coming to your lips:

> Small blame to Trojan or to greaved Achaean,

if such happiness as this was to be the reward of their toils and sufferings. Presently healths are drunk. The host calls for a large beaker, and drinks to 'the Professor,' or whatever your title is to be. You, in your innocence, do not know that you ought to say something in reply; you receive the cup in silence, and are set down as a boor.

17   Apart from this, your host's pledge has secured you the enmity of many of his old friends, with some of whom it was already a grievance, that an acquaintance of a few hours' stand-ing should sit above men who have been drinking the cup of slavery for years. Tongues are busy with you at once. Listen to some of them. 'So! We are to give place to new-comers! It wanted but this. The gates of Rome are open to none but these Greeks. Now what is their claim to be set over our heads? I suppose they think they are conferring a favour on us with their wordy stuff?' 'How he did drink, to be sure!' says another. 'And did you see how he shovelled his food down, hand over hand? Mannerless starveling! He has never so much as dreamt of white bread before. 'Twas the same with the capon and pheasant; much if he left us the bones to pick!' 'My dear sirs' (cries number three), 'I give him five days at

the outside; after which you will see him at our end of the table, making like moan with ourselves. He is a new pair of shoes just now, and is treated with all ceremony. Wait till he has been worn a few times, and the mud has done its work; he will be flung under the bed, poor wretch, like the rest of us, to be a receptacle for bugs.' Such are some among the many comments you excite; and, for all we know, mischief may be brewing at this moment.

Meanwhile, you are the guest of the evening, and the 18 principal theme of conversation. Your unwonted situation has led you on to drink more than was advisable. For some time you have been feeling uncomfortable effects from your host's light, eager wine. To get up before the rest would be bad manners: to remain is perilous. The drinking is prolonged; subject upon subject is started, spectacle after spectacle is produced; for your host is determined that you shall see all he has to show. You suffer the torments of the damned. You see nothing of what is going forward: some favourite singer or musician is performing—you hear him not; and while you force out some complimentary phrase, you are praying that an earthquake may swallow up all, or that the news of a fire may break up the party.

Such, my friend, is your first dinner, the best you will ever 19 get. For my part, give me a dinner of herbs, with liberty to eat when I will and as much as I will. I shall spare you the recital of the nocturnal woes that follow your excess. The next morning, you have to come to terms as to the amount of your salary, and the times of payment. Appearing in answer to his summons, you find two or three friends with him. He bids you be seated, and begins to speak. 'You have now seen the sort of way in which we live—no ostentation, no fuss; everything quite plain and ordinary. Now you will consider everything here as your own. It would be a strange thing, indeed, were I to entrust you with the highest responsibility of all, the moral guidance of myself and my children '—if there are children to be taught—' and yet hesitate to place the rest at your disposal. Something, however, must be settled. I know your moderate, independent spirit. I quite realize that you come to us from no mercenary motive, that you are influenced only by the regard and uniform respect which will be assured to you in this house. Still, as I say, something must be settled. Now, my dear sir, tell me yourself, what you think right ; remembering that there is something to be expected at the great festivals ; for you will not find me remiss in that respect, though I say nothing definite at present ; and these occasions, as you know, come pretty frequently in the course of the year. This consideration will no doubt influence you in settling the amount of your salary ; and apart from that, it sits well on men of culture like yourself, to be above the thought 20 of money.' Your hopes are blasted at the words, and your proud spirit is tamed. The dream of the millionaire and landed proprietor fades away, as you gradually catch his parsimonious drift. Yet you smirk appreciation of the promise. You are to 'consider everything as your own' ; there, surely, is something solid ? 'Tis a draught (did you but know it)

That wets the lips, but leaves the palate dry.

After an interval of embarrassment, you leave the matter to his decision. He declines the responsibility, and calls for the intervention of one of the company : let him name a sum, at once worthy of your acceptance, and not burdensome to his purse, which has so many more urgent calls upon it. ' Sir,' says this officious old gentleman, who has been a toady from his youth, ' Sir, you are the luckiest man in Rome. Deny it if you can ! You have gained a privilege which many a man has longed for, and is not like to obtain at Fortune's hands. You have been admitted to enjoy the company and share the hearth and home of the first citizen of our empire. Used aright, such a privilege will be more to you than the wealth of a Croesus or a Midas. Knowing as I do how many there are—persons of high standing—who would be glad to pay money down, merely for the honour and glory of the acquaintanceship, of being seen in his company, and ranking as his friends and intimates,—knowing this, I am at a loss for words in which to express my sense of your good fortune. You are not only to enjoy this happiness, but to be paid for enjoying it! Under the circumstances, I think we shall satisfy your most extravagant expectations, if we say '—and he names a sum which in itself is of the smallest, quite apart from all reference to your brilliant hopes. However, there is nothing 21 for it but to submit with a good grace. It is too late now for escape; you are in the toils. So you open your mouth for the bit, and are very manageable from the first. You give your rider no occasion to keep a tight rein, or to use the spur; and at last by imperceptible degrees you are quite broken in to him.

The outside world from that time watches you with envy. You dwell within his courts; you have free access; you are become a person of consequence. Yet it is now incomprehensible to you how they can suppose you to be happy. At the same time, you are not without a certain exultation: you cheat yourself from day to day with the thought that there are better things to come. Quite the contrary turns out to be the case. Your prospects, like the proverbial sacrifice of Mandrobulus, dwindle and contract from day to day. Gradually you get 22 some faint glimmerings of the truth. It begins to dawn upon you at last, that those golden hopes were neither more nor less than gilded bubbles: the vexations, on the other hand, are realities; solid, abiding, uncompromising realities. 'And what *are* these vexations?' you will perhaps exclaim; 'I see nothing so vexatious about the matter; I know not what are the hardships and the drudgery alluded to.' Then listen. And do not confine yourself to the article of drudgery, but keep a sharp look-out for ignominy, for degradation, for everything, in short, that is unworthy of a free man.

23   Let me remind you then, to begin with, that you are no longer free-born, no longer a man of family. Birth, freedom, ancestry, all these you will leave on the other side of the door, when you enter upon the fulfilment of your servile contract; for Freedom will never bear you company in that ignoble station. You are a slave, wince as you may at the word; and, be assured, a slave of many masters; a downward-looking drudge, from morning till night

serving for sorry wage.

Then again, you are a backward pupil : Servitude was not the nurse of your childhood; you are getting on in years when she takes you in hand; accordingly, you will do her little credit, and give little satisfaction to your lord. Recollections of Freedom will exercise their demoralizing influence upon you, causing you to jib at times, and you will make villanous work of your new profession. Or will your aspirations after Freedom be satisfied, perhaps, with the thought, that you are no son of a Pyrrhias or a Zopyrion, no Bithynian, to be knocked down under the hammer of a bawling auctioneer ? My dear sir, when pay-day comes round each month, and you mingle in the herd of Pyrrhiases and Zopyrions, and hold out your hand for the wage that is due to you, what is that but a sale ? No need of an auctioneer, for the man who can cry his own wares, and hawks his liberty about from day to day.

24   Wretch ! (one is prompted to exclaim, and particularly when the culprit is a professed philosopher) Wretch ! Were you captured and sold by a pirate or a brigand, you would bewail your lot, and think that Fortune had dealt hardly with you. Were a man to lay violent hands on you, and

claim a master's rights in you, loud and bitter would be your outcry : ' By heaven and earth, 'tis monstrous ! I appeal to the laws ! ' And now, at an age at which a born slave may begin to look towards Freedom, *now* for a few pence do you sell yourself, your virtue and wisdom, in one parcel ? And could Plato's noble words, could all that Chrysippus and Aristotle have said, of the blessings of freedom and the curse of slavery, raise no compunction in you ? Do you count it no shame to be pitted against toadies and vulgar parasites ? no shame to sit at the noisy banquets of a promiscuous, and for the most part a disreputable company, a Greek among Romans, wearing the foreign garb of philosophy, and stammering their tongue with a foreign accent ? How fulsome are your flatteries on these occasions ! how indecent your tipplings ! And next morning the bell rings, and up you must get, losing the best of your sleep, to trudge up and down with yesterday's mud still on your shoes. Were lupines and wild herbs so scarce with you ? had the springs ceased to give their wonted supply, that you were brought to such a pass ? No, the cause of your captivity is too clear. Not water, not lupines were the object of your desire, but dainty viands and fragrant wines ; and your sin has found you out : you are hooked like a pike by your greedy jaws. We have not far to look for the reward of gluttony. Like a monkey with a collar about its neck, you are kept to make amusement for the company ; fancying yourself supremely happy, because you are unstinted in the matter of dried figs. As to freedom and generosity, they are fled, with the memories of Greece, and have left no trace behind them. And would that that were 25 all, the disgrace of falling from freedom to servitude ! Would that your employments were not those of a very menial ! Consider : are your duties any lighter than those of a Dromo or a Tibius ? As to the studies in which your employer professed an interest when he engaged you, they are nothing to him.

Shall an ass affect the lyre ? Remove from these men's minds the gold and the silver, with the cares that these involve, and what remains ? Pride, luxury, sensuality, insolence, wantonness, ignorance. Consuming must be their desire, doubt it not, for the wisdom of Homer, the eloquence of Demosthenes, the sublimity of Plato !

No, your employer has no need of your services in this direction. On the other hand, you have a long beard and a venerable countenance ; the Grecian cloak hangs admirably upon your shoulders, and you are known to be a professor of rhetoric, or literature, or philosophy ; it will not be amiss, he thinks, to have such pursuits represented in the numerous retinue that marches before him. It will give him an air of Grecian culture, of liberal curiosity in fact. Friend, friend ! your stock-in-trade would seem to be not words of wisdom, but a cloak and a beard. If you would do your duty, therefore, be always well in evidence ; begin your unfailing attendance from the early hours of the morning, and never quit his side. Now and again he places a hand upon your shoulder, and mutters some nonsense for the benefit of the passers-by, who are to understand that though he walk abroad the Muses are not forgotten, that in all his comings and goings he can find elegant employment for his mind. Breathless and perspiring, you trot, a pitiable spectacle, at the litter's side ; or if he walks—you know what Rome is—, up hill and down dale after him you tramp. While he is paying a call on a friend, you are left outside, where, for lack of a seat, you are fain to take out your book and read standing.

Night finds you hungry and thirsty. You snatch an apology for a bath ; and it is midnight or near it before you get to dinner. You are no longer an honoured guest ; no longer do you engage the attention of the company. You have retired to make room for some newer capture. Thrust into the most obscure corner, you sit watching the progress of dinner, gnawing in canine sort any bones that come down to you and regaling yourself with hungry zest on such tough mallow-leaves—the wrappers of daintier fare—as may escape the vigilance of those who sit above you. No slight is wanting. You have not so much as an egg to call your own; for there is no reason why you should expect to be treated in the same way as a stranger; that would be absurd. The birds that fall to your lot are not like other birds. Your neighbour gets some plump, luscious affair; you, a poor half-chicken, or lean pigeon, an insult, a positive outrage in poultry. As often as not, an extra guest appears unexpectedly, and the waiter solves the difficulty by removing your share (with the whispered consolation that you are ' one of the family '), and placing it before the new-comer. When the joint, be it pork or venison, is brought in to be carved, let us hope that you stand well with the carver, or you will receive a Promethean helping of ' bones wrapped up in fat.' And the way in which a dish is whisked past you, after remaining with your neighbour till he can eat no more!—what free man would endure it, though he were as innocent of gall as any stag? And I have said nothing yet of the wine. While the other guests are drinking of some rare old vintage, you have vile thick stuff, whose colour you must industriously conceal with the help of a gold or silver cup, lest it should betray the estimation in which the drinker is held. It would be something if you could get enough even of this. Alas! you may call and call: the waiter is

as one that marketh not.

Many are your grievances; nay, all is one huge grievance. 27 And the climax is reached, when you find yourself eclipsed by some minion, some dancing-master, some vile Alexandrian patterer of Ionic lays. How should you hope to rank with the minister of Love's pleasures, with the stealthy conveyer of billets-doux? You cower shamefaced in your corner, and bewail your hard lot, as well you may; cursing your luck that you have never a smattering of such graceful accomplishments yourself. I believe you wish that *you* could turn love-songs, or sing other men's with a good grace; perceiving as you do what a thing it is to be in request. Nay, you could find it in you to play the wizard's, the fortune-teller's part; to deal in thrones and in millions of money. For these, too, you observe, make their way in the world, and are high in favour. Gladly would you enter on any one of these vocations, rather than be a useless castaway. Alas, even these are beyond you; you lack plausibility. It remains for you to give place to others; to endure neglect, and keep your complaints to yourself.

28　Nay, more. Should some slave whisper that you alone withheld your praise, when his mistress's favourite danced or played, the neglect may cost you dear. Then let your dry throat be as busy as any thirsty frog's. See to it, that your voice is heard leading the chorus of applause; and time after time, when all else are silent, throw in some studied servile compliment. The situation is not without humour. Hungry as you are, ay, and thirsty into the bargain, you must anoint yourself with oil of gladness, and crown your head with garlands. It reminds one of the offerings made by recent mourners at a tomb. The tomb gets the ointment and the garlands, while the mourners drink and enjoy the feast.

29　If your patron is of a jealous disposition, and has a young wife or handsome children, and you are not wholly without personal attractions, then beware! you are on dangerous ground. Many are the ears of a king, and many the eyes, that see not the truth only, but ever something over and above the truth, lest they should seem to fail of their office. Imagine yourself, therefore, at a Persian banquet. Keep your eyes downwards, lest a eunuch should catch them resting on one of the concubines. For see, there stands another with his bow ever on the stretch:

one glance at the forbidden object as you raise your cup, and his arrow is through your jaw before you can put it down.

And now dinner is over ; you retire, and snatch a little sleep. 30 But at cock-crow you are aroused. 'Wretch ! Worm that I am ! ' you exclaim. 'To sacrifice the pursuits, the society of former days, the placid life wherein sleep was measured by inclination, and my comings and goings were unfettered, and all to precipitate myself bodily into this hideous gulf ! And why ? What, in God's name, is my glorious recompense ? Was there no other way ? Could I not have provided for myself better than this, and preserved liberty and free-will into the bargain ? Alas ! the lion is fast bound in the net. I am haled hither and thither. Pitiable is my lot, where no honour is to be won, no favour to be hoped for. Untaught, unpractised in the arts of flattery, I am pitted against profes- sionals. I am no choice spirit, no jolly companion ; to raise a laugh is beyond me. My presence (well do I know it) is a vexation to my patron, and then most when he is in his most gracious mood. He finds me sullen ; and how to attune myself to him I know not. If I wear a grim face, I am a sour fellow, scarcely to be endured. If I assume my most cheerful expres- sion, my smiles arouse his contempt and disgust. As well attempt to act a comic part in the mask of tragedy ! And what is the end of it all ? My present life has been another's : do I look to have a new life which shall be my own ? '

Your soliloquy is interrupted by the bell. The old routine 31 awaits you : you must trudge, and you must stand ; and first anoint your limbs, if you would hold out to the end. Dinner will be the same as ever, and go on as late as ever. The change from all your former habits, the wakeful night, the violent exercise, the exhaustion, are slowly undermining your health at this moment, and preparing you for consumption or colic, for asthma or the delights of gout. However, you hold out in spite of all, though many a time your right place would be in bed. But that would never do : that looks like shamming, like shirking your work. The result is that you grow as pallid as a man at the point of death.

32   So much for your city life. And now for an excursion into the country. I will content myself with a single detail. As likely as not it is a wet day. Your turn for the carriage (as might be expected) comes last. You wait and wait, till at last its return is out of the question, and you are squeezed into some vehicle with the cook, or with my lady's *friseur*, without even

33 a proper allowance of straw. I shall make no scruple of relating to you an experience of Thesmopolis the Stoic, which I had from his own mouth ; a most amusing incident, and just the sort of thing one might expect to find happening again. He was in the service of a certain wealthy and luxurious lady of quality, whom on one occasion he had to accompany on a journey from Rome. The fun began at once. The philosopher received as his travelling companion a beardless exquisite of the pitch-plastering persuasion, by whom, you may be certain, my lady set great store; his name, she informed the philosopher, was ' Robinetta.' Is not this a promising start ?—the grave and reverend Thesmopolis, with his hoary beard (you know what a long, venerable affair it is), side by side with this rouged and painted ogler, whose drooping neck and plucked throat suggested the vulture rather than the robin ! 'Twas all that Thesmopolis could do to persuade him not to wear his hair-net ; and as it was he had a sad journey of it, with the fellow singing and whistling all the time—I daresay he would have danced

34 there and then, if Thesmopolis had not prevented him. But there was more to come, as you will see. ' Thesmopolis,' cries my lady, calling him to her, ' I have a great favour to ask of you ; now please don't say no, and don't wait to be asked twice, there 's a good creature.' Of course, he said he would do anything she

wished. ' I only ask you, because I know you are to be trusted ;
you are so good-natured and affectionate ! I want you to take
my little dog Myrrhina in with you, and see that she wants for
nothing. Poor little lady ! she is soon to become a mother.
These hateful, inattentive servants take no notice of *me* when
we are travelling, much less of her. You will be doing me a
great kindness, I assure you, in taking charge of her ; I am so
fond of the sweet little pet ! ' She prayed and almost wept ;
and Thesmopolis promised. Imagine the ludicrous picture.
The little beast peeping out from beneath the philosophic
cloak ; within licking distance of that beard, which perhaps
still held traces of the thick soup of yesterday ; yapping away
with its shrill pipe of a voice, as Maltese terriers will ; and no
doubt taking other liberties, which Thesmopolis did not think
worth mentioning. That night at dinner, the exquisite, his
fellow traveller, after cracking a passable joke here and there at
the expense of the other guests, came to Thesmopolis. ' Of
him,' he remarked, ' I have only this to say, that our Stoic has
turned Cynic.' According to what I heard, the little animal
actually littered in his mantle !

Such are the caprices, nay, the insults, let me rather say, 35
with which the patron gradually breaks the spirit of his dependants. I know myself of an orator, a very free speaker,
who was actually ordered to stand up and deliver a speech at
table ; and a masterly speech it was, trenchant and terse. He
received the congratulations of the company on being timed
by a *wine-* instead of a *water*-clock ; and this affront, it is said,
he was content to put up, for the consideration of £8. But
what of that ? Wait till you get a patron who has poetical or
historical tendencies, and spouts passages of his own works all
through dinner : you must praise, you must flatter, you must
devise original compliments for him,—or die in the attempt.
Then there are the beaux, the Adonises and Hyacinths, as you

must be careful to call them, undeterred by the eighteen inches or so of nose that some of them carry on their faces. Do your praises halt? 'Tis envy, 'tis treason! Away with you, Philoxenus that you are, to Syracusan quarries!—Let them be orators, let them be philosophers, if they will : what matter for a solecism here and there? Find Attic elegance, find honey of Hymettus in every word; and pronounce it law henceforth, to speak as they speak.

36 If we had only men to deal with, it would be something : but there are the women too. For among the objects of feminine ambition is this, of having a scholar or two in their pay, to dance attendance at the litter's side; it adds one more to the list of their adornments, if they can get the reputation of culture and philosophy, of turning a song which will bear comparison with Sappho's. So they too keep their philosopher, their orator, or their *littérateur*; and give him audience—when, think you? Why, at the toilet, by all that is ridiculous, among the rouge-pots and hair-brushes; or else at the dinner-table. They have no leisure at other times. As it is, the philosopher is often interrupted by the entrance of a maid with a billet-doux. Virtue has then to bide her time; for the audience will not be resumed till the gallant has his answer.

37 At rare intervals, at the Saturnalia or the Feast of Minerva, you will be presented with a sorry cloak, or a worn-out tunic; and a world of ceremony will go to the presentation. The first who gets wind of the great man's intention flies to you with the news of what is in store for you; and the bringer of glad tidings does not go away empty-handed. The next morning a dozen of them arrive, conveying the present, each with his tale of how he spoke up for you, or the hints he threw out, or how he was entrusted with the choice, and chose the best. Not a man of them but departs with your money in his pocket, grumbling that it is no more.

As to that salary, it will be paid to you sixpence at a time, 38 and there will be black looks when you ask for it. Still, you must get it somehow. Ply your patron therefore with flatteries and entreaties, and pay due observance to his steward, and let it be the kind of observance that stewards like best ; nor must you forget your kind introducer. You do get something at last ; but it all goes to pay the tailor, the doctor, or the shoe-maker, and you are left the proud possessor of nothing at all.

Meanwhile, jealousy is rife, and some slander is perhaps work- 39 ing its stealthy way to ears which are predisposed to hear any-thing to your discredit. For your employer perceives that by this time incessant fatigues have worn you out ; you are crippled, you are good for nothing more, and gout is coming on. All the profit that was to be had of you, he has effectually sucked out. Your prime has gone by, your bodily vigour is exhausted, you are a tattered remnant. He begins to look about for a con-venient dunghill whereon to deposit you, and for an able-bodied substitute to do your work. You have attempted the honour of one of his minions : you have been trying to corrupt his wife's maid, venerable sinner that you are !—any accusation will serve. You are gagged and turned out neck and crop into the darkness. Away you go, helpless and destitute, with gout for the cheering companion of your old age. Whatever you once knew, you have unlearnt in all these years : on the other hand, you have developed a paunch like a balloon ; a monster insatiable, inexorable, which has acquired a habit of asking for more, and likes not at all the unlearning process. It is not to 40 be supposed that any one else will give you employment, at your age ; you are like an old horse, whose very hide has deterio-rated in value. Not to mention that the worst interpretation will be put upon your late dismissal ; you will be credited with adultery, or poisoning, or something of that kind. Your accuser, you see, is convincing even in silence ; whereas you—you are

a loose-principled, unscrupulous *Greek*. That is the character
we Greeks bear ; and it serves us right ; I see excellent grounds
for the opinion they have of us. Greek after Greek who enters
their service sets up (in default of any other practical knowledge) for wizard or poisoner, and deals in love-charms and evil
spells ; and these are they who talk of culture, who wear grey
beards and philosophic cloaks ! When these, who are accounted
the best of us, stand thus exposed, when men observe their
interested servility, their gross flatteries at table and elsewhere,
it is not to be wondered at that we have all fallen under suspicion.

41 Those whom they have cast off, they hate, and seek to make an
end of them altogether ; arguing, naturally enough, that men
who know their secrets, and have seen them in all their nakedness, may divulge many a foible which will not bear the light ; and
the thought is torment to them. The fact is, that these great
men are for all the world like handsomely bound books. Outside are the gilt edges and the purple cover : and within ?
a Thyestes feasts upon his own children ; an Oedipus commits
incest with his mother ; a Tereus woos two sisters at once.
Such are these human books : their brilliancy attracts all eyes,
but between the purple covers lurks many a horrid tale. Turn
over the pages of any one of them, and you find a drama worthy
the pen of Sophocles or Euripides : close the volume—all is
gilt edge and exquisite tooling. Well may they hate the con-
fidants of such crimes, and plot their destruction ! What if
the outcast should take to rehearsing in public the tragedy that
he has got by heart ?

42 I am minded to give you, after the manner of Cebes, a life-
picture of Dependence ; with this before your eyes, you may
judge for yourself, whether it is the life for you. I would gladly
call in the aid of an Apelles or a Parrhasius, an Aëtion or a
Euphranor, but no such perfect painters are to be found in these
days ; I must sketch you the picture in outline as best I can.

I begin then with tall golden gates, not set in the plain, but high upon a hill. Long and steep and slippery is the ascent; and many a time when a man looks to reach the top, his foot slips, and he is plunged headlong. Within the gates sits Wealth, a figure all of gold (so at least she seems); most fair, most lovely. Her lover painfully scales the height, and draws near to the door; and that golden sight fills him with amazement. The beautiful woman in gorgeous raiment who now takes him by the hand is Hope. As she leads him in, his spirit is stricken with awe. Hope still shows the way; but two others, Despair and Servitude, now take charge of him, and conduct him to Toil, who grinds the poor wretch down with labour, and at last hands him over to Age. He looks sickly now, and all his colour is gone. Last comes Contempt, and laying violent hands on him drags him into the presence of Despair; it is now time for Hope to take wing and vanish. Naked, pot-bellied, pale and old, he is thrust forth, not by those golden gates by which he entered, but by some obscure back-passage. One hand covers his nakedness; with the other he would fain strangle himself. Now let Regret meet him without, dropping vain tears and heaping misery on misery,—and my picture is complete.

Examine it narrowly in all its details, and see whether you like the idea of going in at my golden front door, to be expelled ignominiously at the back. And whichever way you decide, re-member the words of the wise man : ' Blame not Heaven, but your own choice.'   F.

APOLOGY FOR 'THE DEPENDENT SCHOLAR'

DEAR SABINUS,

I have been guessing how you are likely to have expressed yourself upon reading my essay about dependants. I feel pretty sure you read it all and had a laugh over it; but it is your running and general comment in words that I am trying to piece on to it. If I am any good at divination, this is the sort of thing: *To think that a man can set down such a scathing indictment of the life, and then forget it all, get hold of the other end of the stick, and plunge headlong into such manifest conspicuous slavery! Take Midas, Croesus, golden Pactolus, roll them into one, multiply them, and could they induce him to relinquish the freedom which he has loved and consorted with from a child? He is nearly in the clutches of Aeacus, one foot is on the ferryman's boat, and it is now that he lets himself be dragged submissively about by a golden collar*[1]. *There is some slight inconsistency between his life and his treatise; the rivers are running up-hill; topsy-turvydom prevails; our recantations are new-fashioned; the first palinodist*[2] *mended words with words for Helen of Troy; but we spoil words (those words we thought so wise) with deeds.*

2 Such, I imagine, were your inward remarks. And I dare say you will give me some overt advice to the same effect; well, it will not be ill-timed; it will illustrate your friendship, and do you credit as a good man and a philosopher. If I render your part respectably for you, that will do, and we will pay our homage to the God of words[3]; if I fail, you will fill in the deficiency for yourself. There, the stage is ready; I am to hold my tongue, and submit to any necessary carving and

---

[1] Omitting as a scholium, with Dindorf and Fritzsche, the words: οἷά ἐστι τῶν τρυφώντων πλουσίων τὰ σφιγγία καὶ τὰ κουράλλια.

[2] See *Stesichorus* in Notes.

[3] i.e. Hermes.

cauterizing for my good, and you are to plaster me, and have
your scalpel handy, and your iron red-hot. Sabinus takes the
word, and thus addresses me :

My dear friend, this treatise of yours has quite rightly been 3
earning you a fine reputation, from its first delivery before the
great audience I had described to me, to its private use by the
educated who have consulted and thumbed it since. For indeed
it presents the case meritoriously ; there is study of detail and
experience of life in abundance ; your views are the reverse of
vague ; and above all the book is practically useful, chiefly but
not exclusively to the educated whom it might save from an unfore-
seen slavery. However, your mind is changed ; the life you
described is now the better ; good-bye to freedom ; your motto is
that contemptible line :

> *Give me but gain, I'll turn from free to slave.*

Let none hear the lecture from you again, then ; see to it that no
copy of it comes under the eyes of any one aware of your present
life ; ask Hermes to bring Lethe-water from below, enough to drug
your former hearers ; else you will remind us of the Corinthian
tale, and your writing, like Bellerophon's, be your own condemna-
tion. I assure you I see no decent defence you can make, at least
if your detractors have the humour to commend the independence
of the writings while the writer is a slave and a voluntary beast
of burden before their eyes.

They will say with some plausibility : Either the book is some 4
other good man's work, and you a jackdaw strutting in borrowed
plumes ; or, if it is really yours, you are a second Salaethus ; the
Crotoniate legislator made most severe laws against adultery, was
much looked up to on the strength of it, and was shortly after taken
in adultery with his brother's wife. You are an exact reproduc-
tion of Salaethus, they will say ; or rather he was not half so bad
as you, seeing that he was mastered by passion, as he pleaded in

court, and moreover preferred to leap into the flames, like a brave man, when the Crotoniates were moved to compassion and gave him the alternative of exile. The difference between your precept and practice is infinitely more ridiculous ; you draw a realistic word-picture of that servile life ; you pour contempt on the man who runs into the trap of a rich man's house, where a thousand degradations, half of them self-inflicted, await him ; and then in extreme old age, when you are on the border between life and death, you take this miserable servitude upon you and make a sort of circus exhibition of your chains. The conspicuousness of your position will only make the more ridiculous that contrast between your book and your life.

5 *But I need not beat my brains for phrases of reprobation ; there is one good enough in a noble tragedy :*

   Wisdom begins at home ; no wisdom, else.

And your censors will find no lack of illustrations against you ; some will compare you to the tragic actor ; on the stage he is Agamemnon or Creon or great Heracles ; but off it, stripped of his mask, he is just Polus or Aristodemus, a hireling liable to be hissed off, or even whipped on occasion, at the pleasure of the audience. Others will say you have had the experience of Queen Cleopatra's monkey: the docile creature used to dance in perfect form and time, and was much admired for the regularity and decorum of its movements, adapted to the voices and instruments of a bridal chorus ; alas, one day it spied a fig or almond a little way off on the ground ; flutes and measures and steps were all forgotten, the mask was far off in several pieces, and there was he chewing his find.

6 *You, they will say, are the author (for 'actor' would understate the case) who has laid down the laws of noble conduct ; and no sooner is the lump of figs presented than the monkey is revealed ; your lips are the lips of a philosopher, and your heart is quite other ; it is no injustice to say that those sentiments for which you*

claim admiration have 'wetted your lips, and left your palate dry.' You have not had to wait long for retribution; you spoke unadvisedly in scorn of human needs; and, this little while after, behold you making public renunciation of your freedom! Surely Nemesis was standing behind your back as you drank in the flattering tributes to your superiority; did she not smile in her divine fore-knowledge of the impending change, and mark how you forgot to propitiate her before you assailed the victims whom fortune's mutability had reduced to such courses?

Now I want you to imagine a rhetorician writing on the theme 7 *that Aeschines, after his indictment of Timarchus, was himself proved guilty by eyewitnesses of similar iniquity; would, or would not, the amusement of the audience be heightened by the fact that he had got Timarchus punished for offences excused by youth, whereas he was himself an old man at the time of his own guilt? Why, you are like the quack who offered a cough-mixture which was to cure instantaneously, and could hardly get the promise out for coughing.*

Yes, Sabinus, and there is plenty more of the same sort for 8 an accuser like you to urge; the subject is all handles; you can take hold of it anywhere. I have been looking about for my best line of defence. Had I better turn craven, face right-about, confess my sin, and have recourse to the regular plea of Chance, Fate, Necessity? Shall I humbly beseech my critics to pardon me, remembering that nothing is in a man's own choice —we are led by some stronger power, one of the three I mentioned, probably, and are not true agents but guiltless altogether, whatever we say or do? Or will you tell me this might do well enough for one of the common herd, but you cannot have *me* sheltering myself so? *I* must not brief Homer; it will not serve me to plead:

No mortal man e'er yet escaped his fate;

nor again,

His thread was spun, then when his mother bare him.

9   On the other hand, I might avoid that plea as wanting in plausibility, and say that I did not accept this association under the temptation of money or any prospects of that kind, but in pure admiration of the wisdom, strength, and magnanimity of my patron's character, which inspired the wish to partake his activity.   But I fear I should only have brought on myself the additional imputation of flattery.   It would be a case of ' one nail drives out one nail,' and this time the one left in would be the bigger ; for flattery is the most servile, and consequently reckoned the worst, of all vices.

10   Both these pleas, then, being excluded, what is left me but to confess that I have no sound defence to make ?   I have indeed one anchor yet aboard : I may whine over age and ill health, and their attendant poverty, from which a man will purchase escape at any cost.   The situation tempts me to send an invitation to Euripides's *Medea* : will she come and recite certain lines of hers on my behalf, kindly making the slight changes needed ?—

> Too well I know how monstrous is the deed ;
> My poverty, but not my will, consents.

And every one knows the place in Theognis, whether I quote it or not, where he approves of people's flinging themselves to the unplumbed deep from sky-ypointing crags, if one may be quit of poverty that way.

11   That about exhausts the obvious lines of defence ; and none of them is very promising.   But never fear, my friend, I am not going to try any of them.   May never Argos be so hard put to it that Cyllarabis must be sown ! nor ever I be in such straits for a tolerable defence as to be driven upon these evasions ! No, I only ask you to consider the vast difference between being a hireling in a rich man's house, where one is a slave, and must

put up with all that is described in my book—between that and
entering the public service, doing one's best as an administrator,
and taking the Emperor's pay for it.   Go fully into the matter ;
take the two things separately and have a good look at them ;
you will find that they are two octaves apart, as the musical
people say ; the two lives are about as like each other as lead is
to silver, bronze to gold, an anemone to a rose, a monkey to
a man ; there is pay, and there is subordination, in each case ;
but the essence of the two things is utterly different.   In one
we have manifest slavery ; the new-comers who accept the
terms are barely distinguishable from the human chattels a man
has bought or bred ; but persons who have the management of
public business, and give their services to states and nations, are
not to have insinuations aimed at them just because they are
paid ; that single point of resemblance is not to level them
down to the others.   If that is to be the principle, we had
better do away with all such offices at once ; governors of
whole provinces, prefects of cities, commanders of legions and
armies, will all fall under the same condemnation ; for they are
paid.   But of course everything is not to be upset to suit a
single case ; all who receive pay are not to be lumped together.

It is all a mistake ; I never said that all drawers of salaries 12
lived a degraded life ; I only pitied those domestic slaves who
have been caught by compliments on their culture.   My position, you see, is entirely different ; my private relations are as
they were before, though in a public capacity I am now an
active part of the great Imperial machine.   If you care to
inquire, you will find that my charge is not the least important
in the government of Egypt.   I control the cause-list, see that
trials are properly conducted, keep a record of all proceedings
and pleas, exercise censorship over forensic oratory, and edit
the Emperor's rescripts with a view to their official and per-
manent preservation in the most lucid, accurate, and genuine

form. My salary comes from no private person, but from the Emperor; and it is considerable, amounting to many hundreds. In the future too there is before me the brilliant prospect of attaining in due course to a governorship or other distinguished employment.

13 Accordingly I am now going to throw off reserve, come to grips with the charge against me, and prove my case *a fortiori*. I tell you that nobody does anything for nothing; you may point to people in high places—as high as you like; the Emperor himself is paid. I am not referring to the taxes and tribute which flow in annually from subjects; the chief item in the Emperor's pay is panegyrics, world-wide fame, and grateful devotion; the statues, temples, and consecrated ground which their subjects bestow upon them, what are these but pay for the care and forethought which they apply to public policy and improvements? To compare small things with great, if you will begin at the top of the heap and work down through the grains of which it is composed, you will find that we inferior ones differ from the superior in point of size, but all are wage-earners together.

14 If the law I laid down had been that no one should do anything, I might fairly have been accused of transgressing it; but as my book contains nothing of the sort, and as goodness consists in doing good, what better use can you make of yourself than if you join forces with your friends in the cause of progress, come out into the open, and let men see that you are loyal and zealous and careful of your trust, not what Homer calls a vain cumberer of the earth?

15 But before all, my critics are to remember that in me they will be criticizing not a wise man (if indeed there is such a person on earth), but one of the common people, one who has indeed practised rhetoric and won some little reputation therein, but has never been trained up to the perfect virtue

of the really great. Well, I may surely be forgiven for that;
if any one ever did come up to the ideal of the wise man, it has
not been my fortune to meet him. And I confess further that
I should be disappointed if I found you criticizing my present
life; you knew me long ago when I was making a handsome
income out of the public profession of rhetoric; for on that
Atlantic tour of yours which included Gaul, you found me
numbered among those teachers who could command high
fees. Now, my friend, you have my defence; I am exceedingly
busy, but could not be indifferent to securing *your* vote of
acquittal; as for others, let them all denounce me with one
voice if they will; on them I shall waste no more words than,
What cares Hippoclides?   H.

A SLIP OF THE TONGUE
IN SALUTATION [1]

IF a poor mortal has some difficulty in guarding against that
spirit of mischief which dwells aloft, he has still more in clearing
himself of the absurd consequences when that spirit trips him
up. I am in both predicaments at once; coming to make you
my morning salutation, which should have taken the orthodox
form of Rejoice, I bade you, in a very choice fit of absent-
mindedness, Be healthy—a good enough wish in its way, but
a little untimely and unconnected with that early hour. I at

---

[1] This piece, which even in the Greek fails to convince us that Asclepius
heard the prayer with which it concludes, is still flatter in English, because we
have no words of salutation which correspond at once in etymological meaning
and in conventional usage to the Greek. The English reader who cares to
understand a piece so little worth his attention, will obligingly bear in mind
that the Greek word represented here by Joy and Rejoice roughly answered
in Lucian's time to our Good-morning and How do you do, as well as to the
epistolary My dear ——— ; while that represented by Hail or Health did the
work of Good-night, Good-bye, Farewell, and (in letters) Yours truly.

once went moist and red, not quite aware whether I was on my head or my heels; some of the company took me for a lunatic, no doubt, some thought I was in my second childhood, some that I had not quite got over my last night's wine—though you yourself were the pink of good manners, not showing your consciousness of the slip by any ghost of a smile. It occurred to me to write to myself a little something in the way of comfort, and so modify the distress my blunder gave me—prove to myself that it was not absolutely unpardonable for an old man to transgress etiquette so flagrantly before so many witnesses. As to apology, there could be no occasion for that, when one's slip had resulted in so well-omened a wish.

2   I began to write expecting my task to be very difficult, but found plenty of material as I went on. I will defer it, however, till I have cleared the way with a few necessary remarks on the three forms—Rejoice or Joy, Prosper or Prosperity, Hail or Health. Joy is a very ancient greeting; but it was not confined to the morning, or the first meeting. They did use it when they first saw one another:

Joy to thee, Lord of this Tirynthian land!

But again at the moment when the wine succeeded to the meal:

Achilles, Joy! We lack not fair repast—
so says Odysseus discharging his embassy. And even at parting:

Joy be with you! And henceforth know me God,
No longer mortal man.

In fact the apostrophe was not limited to any particular season, as now to the morning alone; indeed they used it on gloomy, nay, on the most lamentable occasions; in Euripides, Polynices ends his life with the words,

Joy with you! for the darkness closes on me.

Nor was it necessarily significative of friendliness; it could express hatred and the determination to see no more of another. To wish much joy to, was a regular form for ceasing to care about.

The modern use of the word dates back to Philippides the 3 dispatch-runner. Bringing the news of Marathon, he found the archons seated, in suspense regarding the issue of the battle. ' Joy, we win ! ' he said, and died upon his message, breathing his last in the word Joy. The earliest letter beginning with it is that in which Cleon the Athenian demagogue, writing from Sphacteria, sends the good news of his victory and capture of Spartans at that place. However, later than that we find Nicias writing from Sicily and keeping to the older custom of coming to business at once with no such introduction.

Now the admirable Plato, no bad authority on such matters, 4 would have us reject the salutation Joy altogether; it is a mean wish, wanting in seriousness, according to him; his substitute is Prosperity, which stands for a satisfactory condition both of body and soul; in a letter to Dionysius, he reproves him for commencing a hymn to Apollo with Joy, which he maintains is unworthy of the Pythian, and not fit even for men of any discretion, not to mention Gods.

Pythagoras the mystic has vouchsafed us no writings of his 5 own; but we may infer from his disciples, Ocellus the Lucanian and Archytas, for instance, that he headed his letters neither with Joy nor Prosperity, but recommended beginning with Hail. At any rate all the Pythagoreans in writing to one another (when their tone is serious, that is) started with wishing Health, which they took to be the prime need of soul and body alike, and to include all human blessings. The Pentagram [1], that interlaced triple triangle which served them as a sort of password, they called by the name Health. They argued that

---

[1] See *Pythagoras* in Notes.

Health included Joy and Prosperity, but that neither of those two was coextensive with Health. Some of them gave to the Quaternion [1], which is their most solemn oath, and sums their perfect number, the name of Beginning of Health. Philolaus might be quoted.

6 But I need hardly go so far back. Epicurus assuredly rejoiced in joy—pleasure was the chief Good in his eyes; yet in his most earnest letters (which are not very numerous), and in those to his most intimate friends, he starts with Hail. And in tragedy and the old comedy you will constantly find it used quite at the beginning. You remember,

> Hail to thee, joy be thine—

which puts health before rejoicing clearly enough. And says Alexis :

> All hail, my lord; after long time thou comest.

Again Achaeus :

> I come in sorry plight, yet wish thee health.

And Philemon :

> Health first I ask, and next prosperity,
> Joy thirdly, and to owe not any man.

As for the writer of the drinking-song mentioned in Plato, what says he ?—'Best is health, and second beauty, and third wealth'; joy he never so much as names. I need hardly adduce the trite saw :

> Chief of them that blessings give,
> Health, with thee I mean to live.

But, if Health is chief, her gift, which is the enjoyment of health, should rank before other Goods.

7 I could multiply these examples by the thousand from poets, historians, philosophers, who give Health the place of honour; but you will not require any such childish pedantry of me,

[1] See *Pythagoras* in Notes.

wiping out my original offence by another; I shall do better to add a historical anecdote or two which occur to me as relevant.

Eumenes of Cardia, writing to Antipater, states that just 8 before the battle of Issus, Hephaestion came at dawn into Alexander's tent. Either in absence of mind and confusion like mine, or else under a divine impulse, he gave the evening salutation like me—'Hail, sire; 'tis time we were at our posts.' All present were confounded at the irregularity, and Hephaestion himself was like to die of shame, when Alexander said, ' I take the omen; it is a promise that we shall come back safe from battle.'

Antiochus Soter, about to engage the Galatians, dreamed that 9 Alexander stood over him and told him to give his men the password Health; and with this word it was that he won that marvellous victory.

Ptolemy, the son of Lagus, in a letter to Seleucus, just re- 10 versed the usual order, bidding him Hail at the beginning, and adding Rejoice at the end instead of wishing him Health; this is recorded by Dionysodorus, the collector of his letters.

The case of Pyrrhus the Epirot is well worth mention; as 11 a general he was only second to Alexander, and he experienced a thousand vicissitudes of fortune. In all his prayers, sacrifices, and offerings, he never asked for victory or increase of his royal dignity, for fame or excessive wealth; his whole prayer was always in one word, Health; as long as he had that, he thought all else would come of itself. And it was true wisdom, in my opinion; he remembered that all other good things are worthless, if health is wanting.

Oh, certainly (says some one); but we have assigned each 12 form to its proper place by this time; and if you disregard that—even though there was no bad meaning in what you did say—you cannot fairly claim to have made no mistake; it is as though one should put a helmet on the shins, or greaves on the head. My dear sir (I reply), your simile would go on all fours if there were any season at all which did not require health; but in point of fact it is needed in the morning and at noonday and at night—especially by busy rulers like you Romans, to whom physical condition is so important. And again, the man who gives you Joy is only beginning auspiciously; it is no more than a prayer; whereas he who bids you Hail is doing you a practical service in reminding you of the means to health; his is more than a prayer, it is a precept.

13 Why, in that book of instructions which you all receive from the Emperor, is not the first recommendation to take care of your health? Quite rightly; that is the condition precedent of efficiency. Moreover, if I know any Latin, you yourselves, in *returning* a salutation, constantly use the equivalent of Health.

14 However, all this does not mean that I have deliberately abandoned Rejoice and substituted Hail for it. I admit that it was quite unintentional; I am not so foolish as to innovate like that, and exchange the regular formulae.

15 No, I only thank Heaven that my stumble had such very fortunate results, landing me in a better position than I had designed; may it not be that Health itself, or Asclepius, inspired me to give you this promise of health? How else should it have befallen me? In the course of a long life I have never been guilty of such a confusion before.

16 Or, if I may not have recourse to the supernatural, it is no wonder that my extreme desire to be known to you for good should so confuse me as to work the contrary effect. Possibly, too, one might be robbed of one's presence of mind by the crowd of military persons pushing for precedence, or treating the salutation ceremony in their cavalier fashion.

17 As to yourself, I feel sure that, however others may have

referred it to stupidity, ignorance, or lunacy, you took it as the sign of a modest, simple, unspoiled, unsophisticated soul. Absolute confidence in such matters comes dangerously near audacity and impudence. My first wish would be to make no such blunder; my second that, if I did, the resulting omen should be good.

There is a story told of the first Augustus. He had given 18 a correct legal decision, which acquitted a maligned person of a most serious charge. The latter expressed his gratitude in a loud voice, thus:—'I thank your majesty for this bad and inequitable verdict.' Augustus's attendants raged, and were ready to tear the man to pieces. But the Emperor restrained them; 'Never mind what he said; it is what he meant that matters.' That was Augustus's view. Well, take my meaning, and it was good; or take my word, and it was auspicious.

And now that I have got to this point, I have reason to fear 19 that I may be suspected of having made the slip on purpose, leading up to this apology. O God of health, only grant me that the quality of my piece may justify the notion that I wanted no more than a peg whereon to hang an essay!   H.

HERMOTIMUS, OR THE
RIVAL PHILOSOPHIES

Lycinus. Hermotimus

Ly. Good morning, Hermotimus; I guess by your book and the pace you are going at that you are on your way to lecture, and a little late. You were conning over something as you walked, your lips working and muttering, your hand flung out this way and that as you got a speech into order in your mind; you were doubtless inventing one of your crooked questions, or pondering some tricky problem; never a vacant mind, even in the streets; always on the stretch and in earnest, bent on advancing in your studies.

Her. I admit the impeachment; I was running over the details of what he said in yesterday's lecture. One must lose no chance, you know; the Coan doctor[1] spoke so truly: *ars longa, vita brevis.* And what *he* referred to was only physic—a simpler matter. As to philosophy, not only will you never attain it, however long you study, unless you are wide awake all the time, contemplating it with intense eager gaze; the stake is so tremendous, too,—whether you shall rot miserably with the vulgar herd, or be counted among philosophers and reach Happiness.

2   *Ly.* A glorious prize, indeed! however, you cannot be far off it now, if one may judge by the time you have given to philosophy, and the extraordinary vigour of your long pursuit. For twenty years now, I should say, I have watched you perpetually

[1] Hippocrates.

going to your professors, generally bent over a book taking notes
of past lectures, pale with thought and emaciated in body.
I suspect you find no release even in your dreams, you are so
wrapped up in the thing. With all this you must surely get
hold of Happiness soon, if indeed you have not found it long
ago without telling us.

Her. Alas, Lycinus, I am only just beginning to get an inkling
of the right way. Very far off dwells Virtue, as Hesiod says,
and long and steep and rough is the way thither, and travellers
must bedew it with sweat.

Ly. And you have not yet sweated and travelled enough ?

Her. Surely not; else should I have been on the summit,
with nothing left between me and bliss ; but I am only starting
yet, Lycinus.

Ly. Ah, but Hesiod, your own authority, tells us, Well begun 3
is half done ; so we may safely call you half-way by this time.

Her. Not even there yet ; that would indeed have been
much.

Ly. Where *shall* we put you, then ?

Her. Still on the lower slopes, just making an effort to get
on ; but it is slippery and rough, and needs a helping hand.

Ly. Well, your master can give you that ; from his station
on the summit, like Zeus in Homer with his golden cord, he can
let you down his discourse, and therewith haul and heave you
up to himself and to the Virtue which he has himself attained
this long time.

Her. The very picture of what he is doing; if it depended
on him alone, I should have been hauled up long ago ; it is
my part that is still wanting.

Ly. You must be of good cheer and keep a stout heart ; gaze 4
at the end of your climb and the Happiness at the top, and
remember that he is working with you. What prospect does
he hold out ? when are you to be up ? does he think you will

be on the top next year—by the Great Mysteries, or the Panathenaea, say ?

Her. Too soon, Lycinus.

Ly. By next Olympiad, then ?

Her. All too short a time, even that, for habituation to Virtue and attainment of Happiness.

Ly. Say two Olympiads, then, for an outside estimate. You may fairly be found guilty of laziness, if you cannot get it done by then ; the time would allow you three return trips from the Pillars of Heracles to India, with a margin for exploring the tribes on the way instead of sailing straight and never stopping. How much higher and more slippery, pray, is the peak on which your Virtue dwells than that Aornos crag which Alexander stormed in a few days ?

5   *Her.* There is no resemblance, Lycinus ; this is not a thing, as you conceive it, to be compassed and captured quickly, though ten thousand Alexanders were to assault it ; in that case, the scalers would have been legion. As it is, a good number begin the climb with great confidence, and do make progress, some very little indeed, others more ; but when they get half-way, they find endless difficulties and discomforts, lose heart, and turn back, panting, dripping, and exhausted. But those who endure to the end reach the top, to be blessed thenceforth with wondrous days, looking down from their height upon the ants which are the rest of mankind.

Ly. Dear me, what tiny things you make us out—not so big as the Pygmies even, but positively grovelling on the face of the earth. I quite understand it ; your thoughts are up aloft already. And we, the common men that walk the earth, shall mingle you with the Gods in our prayers ; for you are translated above the clouds, and gone up whither you have so long striven.

Her. If but that ascent might be, Lycinus ! but it is far yet.

Ly. But you have never told me *how* far, in terms of time.   6

Her. No; for I know not precisely myself.   My guess is that it will not be more than twenty years; by that time I shall surely be on the summit.

Ly. Mercy upon us, you take long views!

Her. Ay; but, as the toil, so is the reward.

Ly. That may be; but about these twenty years—have you your master's promise that you will live so long? is he prophet as well as philosopher? or is it a soothsayer or Chaldean expert that you trust? such things are known to them, I understand. You would never, of course, if there were any uncertainty of your life's lasting to the Virtue-point, slave and toil night and day like this; why, just as you were close to the top, your fate might come upon you, lay hold of you by the heel, and lug you down with your hopes unfulfilled.

Her. God forbid! these are words of ill omen, Lycinus; may life be granted me, that I may grow wise, and have if it be but one day of Happiness!

Ly. For all these toils will you be content with your one day?

Her. Content? yes, or with the briefest moment of it.

Ly. But is there indeed Happiness up there—and worth 7 all the pains? How can you tell? You have never been up yourself.

Her. I trust my master's word; and he knows well; is he not on the topmost height?

Ly. Oh, do tell me what he says about it; what is Happiness like? wealth, glory, pleasures incomparable?

Her. Hush, friend! all these have nought to do with the Virtuous life.

Ly. Well, if these will not do, what *are* the good things he offers to those who carry their course right through?

Her. Wisdom, courage, true beauty, justice, full and firm

knowledge of all things as they are ; but wealth and glory and pleasure and all bodily things — these a man strips off and abandons before he mounts up, like Heracles burning on Mount Oeta before deification ; he too cast off whatever of the human he had from his mother, and soared up to the Gods with his divine part pure and unalloyed, sifted by the fire. Even so those I speak of are purged by the philosophic fire of all that deluded men count admirable, and reaching the summit have Happiness with never a thought of wealth and glory and pleasure—except to smile at any who count them more than phantoms.

8   *Ly.* By Heracles (and his death on Oeta), they quit themselves like men, and have their reward, it seems. But there is one thing I should like to know : are they allowed to come down from their elevation sometimes, and have a taste of what they left behind them ? or when they have once got up, must they stay there, conversing with Virtue, and smiling at wealth and glory and pleasure ?

Her. The latter, assuredly ; more than that, a man once admitted of Virtue's company will never be subject to wrath or fear or desire any more ; no, nor can he feel pain, nor any such sensation.

Ly. Well, but—if one might dare to say what one thinks— but no—let me keep a good tongue in my head—it were irreverent to pry into what wise men do.

Her. Nay, nay ; let me know your meaning.

Ly. Dear friend, I have not the courage.

Her. Out with it, my good fellow ; we are alone.

9   *Ly.* Well, then—most of your account I followed and accepted —how they grow wise and brave and just, and the rest—indeed I was quite fascinated by it ; but then you went on to say they despised wealth and glory and pleasure ; well, just there (quite between ourselves, you know) I was pulled up ; I thought of

a scene t'other day with—shall I tell you whom ? Perhaps we
can do without a name ?

Her. No, no ; we must have that too.

Ly. Your own professor himself, then,—a person to whom all
respect is due, surely, not to mention his years.

Her. Well ?

Ly. You know the Heracleot, quite an old pupil of his in
philosophy by this time—red-haired—likes an argument ?

Her. Yes ; Dion, he is called.

Ly. Well, I suppose he had not paid up punctually ; anyhow
the other day the old man haled him before the magistrate, with
a halter made of his own coat ; he was shouting and fuming,
and if some friends had not come up and got the young man out
of his hands, he would have bitten off his nose, he was in such
a temper.

Her. Ah, *he* is a bad character, always an unconscionable time 10
paying his debts.   There are plenty of others who owe the professor money, and he has never treated any of them so ; they
pay him his interest punctually.

Ly. Not so fast ; what in the world does it matter to him, if
they do not pay up ? he is purified by philosophy, and has no
further need of the cast clothes of Oeta.

Her. Do you suppose his interest in such things is selfish ?
no, but he has little ones ; his care is to save them from in-
digence.

Ly. Whereas he ought to have brought them up to Virtue
too, and let them share his inexpensive Happiness.

Her. Well, I have no time to argue it, Lycinus ; I must not 11
be late for lecture, lest in the end I find myself left behind.

Ly. Don't be afraid, my duteous one ; to-day is a holiday ;
I can save you the rest of your walk.

Her. What do you mean ?

Ly. You will not find him just now, if the notice is to be trusted; there was a tablet over the door announcing in large print, No meeting this day. I hear he dined yesterday with the great Eucrates, who was keeping his daughter's birthday. He talked a good deal of philosophy over the wine, and lost his temper a little with Euthydemus the Peripatetic; they were debating the old Peripatetic objections to the Porch. His long vocal exertions (for it was midnight before they broke up) gave him a bad headache, with violent perspiration. I fancy he had also drunk a little too much, toasts being the order of the day, and eaten more than an old man should. When he got home, he was very ill, they said, just managed to check and lock up carefully the slices of meat which he had conveyed to his servant at table, and then, giving orders that he was not at home, went to sleep, and has not waked since. I overheard Midas his man telling this to some of his pupils; there were a number of them coming away.

12 *Her.* Which had the victory, though, he or Euthydemus—if Midas said anything about that?

Ly. Why, at first, I gathered, it was very even between them; but you Stoics had it in the end, and your master was much too hard for him. Euthydemus did not even get off whole; he had a great cut on his head. He was pretentious, insisted on proving his point, would not give in, and proved a hard nut to crack; so your excellent professor, who had a goblet as big as Nestor's in his hand, brought this down on him as he lay within easy reach, and the victory was his.

Her. Good; so perish all who will not yield to their betters!

Ly. Very reasonable, Hermotimus; what was Euthydemus thinking of, to irritate an old man who is purged of wrath and master of his passions, when he had such a heavy goblet in his hand?

13 But we have time to spare—you might tell a friend like me the story of your start in philosophy; then I might perhaps,

if it is not too late, begin now and join your school ; you are my friends ; you will not be exclusive ?

Her. If only you would, Lycinus ! you will soon find out how much you are superior to the rest of men. I do assure you, you will think them all children, you will be so much wiser.

Ly. Enough for me, if after twenty years of it I am where you are now.

Her. Oh, I was about your age when I started on philosophy ; I was forty ; and you must be about that.

Ly. Just that ; so take and lead me on the same way ; that is but right. And first tell me—do you allow learners to criticize, if they find difficulties in your doctrines, or must juniors abstain from that ?

Her. Why, yes, they must ; but *you* shall have leave to ask questions and criticize ; you will learn easier that way.

Ly. I thank you for it, Hermotimus, by your name-God Hermes.

Now, is there only one road to philosophy—the Stoic way ? 14 they tell me there are a great many other philosophers ; is that so ?

Her. Certainly—Peripatetics, Epicureans, Platonists, followers of Diogenes, Antisthenes, Pythagoras, and more yet.

Ly. Quite so ; numbers of them. Now, are their doctrines the same, or different ?

Her. Entirely different.

Ly. But the truth, I presume, is bound to be in one of them, and not in all, as they differ ?

Her. Certainly.

Ly. Then, as you love me, answer this : when you first went 15 in pursuit of philosophy, you found many gates wide open ; what induced you to pass the others by, and go in at the Stoic gate ? Why did you assume that that was the only true one, which would set you on the straight road to Virtue, while the rest all opened on blind alleys ? What was the test you applied *then* ? Please abolish your present self, the self which is now instructed, or half-instructed, and better able to distinguish between good and bad than we outsiders, and answer in your then character of a layman, with no advantage over me as I am now.

Her. I cannot tell what you are driving at.

Ly. Oh, there is nothing recondite about it. There are a great many philosophers—let us say Plato, Aristotle, Antisthenes, and your spiritual fathers, Chrysippus, Zeno, and all the rest of them ; what was it that induced you, leaving the rest alone, to pick out the school you did from among them all, and pin your philosophic faith to it ? Were you favoured like Chaerephon with a revelation from Apollo ? Did he tell you the Stoics were the best of men, and send you to their school ? I dare say he recommends different philosophers to different persons, according to their individual needs ?

Her. Nothing of the kind, Lycinus ; I never consulted him upon it.

Ly. Why ? was it not a *dignus vindice nodus* ? or were you confident in your own unaided discrimination ?

Her. Why, yes ; I was.

16   *Ly.* Then this must be my first lesson from you—how one can decide out of hand which is the best and the true philosophy to be taken, and the others left.

Her. I will tell you : I observed that it attracted most disciples, and thence inferred that it was superior.

Ly. Give me figures ; how many more of them than of Epicureans, Platonists, Peripatetics ? Of course you took a sort of show of hands.

Her. Well, no ; I didn't count ; I just guessed.

Ly. Now, now ! you are not teaching, but hoaxing me ;

judge by guesswork and impression, indeed, on a thing of this importance! You are hiding the truth.

Her. Well, that was not my only way; every one told me the Epicureans were sensual and self-indulgent, the Peripatetics avaricious and contentious, the Platonists conceited and vain; about the Stoics, on the contrary, many said they had fortitude and an open mind; he who goes their way, I heard, was the true king and millionaire and wise man, alone and all in one.

Ly. And, of course, it was other people who so described 17 them; you would not have taken their own word for their excellences.

Her. Certainly not; it was others who said it.

Ly. Not their rivals, I suppose?

Her. Oh, no.

Ly. Laymen, then?

Her. Just so.

Ly. There you are again, cheating me with your irony; you take me for a blockhead, who will believe that an intelligent person like Hermotimus, at the age of forty, would accept the word of laymen about philosophy and philosophers, and make his own selection on the strength of what they said.

Her. But you see, Lycinus, I did not depend on their judge- 18 ment entirely, but on my own too. I saw the Stoics going about with dignity, decently dressed and groomed, ever with a thoughtful air and a manly countenance, as far from effeminacy as from the utter repulsive negligence of the Cynics, bearing themselves, in fact, like moderate men; and every one admits that moderation is right.

Ly. Did you ever see them behaving like your master, as I described him to you just now? Lending money and clamouring for payment, losing their tempers in philosophic debates, and making other exhibitions of themselves? Or perhaps these are trifles, so long as the dress is decent, the beard long, and the hair close-cropped ? We are provided for the future, then, with an infallible rule and balance, guaranteed by Hermotimus ? It is by appearance and walk and haircutting that the best men are to be distinguished ; and whosoever has not these marks, and is not solemn and thoughtful, shall be condemned and rejected ?

19 Nay, do not play with me like this ; you want to see whether I shall catch you at it.

Her. Why do you say that ?

Ly. Because, my dear sir, this appearance test is one for statues ; *their* decent orderly attire has it easily over the Stoics, because Phidias or Alcamenes or Myron designed them to be graceful. However, granting as much as you like that these are the right tests, what is a blind man to do, if he wants to take up philosophy ? how is he to find the man whose principles are right, when he cannot see his appearance or gait ?

Her. I am not teaching the blind, Lycinus ; I have nothing to do with them.

Ly. Ah, but, my good sir, there ought to have been some universal criterion, in a matter of such great and general use. Still, if you will have it so, let the blind be excluded from philosophy, as they cannot see—though, by the way, they are just the people who most need philosophy to console them for their misfortune ; but now, the people who *can* see—give them the utmost possible acuity of vision, and what can they detect of the spiritual qualities from this external shell ?

20 What I mean is this : was it not from admiration of their *spirit* that you joined them, expecting to have your own spirit purified ?

Her. Assuredly.

Ly. How could you possibly discern the true philosopher from the false, then, by the marks you mentioned ? It is not the way of such qualities to come out like that ; they are hidden and secret ; they are revealed only under long and patient

observation, in talk and debate and the conduct they inspire.
You have probably heard of Momus's indictment of Hephaestus;
if not, you shall have it now. According to the myth, Athene,
Posidon, and Hephaestus had a match in inventiveness. Posidon
made a bull, Athene planned a house, Hephaestus constructed
a man; when they came before Momus, who was to judge, he
examined their productions; I need not trouble you with his
criticisms of the other two; but his objection to the man, and
the fault he found with Hephaestus, was this: he should have
made a window in his chest, so that, when it was opened, his
thoughts and designs, his truth or falsehood, might have been
apparent. Momus must have been blear-eyed, to have such
ideas about men; but you have sharper eyes than Lynceus,
and pierce through the chest to what is inside; all is patent to
you, not merely any man's wishes and sentiments, but the
comparative merits of any pair.

Her. You trifle, Lycinus. I made a pious choice, and do 21
not repent it; that is enough for me.

Ly. And will you yet make a mystery of it to your friend,
and let him be lost with the vulgar herd?

Her. Why, you will not accept anything I say.

Ly. On the contrary, my good sir, it is you who will not say
anything I can accept. Well, as you refuse me your confidence,
and are so jealous of my becoming a philosopher and your
equal, I must even do my best to find out the infallible test
and learn to choose safely for myself. And you may listen, if
you like.

Her. That I will, Lycinus; you will very likely hit on some
good idea.

Ly. Then attend, and do not mock me, if my inquiry is quite
unscientific; it is all I can do, as you, who know better, will not
give me any clearer light.

I conceive Virtue, then, under the figure of a State whose 22 citizens are happy—as your professor, who is one of them, phrases it,—absolutely wise, all of them brave, just, and self-controlled, hardly distinguishable, in fact, from Gods. All sorts of things that go on here, such as robbery, assault, unfair gain, you will never find attempted there, I believe; their relations are all peace and unity; and this is quite natural, seeing that none of the things which elsewhere occasion strife and rivalry, and prompt men to plot against their neighbours, so much as come in their way at all. Gold, pleasures, distinctions, they never regard as objects of dispute; they have banished them long ago as undesirable elements. Their life is serene and blissful, in the enjoyment of legality, equality, liberty, and all other good things.

23   *Her.* Well, Lycinus? Must not all men yearn to belong to a State like that, and never count the toil of getting there, nor lose heart over the time it takes? Enough that one day they will arrive, and be naturalized, and given the franchise.

  Ly. In good truth, Hermotimus, we should devote all our efforts to this, and neglect everything else; we need pay little heed to any claims of our earthly country; we should steel our hearts against the clingings and cryings of children or parents, if we have them; it is well if we can induce them to go with us; but, if they will not or cannot, shake them off and march straight for the city of bliss, leaving your coat in their hands, if they lay hold of it to keep you back, in your hurry to get there; what matter for a coat? You will be admitted there without one.

24   I remember hearing a description of it all once before from an old man, who urged me to go there with him. He would show me the way, enroll me when I got there, introduce me to his own circles, and promise me a share in the universal Happiness. But I was stiff-necked, in my youthful folly (it was some fifteen years ago); else might I have been in the outskirts, nay,

haply at the very gates, by now. Among the noteworthy things he told me, I seem to remember these : all the citizens are aliens and foreigners, not a native among them ; they include numbers of barbarians, slaves, cripples, dwarfs, and poor ; in fact any one is admitted ; for their law does not associate the franchise with income, with shape, size, or beauty, with old or brilliant ancestry ; these things are not considered at all ; any one who would be a citizen needs only understanding, zeal for the right, energy, perseverance, fortitude and resolution in facing all the trials of the road ; whoever proves his possession of these by persisting till he reaches the city is *ipso facto* a full citizen, regardless of his antecedents. Such distinctions as superior and inferior, noble and common, bond and free, simply do not exist there, even in name.

Her. There, now ; you see I am not wasting my pains on 25 trifles ; I yearn to be counted among the citizens of that fair and happy State.

Ly. Why, your yearning is mine too ; there is nothing I would sooner pray for. If the city had been near at hand and plain for all to see, be assured I would never have doubted, nor needed prompting ; I would have gone thither and had my franchise long ago ; but as you tell me—you and your bard Hesiod—that it is set exceeding far off, one must find out the way to it, and the best guide. You agree ?

Her. Of course that is the only thing to do.

Ly. Now, so far as promises and professions go, there is no lack of guides ; there are numbers of them waiting about, all representing themselves as from there. But instead of one single road there seem to be many different and inconsistent ones. North and South, East and West, they go ; one leads through meadows and vegetation and shade, and is well watered and pleasant, with never a stumbling-block or inequality ; another is rough and rocky, threatening heat and drought and toil. Yet all these are supposed to lead to the one city, though they take such different directions.

26   That is where my difficulty lies; whichever of them I try, there is sure to be a most respectable person stationed just at the entrance, with a welcoming hand and an exhortation to go his way; each of them says he is the only one who knows the straight road; his rivals are all mistaken, have never been themselves, nor learnt the way from competent guides. I go to his neighbour, and he gives the same assurances about *his* way, abusing the other respectable persons; and so the next, and the next, and the next. This multiplicity and dissimilarity of the roads gives me searchings of heart, and still more the assertiveness and self-satisfaction of the guides; I really cannot tell which turning or whose directions are most likely to bring me to the city.

27   *Her.* Oh, but I can solve that puzzle for you; you cannot go wrong, if you trust those who have been already.

Ly. Which do you mean? those who have been by which road, and under whose guidance? It is the old puzzle in a new form; you have only substituted men for measures.

Her. How do you mean?

Ly. Why, the man who has taken Plato's road and travelled with him will recommend that road; so with Epicurus and the rest; and *you* will recommend your own. How else, Hermotimus? it must be so.

Her. Well, of course.

Ly. So you have not solved my puzzle; I know just as little as before which traveller to trust; I find that each of them, as well as his guide, has tried one only, which he now recommends and will have to be the only one leading to the city. Whether he tells the truth I have no means of knowing; that he has attained *some* end, and seen *some* city, I may perhaps allow; but whether he saw the right one, or whether, Corinth being

the real goal, he got to Babylon and thought he had seen Corinth
—that is still undecided; for surely every one who has seen
a city has not seen Corinth, unless Corinth is the only city
there is.   But my greatest difficulty of all is the absolute certainty that the true road is one; for Corinth is one, and the
other roads lead anywhere but to Corinth, though there may
be people deluded enough to suppose that the North road
and the South road lead equally to Corinth.

Her. But that is absurd, Lycinus; they go opposite ways,
you see.

Ly. Then, my dear good man, this choice of roads and guides 28
is quite a serious matter; we can by no means just follow our
noses; we shall be discovering that we are well on the way to
Babylon or Bactria instead of to Corinth.   Nor is it advisable
to toss up, either, on the chance that we may hit upon the
right way if we start upon any one at a venture.   That is no
impossibility; it may have come off once and again in a cycle;
but I cannot think we ought to gamble recklessly with such
high stakes, nor commit our hopes to a frail craft, like the wise
men who went to sea in a bowl; we should have no fair complaint against Fortune, if her arrow or dart did not precisely
hit the centre; the odds are ten thousand to one against her;
just so the archer in Homer—Teucer, I suppose it was—when
he meant to hit the dove, only cut the string, which held it;
of course it is infinitely more likely that the point of the arrow
will find its billet in one of the numberless other places, than
just in that particular central one.   And as to the perils of
blundering into one of the wrong roads instead of the right one,
misled by a belief in the discretion of Fortune, here is an illustration :—it is no easy matter to turn back and get safe into
port when you have once cast loose your moorings and committed yourself to the breeze; you are at the mercy of the sea,
frightened, sick and sorry with your tossing about, most likely.

Your mistake was at the beginning: before leaving, you should have gone up to some high point, and observed whether the wind was in the right quarter, and of the right strength for a crossing to Corinth, not neglecting, by the way, to secure the very best pilot obtainable, and a seaworthy craft equal to so high a sea.

29   *Her.* Much better so, Lycinus. However, I know that, if you go the whole round, you will find no better guides or more expert pilots than the Stoics ; if you mean ever to get to Corinth, you will follow them, in the tracks of Chrysippus and Zeno. It is the only way to do it.

  Ly. Ah, many can play at the game of assertion. Plato's fellow traveller, Epicurus's follower, and all the rest, will tell me just what you do, that I shall never get to Corinth except with whichever of them it is. So I must either believe them all, or disbelieve impartially. The latter is much the safest, until we have found out the truth.

30   Put a case, now : just as I am, as uncertain as ever which of the whole number has the truth, I choose your school ; I rely on you, who are my friend, but who still know only the Stoic doctrine, and have not travelled any way but that. Now some God brings Plato, Pythagoras, Aristotle, and the rest to life again ; they gather round and cross-examine me, or actually sue me in court for constructive defamation ; *Good Lycinus,* they say, *what possessed or who induced you to exalt Chrysippus and Zeno at our expense ? we are far older established ; they are mere creatures of yesterday ; yet you never gave us a hearing, nor inquired into our statements at all.* Well, what am I to plead ? will it avail me to say I trusted my friend Hermotimus ? I feel sure they will say, *We know not this Hermotimus, who he is, nor he us ; you had no right to condemn us all, and give judgement by default against us, on the authority of a man who knew only one of the philosophic roads, and even that, perhaps, imper-*

fectly. These are not the instructions issued to juries, Lycinus;
they are not to hear one party, and refuse the other permission to
say what he deems advisable; they are to hear both sides alike,
with a view to the better sifting of truth from falsehood by comparison of the arguments; if they fail in these duties, the law
allows an appeal to another court. That is what we may expect
them to say.

Then one of them might proceed to question me like this : 31
*Suppose, Lycinus, that an Ethiopian who had never been abroad
in his life, nor seen other men like us, were to state categorically
in an Ethiopian assembly that there did not exist on earth any
white or yellow men—nothing but blacks—, would his statement
be accepted? or would some Ethiopian elder remark, How do you
know, my confident friend? you have never been in foreign parts,
nor had any experience of other nations.* Shall I tell him the old
man's question was justified? what do you advise, my counsel?

Her. Say that, certainly; I consider the old man's rebuke
quite reasonable.

Ly. So do I. But I am not so sure you will approve what
comes next; as for me, I have as little doubt of that as of the
other.

Her. What is it?

Ly. The next step will be the application; my questioner 32
will say, *Now Lycinus, let us suppose an analogue, in a person
acquainted only with the Stoic doctrine, like your friend Hermotimus; he has never travelled in Plato's country, or to Epicurus,
or any other land; now, if he were to state that there was no such
beauty or truth in those many countries as there is in the Porch
and its teaching, would you not be justified in considering it bold
of him to give you his opinion about them all, whereas he knew only
one, having never set foot outside the bounds of Ethiopia?* What
reply do you advise to that?

Her. The perfectly true one, of course, that it is indeed the

Stoic doctrine that we study fully, being minded to sink or swim with that, but still we do know what the others say also ; our teacher rehearses the articles of their beliefs to us incidentally, and demolishes them with his comments.

33 *Ly.* Do you suppose the Platonists, Pythagoreans, Epicureans, and other schools, will let that pass ? or will they laugh out loud and say, *What remarkable methods your friend has, Lycinus ! he accepts our adversaries' character of us, and gathers our doctrines from the description of people who do not know, or deliberately misrepresent them. If he were to see an athlete getting his muscles in trim by kicking high, or hitting out at empty space as though he were getting a real blow home, would he (in the capacity of umpire) at once proclaim him victor, because* he could not help winning? *No ; he would reflect that these displays are easy and safe, when there is no defence to be reckoned with, and that the real decision must wait till he has beaten and mastered his opponent, and the latter ' has had enough.' Well then, do not let Hermotimus suppose from his teachers' sparrings with our shadows (for we are not there) that they have the victory, or that our doctrines are so easily upset ; tell him the business is too like the sand houses which children, having built them weak, have no difficulty in overturning, or, to change the figure, like people practising archery ; they make a straw target, hang it to a post, plant it a little way off, and then let fly at it ; if they hit and get through the straw, they burst into a shout, as if it were a great triumph to have driven through the dry stuff. That is not the way the Persians take, or those Scythian tribes which use the bow. Generally, when they shoot, in the first place they are themselves mounted and in motion, and secondly, they like the mark to be moving too ; it is not to be stationary, waiting for the arrival of the arrow, but passing at full speed ; they can usually kill beasts, and their marksmen hit birds. If it ever happens that they want to test the actual impact on a target, they set up one of*

stout wood, or a shield of raw hide ; piercing that, they reckon that their shafts will go through armour too. So, Lycinus, tell Hermotimus from us that his teachers pierce straw targets, and then say they have disposed of armed men ; or paint up figures of us, spar at them, and, after a not surprising success, think they have beaten us. But we shall severally quote against them Achilles's words against Hector :

> *They dare not face the nodding of my plume.*

So say all of them, one after the other.   34

I suspect that Plato, with his intimate knowledge of Sicily, will add an anecdote from there. Gelo of Syracuse had disagreeable breath, but did not find it out himself for a long time, no one venturing to mention such a circumstance to a tyrant. At last a foreign woman who had a connexion with him dared to tell him ; whereupon he went to his wife and scolded her for never having, with all her opportunities of knowing, warned him of it ; she put in the defence that, as she had never been familiar or at close quarters with any other man, she had supposed all men were like that. So Hermotimus (Plato will say) after his exclusive association with Stoics, cannot be expected to know the savour of other people's mouths. Chrysippus, on the other hand, might say as much or more if I were to put *him* out of court and betake myself to Platonism, in reliance upon some one who had conversed with Plato alone. And in a word, as long as it is uncertain which is the true philosophic school, I choose none ; choice of one is insult to the rest.

Her. For Heaven's sake, Lycinus, let us leave Plato, Aristotle, 35 Epicurus, and the rest of them alone ; to argue with them is not for me. Why not just hold a private inquiry, you and I, whether philosophy is what I say it is ? As for the Ethiopians and Gelo's wife, what a long way you have brought them on none of their business !

Ly. Away with them, then, if you find their company super-
fluous. And now do you proceed; my expectations are high.

Her. Well, it seems to me perfectly possible, Lycinus, after
studying the Stoic doctrines alone, to get at the truth from
them, without going through a course of all the others too.
Look at it this way : if any one tells you simply, Twice two is
four, need you go round all the mathematicians to find out
whether there is one who makes it five, or seven ; or would you
know at once that the man was right ?

Ly. Certainly I should.

Her. Then why should you think it impossible for a man
who finds, without going further, that the Stoics make true
statements, to believe them and dispense with further witness ?
He knows that four can never be five, though ten thousand
Platos or Pythagorases said it was.

36 *Ly.* Not to the point. You compare accepted with disputed
facts, whereas they are completely different. Tell me, did you
ever meet a man who said twice two was seven or eleven ?

Her. Not I ; any one who did not make four of it must be
mad.

Ly. But on the other hand—try to tell the truth, I adjure
you—, did you ever meet a Stoic and an Epicurean who did *not*
differ about principles or ends ?

Her. No.

Ly. You are an honest man ; now ask yourself whether you
are trapping a friend with false logic. We are trying to find
out with whom philosophic truth lies ; and you beg the question
and make a present of that same truth to the Stoics ; for you
say (what is quite unproved) that they are the people who
make twice two four ; the Epicureans or Platonists would say
that *they* bring out that result, whereas you get five or seven.
Does it not amount to that, when your school reckon goodness
the only end, and the Epicureans pleasure ? or again when you

say everything is material, and Plato recognizes an immaterial element also in all that exists ?   As I said, you lay hold of the thing in dispute, as though it were the admitted property of the Stoics, and put it into their hands, though the others claim it and maintain that it is theirs ; why, it is the very point at issue.   If it is once established that Stoics have the monopoly of making four out of twice two, it is time for the rest to hold their tongues ; but as long as they refuse to yield that point, we must hear all alike, or be prepared for people's calling us partial judges.

Her. It seems to me, Lycinus, you do not understand what 37 I mean.

Ly. Very well, put it plainer, if it is something different from that.

Her. You will see in a minute.   Let us suppose two people have gone into the temple of Asclepius or Dionysus, and subsequently one of the sacred cups is missing.   Both of them will have to be searched, to see which has it about him.

Ly. Clearly.

Her. Of course one of them has it.

Ly. Necessarily, if it is missing.

Her. Then, if you find it on the first, you will not strip the other ; it is clear he has not got it.

Ly. Quite.

Her. And if we fail to find it on the first, the other certainly has it ; it is unnecessary to search him that way either.

Ly. Yes, he has it.

Her. So with us ; if we find the cup in the possession of the Stoics, we shall not care to go on and search the others ; we have what we were looking for ; why trouble further ?

Ly. There is no why, if you really find it, and can be certain 38 it is the missing article, the sacred object being unmistakable. But there are some differences in this case, friend ; the temple-visitors are not two, so that if one has not got the booty the other has; but many; and the identity of the missing object is also uncertain; it may be cup, or bowl, or garland; every priest gives a different description of it; they do not agree even about the material; bronze, say these, silver, say those—anything from gold to tin. So there is nothing for it but to strip the visitors, if you want to find it; even if you discover a gold cup on the first man, you must go on to the others.

Her. What for?

Ly. Because it is not certain that the thing was a cup. And even if that is generally admitted, they do not all agree that it was gold; and if it is well known that a gold cup is missing, and you find a gold cup on your first man, even so you are not quit of searching the others; it is not clear that this is *the* sacred cup; do you suppose there is only one gold cup in the world?

Her. No, indeed.

Ly. So you will have to go the round, and then collect all your finds together and decide which of them is most likely to be divine property.

39 For the source of all the difficulty is this: every one who is stripped has something or other on him, one a bowl, one a cup, one a garland, which again may be bronze, gold, or silver; but whether the one he has is the sacred one, is not yet clear. It is absolutely impossible to know which man to accuse of sacrilege; even if all the objects were similar, it would be uncertain who had robbed the God; for such things may be private property too. Our perplexity, of course, is simply due to the fact that the missing cup—assume it to be a cup—has no inscription; if either the God's or the donor's name had been on it, we should not have had all this trouble; when we found the inscribed one, we should have stopped stripping and inconveniencing other visitors. I suppose, Hermotimus, you have often been at athletic meetings?

Her. You suppose right ; and in many places too.

Ly. Did you ever have a seat close by the judges ?

Her. Dear me, yes ; last Olympia, I was on the left of the stewards ; Euandridas of Elis had got me a place in the Elean enclosure ; I particularly wanted to have a near view of how things are done there.

Ly. So you know how they arrange ties for the wrestling or the pancratium ?

Her. Yes.

Ly. Then you will describe it better than I, as you have seen it so close.

Her. In old days, when Heracles presided, bay leaves——   40

Ly. No old days, thank you ; tell me what you saw with your own eyes.

Her. A consecrated silver urn is produced, and into it are thrown little lots about the size of a bean, with letters on them. Two are marked alpha[1], two beta, two more gamma, and so on, if the competitors run to more than that—two lots always to each letter. A competitor comes up, makes a prayer to Zeus, dips his hand into the urn, and pulls out one lot ; then another does the same ; there is a policeman to each drawer, who holds his hand so that he cannot see what letter he has drawn. When all have drawn, the chief police officer, I think it is, or one of the stewards themselves—I cannot quite remember this detail—, goes round and examines the lots while they stand in a circle, and puts together the two alphas for the wrestling or pancratium, and so for the two betas, and the rest. That is the procedure when the number of competitors is even, as eight, four, or twelve. If it is five, seven, nine, or other odd number, an odd letter is marked on one lot, which is put in with the

[1] The Greek alphabet runs : alpha, beta, gamma, delta, epsilon, zeta, eta, theta, iota, kappa, lambda, mu, nu, xi, omicron, pi, rho, sigma, tau, upsilon, phi, chi, psi, omega.

others, not having a duplicate. Whoever draws this is a bye, and waits till the rest have finished their ties; no duplicate turns up for him, you see; and it is a considerable advantage to an athlete, to know that he will come fresh against tired competitors.

41   *Ly.* Stop there; that is just what I wanted. There are nine of them, we will say, and they have all drawn, and the lots are in their hands. You go round—for I promote you from spectator to steward—examining the letters; and I suppose you will not know who is the bye till you have been to them all and paired them.

Her. How do you mean?

Ly. It is impossible for you to hit straight upon the letter which indicates the bye; at least, you may hit upon the letter, but you will not know about the bye; it was not announced beforehand that kappa or mu or iota had the appointment in its gift; when you find alpha, you look for the holder of the other alpha, whom finding, you pair the two. Again finding beta, you inquire into the whereabouts of the second beta which matches it; and so all through, till there is no one left but the holder of the single unpaired letter.

42   *Her.* But suppose you come upon it first or second, what will you do then?

Ly. Never mind me; I want to know what *you* will do, Mr. Steward. Will you say at once, Here is the bye? or will you have to go round to all, and see whether there is a duplicate to be found, it being impossible to know the bye till you have seen all the lots?

Her. Why, Lycinus, I shall know quite easily; nine being the number, if I find the epsilon first or second, I know the holder of it for the bye

Ly. But how?

Her. How? Why, two of them must have alpha, two beta,

and of the next two pairs one has certainly drawn gammas and the other deltas, so that four letters have been used up over eight competitors. Obviously, then, the next letter, which is epsilon, is the only one that can be odd, and the drawer of it is the bye.

Ly. Shall I extol your intelligence, or would you rather I explained to you my own poor idea, which differs?

Her. The latter, of course, though I cannot conceive how you can reasonably differ.

Ly. You have gone on the assumption that the letters are 43 taken in alphabetical order, until at a particular one the number of competitors runs short; and I grant you it may be done so at Olympia. But suppose we were to pick out five letters at random, say chi, sigma, zeta, kappa, theta, and duplicate the other four on the lots for eight competitors, but put a single zeta on the ninth, which we meant to indicate the bye—what then would you do if you came on the zeta first? How can you tell that its holder is the bye till you have been all round and found no counterpart to it? for you could not tell by the alphabetical order, as at Olympia.

Her. A difficult question.

Ly. Look at the same thing another way. Suppose we put 44 no letters at all on the lots, but, instead of them, signs and marks such as the Egyptians use for letters, men with dogs' or lions' heads. Or no, those are rather too strange; let us avoid hybrids, and put down simple forms, as well as our draughts- manship will allow—men on two lots, horses on two, a pair of cocks, a pair of dogs, and let a lion be the mark of the ninth. Now, if you hit upon the lion at the first try, how can you tell that this is the bye-maker, until you have gone all round and seen whether any one else has a lion to match?

Her. Your question is too much for me.

Ly. No wonder; there is no plausible answer. Consequently, 45 if we mean to find either the man who has the sacred cup, or the bye, or our best guide to the famous city of Corinth, we must absolutely go to and examine them all, trying them carefully, stripping and comparing them; the truth will be hard enough to find, even so. If I am to take any one's advice upon the right philosophy to choose, I insist upon his knowing what they all say; every one else I disqualify; I will not trust him while there is one philosophy he is unacquainted with; that one may possibly be the best of all. If some one were to produce a handsome man, and state that he was the handsomest of mankind, we should not accept that, unless we knew he had seen all men; very likely his man is handsome, but whether the handsomest, he has no means of knowing without seeing all. Now we are looking not simply for beauty, but for the greatest beauty, and if we miss that, we shall account ourselves no further than we were; we shall not be content with chancing upon some sort of beauty; we are in search of a definite thing, the supreme beauty, which must necessarily be *one*.

46 *Her*. True.

Ly. Well then, can you name me a man who has tried every road in philosophy? one who, knowing the doctrine of Pythagoras, Plato, Aristotle, Chrysippus, Epicurus, and the rest, has ended by selecting one out of all these roads, because he has proved it genuine, and had found it by experience to be the only one that led straight to Happiness? If we can meet with such a man, we are at the end of our troubles.

Her. Alas, that is no easy matter.

47 *Ly*. What shall we do, then? I do not think we ought to despair, in the momentary absence of such a guide. Perhaps the best and safest plan of all is to set to work oneself, go through every system, and carefully examine the various doctrines.

Her. That is what seems to be indicated. I am afraid, though, there is an obstacle in what you said just now: it is not

easy, when you have committed yourself with a spread of canvas
to the wind, to get home again. How can a man try all the
roads, when, as you said, he will be unable to escape from the
first of them ?

Ly. My notion is to copy Theseus, get dame Ariadne to
give us a skein, and go into one labyrinth after another, with
the certainty of getting out by winding it up.

Her. Who is to be our Ariadne ? Where shall we find the
skein ?

Ly. Never despair ; I fancy I have found something to hold
on to and escape.

Her. And what is that ?

Ly. It is not original ; I borrow it from one of the wise
men : 'Be sober and doubt all things,' says he. If we do not
believe everything we are told, but behave like jurymen who
suspend judgement till they have heard the other side, we may
have no difficulty in getting out of the labyrinths.

Her. A good plan ; let us try it.

Ly. Very well, which shall we start with ? However, that will
make no difference ; we may begin with whomsoever we fancy,
Pythagoras, say ; how long shall we allow for learning the
whole of Pythagoreanism ? and do not omit the five years of
silence ; including those, I suppose thirty altogether will do ;
or, if you do not like that, still we cannot put it lower than
twenty.

Her. Put it at that.

Ly. Plato will come next with as many more, and then
Aristotle cannot do with less.

Her. No.

Ly. As to Chrysippus, I need not ask you ; you have told me
already that forty is barely enough.

Her. That is so.

Ly. And we have still Epicurus and the others. I am not

48

taking high figures, either, as you will see if you reflect upon the number of octogenarian Stoics, Epicureans, and Platonists who confess that they have not yet completely mastered their own systems. Or, if they did not confess it, at any rate Chrysippus, Aristotle, and Plato would for them ; still more Socrates, who is as good as they ; he used to proclaim to all comers that, so far from knowing all, he knew nothing whatever, except the one fact of his own ignorance. Well, let us add up. Twenty years we gave Pythagoras, the same to Plato, and so to the others. What will the total come to, if we assume only ten schools ?

Her. Over two hundred years.

Ly. Shall we deduct a quarter of that, and say a hundred and fifty will do ? or can we halve it ?

49 *Her.* You must decide about that ; but I see that, at the best, it will be but few who will get through the course, though they begin philosophy and life together.

Ly. In that case, what are we to do ? Must we withdraw our previous admission, that no one can choose the best out of many without trying all ? We thought selection without experiment a method of inquiry savouring more of divination than of judgement, did we not ?

Her. Yes.

Ly. Without such longevity, then, it is absolutely impossible for us to complete the series—experiment, selection, philosophy, Happiness. Yet anything short of that is a mere game of blindman's-buff ; whatever we knock against and get hold of we shall be taking for the thing we want, because the truth is hidden from us. Even if a mere piece of luck brings us straight to it, we shall have no grounded conviction of our success ; there are so many similar objects, all claiming to be the real thing.

50 *Her.* Ah, Lycinus, your arguments seem to me more or less logical, but—but—to be frank with you—I hate to hear you going through them and wasting your acuteness. I suspect it

was in an evil hour that I came out to-day and met you ; my
hopes were almost in my grasp ; and now here are you plunging
me into a slough of despond with your demonstrations ; truth
is undiscoverable, if the search needs so many years.

Ly. My dear friend, it would be much fairer to blame your
parents, Menecrates and whatever your mother's name may have
been—or indeed to go still further back to human nature. Why
did not they make you a Tithonus for years and durability ?
instead of which, they limited you like other men to a century
at the outside. As for me, I have only been helping you to
deduce results.

Her. No, no ; it is just your way ; you want to crow over 51
me ; you detest philosophy—I cannot tell why—and poke fun
at philosophers.

Ly. Hermotimus, I cannot show what truth is, so well as wise
people like you and your professor ; but one thing I do know
about it, and that is that it is not pleasant to the ear ; falsehood
is far more esteemed ; it is prettier, and therefore pleasanter ;
while Truth, conscious of its purity, blurts out downright
remarks, and offends people. Here is a case of it : even you
are offended with me for having discovered (with your assistance) how this matter really stands, and shown that our common
object is hard of attainment. Suppose you had been in love
with a statue and hoped to win it, under the impression that it
was human, and I had realized that it was only bronze or marble,
and given you a friendly warning that your passion was hopeless
—you might just as well have thought I was your enemy then,
because I would not leave you a prey to extravagant and imprac-
ticable delusions.

Her. Well, well ; are we to give up philosophy, then, and idle 52
our lives away like the common herd ?

Ly. What have I said to justify that ? My point is not that
we are to give up philosophy, but this : whereas we are to

pursue philosophy, and whereas there are many roads, each professing to lead to philosophy and Virtue, and whereas it is uncertain which of these is the true road, therefore the selection shall be made with care. Now we resolved that it was impossible out of many offers to choose the best, unless a man should try all in turn; and then the process of trial was found to be long. What do *you* propose?—It is the old question again. To follow and join philosophic forces with whomsoever you first fall in with, and let him thank Fortune for his proselyte?

53   *Her.* What is the good of answering your questions? You say no one can judge for himself, unless he can devote the life of a phoenix to going round experimenting; and on the other hand you refuse to trust either previous experience or the multitude of favourable testimony.

Ly. Where is your multitude, with knowledge and experience *of all*? Never mind the multitude; one man who answers the description will do for me. But if you mean the people who do *not* know, their mere numbers will never persuade me, as long as they pronounce upon all from knowledge of, at the most, one.

Her. Are you the only man who has found the truth, and are all the people who go in for philosophy fools?

Ly. You wrong me, Hermotimus, when you imply that I put myself above other people, or rank myself at all with those who know; you forget what I said; I never claimed to know the truth better than others, only confessed that I was as ignorant of it as every one else.

54   *Her.* Well, but, Lycinus, it may be all very well to insist on going the round, testing the various statements, and eschewing any other method of choice; but it is ridiculous to spend so many years on each experiment, as though there were no such thing as judging from samples. That device seems to me quite

simple, and economical of time. There is a story that some sculptor, Phidias, I think, seeing a single claw, calculated from it the size of the lion, if it were modelled proportionally. So, if some one were to let you see a man's hand, keeping the rest of his body concealed, you would know at once that what was behind was a man, without seeing his whole body. Well, it is easy to find out in a few hours the essential points of the various doctrines, and, for selecting the best, these will suffice, without any of your scrupulous exacting investigation.

Ly. Upon my word, how confident you are in your faculty 55 of divining the whole from the parts! and yet I remember being told just the opposite—that knowledge of the whole includes that of the parts, but not vice versa. Well, but tell me; when Phidias saw the claw, would he ever have known it for a lion's, if he had never seen a lion? Could you have said the hand was a man's, if you had never known or seen a man? Why are you dumb? Let me make the only possible answer for you—that you could *not*; I am afraid Phidias has modelled his lion all for nothing; for it proves to be neither here nor there. What resemblance is there? What enabled you and Phidias to recognize the parts was just your knowledge of the wholes— the lion and the man. But in philosophy—the Stoic, for instance—how will the part reveal the other parts to you, or how can you conclude that they are beautiful? You do not know the whole to which the parts belong.

Then you say it is easy to hear in a few hours the essentials 56 of all philosophy—meaning, I suppose, their principles and ends, their accounts of God and the soul, their views on the material and the immaterial, their respective identification of pleasure or goodness with the desirable and the Happy; well, it is easy—it is quite a trifle—to deliver an opinion after such a hearing; but really to *know* where the truth lies will be work, I suspect, not for a few hours, but for a good many days. If not, what can have induced them to enlarge on these rudiments to the tune of a hundred or a thousand volumes apiece? I imagine they only wanted to establish the truth of those few points which you thought so easy and intelligible. If you refuse to spend your time on a conscientious selection, after personal examination of each and all, in sum and in detail, it seems to me you will still want your soothsayer to choose the best for you. It would be a fine short cut, with no meanderings or wastings of time, if you sent for him, listened to the summaries, and killed a victim at the end of each; by indicating in its liver which is the philosophy for you, the God would save you a pack of troubles.

57 Or, if you like, I can suggest a still simpler way; you need not shed all this blood in sacrifice to any God, nor employ an expensive priest; put into an urn a set of tablets, each marked with a philosopher's name, and tell a boy (he must be quite young, and his parents both be living) to go to the urn and pick out whichever tablet his hand first touches; and live a philosopher ever after, of the school which then comes out triumphant.

58 *Her.* This is buffoonery, Lycinus; I should not have expected it of you. Now tell me, did you ever buy wine? in person, I mean.

Ly. Many a time.

Her. Well, did you go to every wine vault in town, one after another, tasting and comparing?

Ly. Certainly not.

Her. No; as soon as you find good sound stuff, you have only to get it sent home.

Ly. To be sure.

Her. And from that little taste you could have answered for the quality of the whole?

Ly. Yes.

Her. Now suppose you had gone to all the wine-merchants
and said : I want to buy a pint of wine ; I must ask you, gentlemen, to let me drink the whole of the cask which each of you
has on tap ; after that exhaustive sampling, I shall know which
of you keeps the best wine, and is the man for my money.   If
you had talked like that, they might have laughed at you, and,
if you persisted in worrying them, have tried how you liked
water.

Ly. Yes ; it would be no more than my deserts.

Her. Apply this to philosophy. What need to drink the
whole cask, when you can judge the quality of the whole from
one little taste ?

Ly. What an adept at evasion you are, Hermotimus ! How
you slip through one's fingers !   However, it is all the better
this time ; you fancied yourself out, but you have flopped into
the net again.

Her. What do you mean ?

Ly. You take a thing whose nature is self-evident and universally admitted, like wine, and argue from it to perfectly unlike
things, whose nature is obscure and generally debated.   In
fact I cannot tell what analogy you find between philosophy
and wine ; there *is* just one, indeed : philosophers and wine-
merchants both sell their wares, mostly resorting to adultera-
tion, fraud, and false measures, in the process.   But let us look
into your real meaning. You say all the wine in a cask is of
the same quality—which is perfectly reasonable ; further, that
any one who draws and tastes quite a small quantity will know
at once the quality of the whole—of which the same may be
said ; I should never have thought of objecting.   But mark
what comes now : do philosophy and its professors (your own,
for instance) give you every day the same remarks on the same
subjects, or do they vary them ?   They vary them a great deal,
friend ; you would never have stuck to your master through

your twenty years' wandering—quite a philosophic Odyssey—
if he had always said the same thing; one hearing would have
been enough.

60   *Her.* So it would.

  Ly. How could you have known the whole of his doctrines
from the first taste, then? They were not homogeneous, like
the wine; novelty to-day, and novelty to-morrow on the top
of it. Consequently, dear friend, short of drinking the whole
cask, you might soak to no purpose; Providence seems to me to
have hidden the philosophic Good right at the bottom, under-
neath the lees. So you will have to drain it dry, or you will
never get to that nectar for which I know you have so long
thirsted. According to your idea, it has such virtue that,
could you once taste it and swallow the very least drop, you
would straightway have perfect wisdom; so they say the Delphian prophetess is inspired by one draught of the sacred spring
with answers for those who consult the oracle. But it seems
not to be so; you have drunk more than half the cask; yet
you told me you were only beginning yet.

61   Now see whether this is not a better analogy. You shall
keep your merchant, and your cask; but the contents of the
latter are not to be wine, but assorted seeds. On the top is
wheat, next beans, then barley, below that lentils, then peas—
and other kinds yet. You go to buy seeds, and he takes some
wheat out of that layer, and puts it in your hand as a sample;
now, could you tell by looking at that whether the peas were
sound, the lentils tender, and the beans full?

  Her. Impossible.

  Ly. No more can you tell the quality of a philosophy from
the first statements of its professor; it is not uniform, like the
wine to which you compared it, claiming that it must resemble
the sample glass; it is heterogeneous, and it had better not be
cursorily tested. If you buy bad wine, the loss is limited to

a few pence; but to rot with the common herd (in your own words) is not so light a loss. Moreover, your man who wants to drink up the cask as a preliminary to buying a pint will injure the merchant, with his dubious sampling; but philosophy knows no such danger; you may drink your fill, but this cask grows no emptier, and its owner suffers no loss. It is cut and come again here; we have the converse of the Danaids' cask; that would not hold what was put into it; it ran straight through; but here, the more you take away, the more remains.

And I have another similar remark to make about these 62 specimen drops of philosophy. Do not fancy I am libelling it, if I say it is like hemlock, aconite, or other deadly poison. Those too, though they have death in them, will not kill if a man scrapes off the tiniest particle with the edge of his nail and tastes it; if they are not taken in the right quantity, the right manner, and the right vehicle, the taker will not die; you were wrong in claiming that the least possible quantity is enough to base a generalization on.

Her. Oh, have it your own way, Lycinus. Well then, we 63 have got to live a hundred years, and go through all this trouble? There is no other road to philosophy?

Ly. No, none; and we need not complain; as you very truly said, *ars longa, vita brevis.* But I do not know what has come over you; you now make a grievance of it, if you cannot before set of sun develop into a Chrysippus, a Plato, a Pythagoras.

Her. You trap me, and drive me into a corner, Lycinus; yet I never provoked you; it is all envy, I know, because I have made some progress in my studies, whereas you have neglected yourself, when you were old enough to know better.

Ly. Seest, then, thy true course? never mind me, but leave me as a lunatic to my follies, and you go on your way and accomplish what you have intended all this time.

Her. But you are so masterful, you will not let me make a choice, till I have proved all.

Ly. Why, I confess, you will never get me to budge from that. But when you call me masterful, it seems to me you blame the blameless, as the poet says; for I am myself being dragged along by reason, until you bring up some other reason to release me from durance. And here is reason about to talk more masterfully still, you will see; but I suppose you will exonerate it, and blame me.

Her. What can it be? I am surprised to hear it still has anything in reserve.

64 *Ly.* It says that seeing and going through all philosophies will not suffice, if you want to choose the best of them; the most important qualification is still missing.

Her. Indeed? Which?

Ly. Why (bear with me), a critical investigating faculty, mental acumen, intellectual precision and independence equal to the occasion; without this, the completest inspection will be useless. Reason insists that the owner of it must further be allowed ample time; he will collect the rival candidates together, and make his choice with long, lingering, repeated deliberation; he will give no heed to the candidate's age, appearance, or repute for wisdom, but perform his functions like the Areopagites, who judge in the darkness of night, so that they must regard not the pleaders, but the pleadings. Then and not till then will you be able to make a sound choice and live a philosopher.

Her. Live? an after life, then. No mortal span will meet your demands; let me see: go the whole round, examine each with care, on that examination form a judgement, on that judgement make a choice, on that choice be a philosopher; so and no otherwise you say the truth may be found.

65 *Ly.* I hardly dare tell you—even that is not exhaustive; I am afraid, after all, the solid basis we thought we had found

was imaginary. You know how fishermen often let down their nets, feel a weight, and pull them up expecting a great haul; when they have got them up with much toil, behold, a stone, or an old pot full of sand. I fear our catch is one of those.

Her. I don't know what this particular net may be; your nets are all round me, anyhow.

Ly. Well, try and get through; providentially, you are as good a swimmer as can be. Now, this is it: granted that we go all round experimenting, and get it done at last, too, I do not believe we shall have solved the elementary question, whether *any* of them has the much-desired; perhaps they are all wrong together.

Her. Oh, come now! not one of *them* right either?

Ly. I cannot tell. Do you think it impossible they may all be deluded, and the truth be something which none of them has yet found?

Her. How can it possibly be?   66

Ly. This way: take a correct number, twenty; suppose, I mean, a man has twenty beans in his closed hand, and asks ten different persons to guess the number; they guess seven, five, thirty, ten, fifteen—various numbers, in short. It is possible, I suppose, that one may be right?

Her. Yes.

Ly. It is not impossible, however, that they may all guess different incorrect numbers, and not one of them suggest twenty beans. What say you?

Her. It is not impossible.

Ly. In the same way, all philosophers are investigating the nature of Happiness; they get different answers, one Pleasure, another Goodness, and so through the list. It is probable that Happiness *is* one of these; but it is also not improbable that it is something else altogether. We seem to have reversed the proper procedure, and hurried on to the end before we had found the beginning. I suppose we ought first to have ascertained that the truth has actually been discovered, and that some philosopher or other has it, and only then to have gone on to the next question, *which* of them is to be believed.

Her. So that, even if we go all through all philosophy, we shall have no certainty of finding the truth even then ; that is what you say.

Ly. Please, please do not ask *me* ; once more, apply to reason itself. Its answer will perhaps be that there can be no certainty yet—as long as we cannot be sure that it is one or other of the things they say it is.

67   *Her.* Then, according to you, we shall never finish our quest nor be philosophers, but have to give it up and live the life of laymen. What you say amounts to that : philosophy is impossible and inaccessible to a mere mortal ; for you expect the aspirant first to choose the best philosophy ; and you considered that the only guarantee of such choice's being correct was to go through all philosophy before choosing the truest. Then in reckoning the number of years required by each you spurned all limits, extended the thing to several generations, and made out the quest of truth too long for the individual life ; and now you crown all by proving success doubtful even apart from all that ; you say it is uncertain whether the philosophers have ever found truth at all.

Ly. Could you state on oath that they have ?

Her. Not on oath, no.

Ly. And yet there is much that I have intentionally spared you, though it merits careful examination too.

68   *Her.* For instance ?

Ly. Is it not said that, among the professed Stoics, Platonists, and Epicureans, some do know their respective doctrines, and some do not (without prejudice to their general respectability) ?

Her. That is true.

Ly. Well, don't you think it will be a troublesome business to distinguish the first, and know them from the ignorant professors ?

Her. Very.

Ly. So, if you are to recognize the best of the Stoics, you will have to go to most, if not all, of them, make trial, and appoint the best your teacher, first going through a course of training to provide you with the appropriate critical faculty ; otherwise you might mistakenly prefer the wrong one. Now reflect on the additional time this will mean ; I purposely left it out of account, because I was afraid you might be angry ; all the same, it is the most important and necessary thing of all in questions like this—so uncertain and dubious, I mean. For the discovery of truth, your one and only sure or well-founded hope is the possession of this power : you *must* be able to judge and sift truth from falsehood ; you must have the assayer's sense for sound and true or forged coin ; if you could have come to your examination of doctrines equipped with a technical skill like that, I should have nothing to say ; but without it there is nothing to prevent their severally leading you by the nose ; you will follow a dangled bunch of carrots like a donkey ; or, better still, you will be water spilt on a table, trained whichever way one chooses with a finger-tip ; or again, a reed growing on a river's bank, bending to every breath, however gentle the breeze that shakes it in its passage.

If you could find a teacher, now, who understood demonstra- 69 tion and controversial method, and would impart his knowledge to you, you would be quit of your troubles ; the best and the true would straightway be revealed to you, at the bidding of this art of demonstration, while falsehood would stand convicted ; you would make your choice with confidence ; judgement would be followed by philosophy ; you would reach your long-desired Happiness, and live in its company, which sums up all good things.

Her. Thank you, Lycinus; that is a much better hearing; there is more than a glimpse of hope in that. We must surely look for a man of that sort, to give us discernment, judgement, and, above all, the power of demonstration; then all will be easy and clear, and not too long. I am grateful to you already for thinking of this short and excellent plan.

Ly. Ah, no, I cannot fairly claim gratitude yet. I have not discovered or revealed anything that will bring you nearer your hope; on the contrary, we are further off than ever; it is a case of much cry and little wool.

Her. Bird of ill omen, pessimist, explain yourself.

70 *Ly.* Why, my friend, even if we find some one who claims to know this art of demonstration, and is willing to impart it, we shall surely not take his word for it straight off; we shall look about for another man to resolve us whether the first is telling the truth. Finding number two, we shall still be uncertain whether our guarantor really knows the difference between a good judge and a bad, and shall need a number three to guarantee number two; for how can we possibly know ourselves how to select the best judge? You see how far this must go; the thing is unending; its nature does not allow us to draw the line and put a stop to it; for you will observe that all the demonstrations that can possibly be thought of are themselves unfounded and open to dispute; most of them struggle to establish their certainty by appealing to facts as questionable as themselves; and the rest produce certain truisms with which they compare, quite illegitimately, the most speculative theories, and then say they have demonstrated the latter: our eyes tell us there are altars to the Gods; therefore there must be Gods; that is the sort of thing.

71 *Her.* How unkindly you treat me, Lycinus, turning my treasure into ashes; I suppose all these years are to have been lost labour.

Ly. At least your chagrin will be considerably lessened by the
thought that you are not alone in your disappointment; practically all who pursue philosophy do no more than disquiet
themselves in vain. Who could conceivably go through all the
stages I have rehearsed ? you admit the impossibility yourself.
As to your present mood, it is that of the man who cries and
curses his luck because he cannot climb the sky, or plunge into
the depths of the sea at Sicily and come up at Cyprus, or soar
on wings and fly within the day from Greece to India; what is
responsible for his discontent is his basing of hopes on a dream-
vision or his own wild fancy, without ever asking whether his
aspirations were realizable or consistent with humanity. You
too, my friend, have been having a long and marvellous dream;
and now reason has stuck a pin into you and startled you out of
your sleep; your eyes are only half open yet, you are reluctant
to shake off a sleep which has shown you such fair visions, and
so you scold. It is just the condition of the day-dreamer; he
is rolling in gold, digging up treasure, sitting on his throne, or
somehow at the summit of bliss; for dame *How-I-wish* is a
lavish facile Goddess, that will never turn a deaf ear to her
votary, though he have a mind to fly, or change statures with
Colossus, or strike a gold-reef; well, in the middle of all this,
in comes his servant with some every-day question, wanting to
know where he is to get bread, or what he shall say to the
landlord, tired of waiting for his rent; and then he flies into
a temper, as though the intrusive questioner had robbed him
of all his bliss, and is ready to bite the poor fellow's nose off.

As you love me, do not treat me like that. I see you digging 72
up treasure, spreading your wings, nursing extravagant ideas,
indulging impossible hopes; and I love you too well to leave you
to the company of a life-long dream—a pleasant one, if you will,
but yet a dream; I beseech you to get up and take to some
every-day business, such as may direct the rest of your life's

course by common sense. Your acts and your thoughts up
to now have been no more than Centaurs, Chimeras, Gorgons, or what else is figured by dreams and poets and painters,
chartered libertines all, who reck not of what has been or may
be. Yet the common folk believe them, bewitched by tale and
picture just because they are strange and monstrous.

73 I fancy you hearing from some teller of tales how there is
a certain lady of perfect beauty, beyond the Graces themselves
or the Heavenly Aphrodite, and then, without ever an inquiry
whether his tale is true, and such a person to be found on earth,
falling straight in love with her, like Medea in the story en-
amoured of a dream-Jason. And what most drew you on to
love, you and the others who worship the same phantom, was,
if I am not mistaken, the consistent way in which the inventor
of the lady added to his picture, when once he had got your
ear. That was the only thing you all looked to, with that he
turned you about as he would, having got his first hold upon
you, averring that he was leading you the straight way to your
beloved. After the first step, you see, all was easy ; none of
you ever looked round when he came to the entrance, and
inquired whether it was the right one, or whether he had
accidentally taken the wrong ; no, you all followed in your
predecessors' footsteps, like sheep after the bell-wether, whereas
the right thing was to decide at the entrance whether you
should go in.

74 Perhaps an illustration will make my meaning clearer : when
one of those audacious poets affirms that there was once a three-
headed and six-handed man, if you accept that quietly without
questioning its possibility, he will proceed to fill in the picture
consistently—six eyes and ears, three voices talking at once, three
mouths eating, and thirty fingers instead of our poor ten all told ;
if he has to fight, three of his hands will have a buckler, wicker
targe, or shield apiece, while of the other three one swings an

axe, another hurls a spear, and the third wields a sword. It is too late to carp at these details, when they come ; they are consistent with the beginning ; it was about that that the question ought to have been raised whether it was to be accepted and passed as true. Once grant that, and the rest comes flooding in, irresistible, hardly now susceptible of doubt, because it is consistent and accordant with your initial admissions. That is just your case ; your love-yearning would not allow you to look into the facts at each entrance, and so you are dragged on by consistency ; it never occurs to you that a thing may be self-consistent and yet false ; if a man says twice five is seven, and you take his word for it without checking the sum, he will naturally deduce that four times five is fourteen, and so on *ad libitum*. This is the way that weird geometry proceeds : it sets before beginners certain strange assumptions, and insists on their granting the existence of inconceivable things, such as points having no parts, lines without breadth, and so on, builds on these rotten foundations a superstructure equally rotten, and pretends to go on to a demonstration which is true, though it starts from premisses which are false.

Just so you, when you have granted the principles of any 75 school, believe in the deductions from them, and take their consistency, false as it is, for a guarantee of truth. Then with some of you, hope travels through, and you die before you have seen the truth and detected your deceivers, while the rest, disillusioned too late, will not turn back for shame : what, confess at their years that they have been abused with toys all this time ? so they hold on desperately, putting the best face upon it and making all the converts they can, to have the consolation of good company in their deception ; they are well aware that to speak out is to sacrifice the respect and superiority and honour they are accustomed to ; so they will not do it if it may be helped, knowing the height from which they will fall to the common level. Just a few are found with the courage to say they were deluded, and warn other aspirants. Meeting such a one, call him a good man, a true and an honest; nay, call him philosopher, if you will; to my mind, the name is his or no one's; the rest either have no knowledge of the truth, though they think they have, or else have knowledge and hide it, shamefaced cowards clinging to reputation.

76 But now for goodness' sake let us drop all this, cover it up with an amnesty, and let it be as if it had not been said; let us assume that the Stoic philosophy, and no other, is correct; then we can examine whether it is practicable and possible, or its disciples wasting their pains; it makes wonderful promises, I am told, about the Happiness in store for those who reach the summit; for none but they shall enter into full possession of the true Good. The next point you must help me with— whether you have ever met such a Stoic, such a pattern of Stoicism, as to be unconscious of pain, untempted by pleasure, free from wrath, superior to envy, contemptuous of wealth, and, in one word, Happy; such should the example and model of the Virtuous life be; for any one who falls short in the slightest degree, even though he is better than other men at all points, is not complete, and in that case not yet Happy.

77 *Her.* I never saw such a man.

Ly. I am glad you do not palter with the truth. But what are your hopes in pursuing philosophy, then? You see that neither your own teacher, nor his, nor his again, and so on to the tenth generation, has been absolutely wise and so attained Happiness. It will not serve you to say that it is enough to get near Happiness; that is no good; a person on the doorstep is just as much outside and in the air as another a long way off, though with the difference that the former is tantalized by a nearer view. So it is to get into the neighbourhood of Happiness—I will grant you so much—that you toil like this, wearing yourself away, letting this great portion of your life slip from you, while you are sunk in dullness and wakeful weariness ; and you are to go on with it for twenty more years at the least, you tell me, to take your place when you are eighty—always assuming some one to assure you that length of days—in the ranks of the not yet Happy. Or perhaps you reckon on being the exception ; you are to crown your pursuit by attaining what many a good man before you, swifter far, has pursued and never overtaken.

Well, overtake it, if that is your plan, grasp it and have it 78 whole, this something, mysterious to me, of which the possession is sufficient reward for such toils ; this something which I wonder how long you will have the enjoyment of, old man that you will be, past all pleasure, with one foot in the grave ; ah, but perhaps, like a brave soul, you are getting ready for another life, that you may spend it the better when you come to it, having learned how to live : as though one should take so long preparing and elaborating a superlative dinner that he fainted with hunger and exhaustion !

However, there is another thing I do not think you have 79 observed : Virtue is manifested, of course, in action, in doing what is just and wise and manly ; but you—and when I say you, I mean the most advanced philosophers—you do not seek these things and ensue them, but spend the greater part of your life conning over miserable sentences and demonstrations and problems ; it is the man who does best at these that you hail a glorious victor. And I believe that is why you admire this experienced old professor of yours : he nonplusses his associates, knows how to put crafty questions and inveigle you into pitfalls ; so you pay no attention to the fruit—which consists in action—, but are extremely busy with the husks, and smother each other with the leaves in your debates ; come now, Hermotimus, what else are you about from morning to night ?

Her. Nothing; that is what it comes to.

Ly. Is it wronging you to say that you hunt the shadow or the snake's dead slough, and neglect the solid body or the creeping thing itself? You are no better than a man pouring water into a mortar and braying it with an iron pestle; he thinks he is doing a necessary useful job, whereas, let him bray till all 's blue (excuse the slang), the water is as much water as ever it was.

80   And here let me ask you whether, putting aside his discourse, you would choose to resemble your master, and be as passionate, as sordid, as quarrelsome, ay, and as addicted to pleasure (though that trait of his is not generally known). Why no answer, Hermotimus? Shall I tell you a plea for philosophy which I lately heard? It was from the mouth of an old, old man, who has quite a company of young disciples. He was angrily demanding his fees from one of these; they were long overdue, he said; the day stated in the agreement was the first of the month, and it was now the fifteenth.

81   The youth's uncle was there, a rustic person without any notion of your refinements; and by way of stilling the storm, *Come, come, sir,* says he, *you need not make such a fuss because we have bought words of you and not yet settled the bill. As to what you have sold us, you have got it still; your stock of learning is none the less; and in what I really sent the boy to you for, you have not improved him a bit; he has carried off and seduced neighbour Echecrates's daughter, and there would have been an action for assault, only Echecrates is a poor man; but the prank cost me a couple of hundred. And the other day he struck his mother; she had tried to stop him when he was smuggling wine out of the house, for one of his club-dinners, I suppose. As to temper and conceit and impudence and brass and lying, he was not half so bad twelve months ago as he is now. That is where I should have liked him to profit by your teaching; and we could have done without his knowing the stuff he reels off at table every day: ' a*

crocodile [1] *seized hold of a baby,' says he, ' and promised to give
it back if its father could answer'—the Lord knows what ; or
how, ' day [1] being, night cannot be ' ; and sometimes his worship
twists round what we say somehow or other, till there we are with
horns [1] on our heads ! We just laugh at it—most of all when he
stuffs up his ears and repeats to himself what he calls temperaments
and conditions and conceptions and impressions, and a lot more like
that. And he tells us God is not in heaven, but goes about in everything, wood and stone and animals—the meanest of them, too ; and
if his mother asks him why he talks such stuff, he laughs at her and
says if once he gets the 'stuff' pat off, there will be nothing to
prevent him from being the only rich man, the only king, and counting every one else slaves and offscourings.*

When he had finished, mark the reverend philosopher's
answer. *You should consider,* he said, *that if he had never come
to me, he would have behaved far worse—very possibly have come
to the gallows. As it is, philosophy and the respect he has for it
have been a check upon him, so that you find he keeps within bounds
and is not quite unbearable ; the philosophic system and name tutor
him with their presence, and the thought of disgracing them shames
him. I should be quite justified in taking your money, if not for
any positive improvement I have effected, yet for the abstentions
due to his respect for philosophy ; the very nurses will tell you as
much : children should go to school, because, even if they are not
old enough to learn, they will at least be out of mischief there. My
conscience is quite easy about him ; if you like to select any of
your friends who is acquainted with Stoicism and bring him here
to-morrow, you shall see how the boy can question and answer,
how much he has learnt, how many books he has read on axioms,
syllogisms, conceptions, duty, and all sorts of subjects. As for
his hitting his mother or seducing girls, what have I to do with
that ? am I his keeper ?*

[1] See *Puzzles* in Notes.

83   A dignified defence of philosophy for an old man! Perhaps *you* will say too that it is a good enough reason for pursuing it, if it will keep us from worse employments. Were our original expectations from philosophy at all of a different nature, by the way? did they contemplate anything beyond a more decent behaviour than the average? Why this obstinate silence?

Her. Oh, why but that I could cry like a baby? It cuts me to the heart, it is all so true; it is too much for me, when I think of my wretched, wasted years—paying all that money for my own labour, too! I am sober again after a debauch, I see what the object of my maudlin affection is like, and what it has brought upon me.

84   *Ly.* No need for tears, dear fellow; that is a very sensible fable of Aesop's. A man sat on the shore and counted the waves breaking; missing count, he was excessively annoyed. But the fox came up and said to him: 'Why vex yourself, good sir, over the past ones? you should let them go, and begin counting afresh.' So you, since this is your mind, had better reconcile yourself now to living like an ordinary man; you will give up your extravagant haughty hopes and put yourself on a level with the commonalty; if you are sensible, you will not be ashamed to unlearn in your old age, and change your course for a better.

85   Now I beg you not to fancy that I have said all this as an anti-Stoic, moved by any special dislike of your school; my arguments hold against all schools. I should have said just the same if you had chosen Plato or Aristotle, and condemned the others unheard. But, as Stoicism was your choice, the argument has seemed to be aimed at that, though it had no such special application.

86   *Her.* You are quite right. And now I will be off to metamorphose myself. When we next meet, there will be no long, shaggy beard, no artificial composure; I shall be natural, as

a gentleman should. I may go as far as a fashionable coat, by way of publishing my renunciation of nonsense. I only wish there were an emetic that would purge out every doctrine they have instilled into me; I assure you, if I could reverse Chrysippus's plan with the hellebore, and drink forgetfulness, not of the world but of Stoicism, I would not think twice about it. Well, Lycinus, I owe you a debt indeed; I was being swept along in a rough turbid torrent, unresisting, drifting with the stream; when lo, you stood there and fished me out, a true *deus ex machina*. I have good enough reason, I think, to shave my head like the people who get clear off from a wreck; for I am to make votive offerings to-day for the dispersion of that thick cloud which was over my eyes. Henceforth, if I meet a philosopher on my walks (and it will not be with my will), I shall turn aside and avoid him as I would a mad dog.

H.

HERODOTUS AND AËTION

I DEVOUTLY wish that Herodotus's other characteristics were imitable; not all of them, of course—that is past praying for—, but any one of them: the agreeable style, the constructive skill, the native charm of his Ionic, the sententious wealth, or any of a thousand beauties which he combined into one whole, to the despair of imitators. But there is one thing—the use he made of his writings, and the speed with which he attained the respect of all Greece; from that you, or I, or any one else, might take a hint. As soon as he had sailed from his Carian home for Greece, he concentrated his thoughts on the quickest and easiest method of winning a brilliant reputation for himself and his works. He might have gone the round, and read them successively at Athens, Corinth, Argos, and Sparta; but that would be a long toilsome business, he thought, with no end to it; so he would not do it in detail, collecting his recognition by degrees, and scraping it together little by little; his idea was, if possible, to catch all Greece together. The great Olympic Games were at hand, and Herodotus bethought him that here was the very occasion on which his heart was set. He seized the moment when the gathering was at its fullest, and every city had sent the flower of its citizens; then he appeared in the temple hall, bent not on sight-seeing, but on bidding for an Olympic victory of his own; he recited his *Histories*, and bewitched his hearers; nothing would do but each book must be named after one of the Muses, to whose number they corresponded.

2   He was straightway known to all, better far than the Olympic winners. There was no man who had not heard his name; they had listened to him at Olympia, or they were told of him by those who had been there; he had only to appear, and fingers were pointing at him: 'There is the great Herodotus, who wrote the Persian War in Ionic, and celebrated our victories.' That was what he made out of his *Histories*; a single meeting sufficed, and he had the general unanimous acclamation of all Greece; his name was proclaimed, not by a single herald; every spectator did that for him, each in his own city.

3   The royal road to fame was now discovered; it was the regular practice of many afterwards to deliver their discourses at the festival; Hippias the rhetorician was on his own ground there; but Prodicus came from Ceos, Anaximenes from Chios, Polus from Agrigentum; and a rapid fame it brought, to them and many others.

4   However, I need not have cited ancient rhetoricians, historians, and chroniclers like these; in quite recent times the painter Aëtion is said to have brought his picture, *Nuptials of Roxana and Alexander*, to exhibit at Olympia; and Proxenides, High Steward of the Games on the occasion, was so delighted with his genius that he gave him his daughter.

It must have been a very wonderful picture, I think I hear 5
some one say, to make the High Steward give his daughter to
a stranger. Well, I have seen it—it is now in Italy—, so I can
tell you. A fair chamber, with the bridal bed in it; Roxana
seated—and a great beauty she is—with downcast eyes, troubled
by the presence of Alexander, who is standing. Several smiling
Loves; one stands behind Roxana, pulling away the veil on her
head to show her to Alexander; another obsequiously draws
off her sandal, suggesting bed-time; a third has hold of Alexander's mantle, and is dragging him with all his might towards
Roxana. The King is offering her a garland, and by him as sup-
porter and groom's-man is Hephaestion, holding a lighted torch
and leaning on a very lovely boy; this is Hymenaeus, I conjecture, for there are no letters to show. On the other side
of the picture, more Loves playing among Alexander's armour;
two are carrying his spear, as porters do a heavy beam; two
more grasp the handles of the shield, tugging it along with
another reclining on it, playing king, I suppose; and then
another has got into the breast-plate, which lies hollow part
upwards; he is in ambush, and will give the royal equipage
a good fright when it comes within reach.

All this is not idle fancy, on which the painter has been 6
lavishing needless pains; he is hinting that Alexander has also
another love, in War; though he loves Roxana, he does not
forget his armour. And, by the way, there was some extra
nuptial virtue in the picture itself, outside the realm of fancy;
for it did Aëtion's wooing for him. He departed with a wedding
of his own as a sort of pendant to that of Alexander; *his* groom's-
man was the King; and the price of his marriage-piece was a
marriage.

Herodotus, then (to return to him), thought that the Olympic 7
festival would serve a second purpose very well—that of revealing
to the Greeks a wonderful historian who had related their vic-

tories as he had done. As for me—and in Heaven's name do
not suppose me so beside myself as to intend any comparison
between my works and his; I desire his favour too much for
that—but one experience I have in common with him. On
my first visit to Macedonia, *my* thoughts too were busy with
my best policy. My darling wish was to be known to you all,
and to exhibit my writings to as many Macedonians as might
be; I decided that it would be too great an undertaking at
such a time of year to go round in person visiting city by city;
but if I seized the occasion of this your meeting, appeared before
you all, and delivered my discourse, my aspirations, I thought,
might be realized that way.

8   And now here are you met together, the *élite* of every city,
the true soul of Macedonia; the town which lodges you is the
chief of all, little enough resembling Pisa, with its crowding, its
tents and hovels and stifling heat; there is as great a difference
between this audience and that promiscuous crowd, mainly
intent upon mere athletics, and thinking of Herodotus only as
a stop-gap; here we have orators, historians, professors, the first
in each kind—that is much in itself; my arena, it seems, need
not suffer from comparison with Olympia. And though, if you
insist on matching me with the Polydamases, Glauceses, and
Milos of literature, you must think me a very presumptuous
person, it is open to you on the other hand to put them out of
your thoughts altogether; and if you strip and examine me
independently, you may decide that at least I need not be
whipped [1]. Considering the nature of the contest, I may well
be satisfied with that measure of success.   H.

---

[1] Cf. *Remarks addressed to an Illiterate Book-fancier*, 9.

ZEUXIS AND ANTIOCHUS

I was lately walking home after lecturing, when a number of my audience (you are now my friends, gentlemen, and there can be no objection to my telling you this)—these persons, then, came to me and introduced themselves, with the air of admiring hearers. They accompanied me a considerable way, with such laudatory exclamations that I was reduced to blushing at the discrepancy between praise and thing praised. Their chief point, which they were absolutely unanimous in emphasizing, was that the substance of my work was so fresh, so crammed with novelty. I had better give you their actual phrases : ' How new! What paradoxes, to be sure! What invention the man has! His ideas are quite unequalled for originality.' They said a great deal of this sort about my fascinating lecture, as they called it ; they could have had no motive for pretending, or addressing such flatteries to a stranger who had no independent claims on their attention.

These commendations, to be quite frank, were very far from gratifying to me ; when at length they left me to myself, my reflections took this course :—*So the only attraction in my work is that it is unusual, and does not follow the beaten track ; good vocabulary, orthodox composition, insight, subtlety, Attic grace, general constructive skill—these may for aught I know be completely wanting ; else indeed they would hardly have left them unnoticed, and approved my method only as new and startling. Fool that I was, I did indeed guess, when they jumped up to applaud, that novelty was* part *of the attraction ; I knew that Homer spoke truly when he said there is favour for the new song ; but I did not see that novelty was to have so vast a share—the whole, indeed—of the credit ; I thought it gave a sort of adventitious charm, and*

contributed its part to the success, but that the real object of com-
mendation—what extracted the cheers—was those other qualities.
Why, I have been absurdly self-satisfied, and come very near
believing them when they called me the one and only real Greek,
and such nonsense. But behold, my gold is turned to ashes ; my
fame, after all, is little different from that enjoyed by a conjuror.

3   Now I should like to give you an illustration from painting.
The great Zeuxis, after he had established his artistic supremacy,
seldom or never painted such common popular subjects as Heroes,
Gods, and battle-pieces ; he was always intent on novelty ; he
would hit upon some extravagant and strange design, and then
use it to show his mastery of the art. One of these daring
pieces of his represented a female Centaur, nursing a pair of
infant Centaur twins. There is a copy of the picture now at
Athens, taken exactly from the original. The latter is said to
have been put on ship-board for Italy with the rest of Sulla's
art treasures, and to have been lost with them by the sinking
of the ship, off Malea, I think it was. The picture of the
picture I have seen, and the best word-picture I can manage
of that I am now to give you ; I am no connoisseur, you must
understand, but I have a vivid recollection of it as I saw it in
an Athenian studio not long ago ; and my warm admiration
of it as a work of art may perhaps inspire me with a clear description.

4   On fresh green-sward appears the mother Centaur, the whole
equine part of her stretched on the ground, her hoofs extended
backwards ; the human part is slightly raised on the elbows ;
the fore feet are not extended like the others, for she is only
partially on her side ; one of them is bent as in the act of kneel-
ing, with the hoof tucked in, while the other is beginning to
straighten and take a hold on the ground—the action of a horse
rising. Of the cubs she is holding one in her arms suckling it
in the human fashion, while the other is drawing at the mare's

dug like a foal. In the upper part of the picture, as on higher ground, is a Centaur who is clearly the husband of the nursing mother ; he leans over laughing, visible only down to the middle of his horse body ; he holds a lion whelp aloft in his right hand, terrifying the youngsters with it in sport.

There are no doubt qualities in the painting which evade 5 analysis by a mere amateur, and yet involve supreme craftsman-ship—such things as precision of line, perfect mastery of the palette, clever brush-work, management of shadow, perspective, proportion, and relation of the parts to the whole ; but I leave all that to the professionals whose business it is to appreciate it ; what strikes *me* especially about Zeuxis is the manifold scope which he has found for his extraordinary skill, in a single subject. You have in the husband a truly terrible savage creature ; his locks toss about, he is almost covered with hair, human part as well as equine ; the shoulders high to monstro-sity ; the look, even in his merry mood, brutal, uncivilized, wild.

In contrast with him, the animal half of the female is lovely ; 6 a Thessalian filly, yet unbroken and unbacked, might come nearest ; and the human upper half is also most beautiful, with the one exception of the ears, which are pointed as in a satyr. At the point of junction which blends the two natures, there is no sharp line of division, but the most gradual of transitions ; a touch here, a trait there, and you are surprised to find the change complete. It was perfectly wonderful, again, to see the combination of wildness and infancy, of terrible and tender, in the young ones, looking up in baby curiosity at the lion-cub, while they held on to breast and dug, and cuddled close to their dam.

Zeuxis imagined that when the picture was shown the tech- 7 nique of it would take visitors by storm. Well, they did acclaim him ; they could hardly help that, with such a masterpiece before them; but their commendations were all in the style of those given to me the other night; it was the strangeness of the idea, the fresh unhackneyed sentiment of the picture, and so on. Zeuxis saw that they were preoccupied with the novelty of his subject, art was at a discount, and truth of rendering quite a minor matter. 'Oh, pack it up, Miccio,' he said to his pupil, 'and you and the others take it home; these people are delighted with the earthy part of the work; the questions of its aim, its beauty, its artistic merit, are of no importance whatever; novelty of subject goes for much more than truth of rendering.'

8 So said Zeuxis, not in the best of tempers. Antiochus Soter had a somewhat similar experience about his battle with the Galatians. If you will allow me, I propose to give you an account of that event also. These people were good fighters, and on this occasion in great force; they were drawn up in a serried phalanx, the first rank, which consisted of steel-clad warriors, being supported by men of the ordinary heavy-armed type to the depth of four-and-twenty; twenty thousand cavalry held the flanks; and there were eighty scythed, and twice that number of ordinary war chariots ready to burst forth from the centre. These dispositions filled Antiochus with apprehension, and he thought the task was too hard for him. His own preparations had been hurried, on no great scale, and inadequate to the occasion; he had brought quite a small force, mostly of skirmishers and light-armed troops; more than half his men were without defensive armour. He was disposed to negotiate and find some honourable composition.

9 Theodotas of Rhodes, however, a brave and skilful officer, put him in heart again. Antiochus had sixteen elephants; Theodotas advised him to conceal these as well as he could for the present, not letting their superior height betray them; when the signal for battle was given, the shock just at hand,

the enemy's cavalry charging, and their phalanx opening to give free passage to the chariots, then would be the time for the elephants. A section of four was to meet the cavalry on each flank, and the remaining eight to engage the chariot squadron. 'By this means,' he concluded, 'the horses will be frightened, and there will be a stampede into the Galatian infantry.' His anticipations were realized, thus:

Neither the Galatians nor their horses had ever seen an elephant, and they were so taken aback by the strange sight that, long before the beasts came to close quarters, the mere sound of their trumpeting, the sight of their gleaming tusks relieved against dark bodies, and minatory waving trunks, was enough; before they were within bow-shot, the enemy broke and ran in utter disorder; the infantry were spitted on each other's spears, and trampled by the cavalry who came scurrying on to them. The chariots, turning in like manner upon their own friends, whirled about among them by no means harmlessly; it was a Homeric scene of 'rumbling tumbling cars'; when once the horses shied at those formidable elephants, off went the drivers, and 'the lordless chariots rattled on,' their scythes maiming and carving any of their late masters whom they came within reach of; and, in that chaos, many were the victims. Next came the elephants, trampling, tossing, tearing, goring; and a very complete victory they had made of it for Antiochus.

The carnage was great, and all the Galatians were either killed or captured, with the exception of a quite small band which got off to the mountains; Antiochus's Macedonians sang the Paean, gathered round, and garlanded him with acclamations on the glorious victory. But the King—so the story goes—was in tears; 'My men,' he said, 'we have more reason for shame; saved by those sixteen brutes! if their strangeness had not produced the panic, where should we have been?'

And on the trophy he would have nothing carved except just an elephant.

12   Gentlemen, *de me fabula*; are my resources like those of Antiochus—quite unfit for battle on the whole, but including some elephants, some queer impositions, some jugglery, in fact? That is what all the praise I hear points at. The things I really relied upon seem to be of little account; the mere fact that my picture is of a female Centaur exercises fascination; it passes for a novelty and a marvel, as indeed it is. The rest of Zeuxis's pains is thrown away, I suppose. But ah, no, not thrown away; *you* are connoisseurs, and judge by the rules of art. I only hope the show may be worthy of the spectators.

H.

HARMONIDES

'TELL me, Timotheus,' said Harmonides the flute-player one day to his teacher, 'tell me how I may win distinction in my art. What can I do to make myself known all over Greece? Everything but this you have taught me. I have a correct ear, thanks to you, and a smooth, even delivery, and have acquired the light touch so essential to the rendering of rapid measures; rhythmical effect, the adaptation of music to dance, the true character of the different moods—exalted Phrygian, joyous Lydian, majestic Dorian, voluptuous Ionic—all these I have mastered with your assistance. But the prime object of my musical aspirations seems out of my reach: I mean popular esteem, distinction, and notoriety; I would have all eyes turn in my direction, all tongues repeat my name: "There goes Harmonides, the great flute-player." Now when *you* first came from your home in Boeotia, and performed in the *Procne*, and won the prize for your rendering of the *Ajax Furens*, composed by your namesake, there was not a man who did not

know the name of Timotheus of Thebes; and in these days
you have only to show yourself, and people flock together as
birds do at the sight of an owl in daylight. It is for this that
I sought to become a flute-player; this was to be the reward
of all my toil. The skill without the glory I would not take at
a gift, not though I should prove to be a Marsyas or an Olympus
in disguise. What is the use of a light that is to be hidden under
a bushel? Show me then, Timotheus, how I may avail myself
of my powers and of my art. I shall be doubly your debtor:
not for my skill alone, but for the glory that skill confers.'

'Why, really,' says Timotheus, 'it is no such easy matter, 2
Harmonides, to become a public character, or to gain the prestige and distinction to which you aspire; and if you propose
to set about it by performing in public, you will find it a long
business, and at the best will never achieve a universal reputation. Where will you find a theatre or circus large enough to
admit the whole nation as your audience? But if you would
attain your object and become known, take this hint. By all
means perform occasionally in the theatres, but do not concern
yourself with the public. Here is the royal road to fame: get
together a small and select audience of connoisseurs, real experts,
whose praise, whose blame are equally to be relied upon; display
your skill to these; and if you can win *their* approval, you may
rest content that in a single hour you have gained a national
reputation. I argue thus. If you are known to be an admirable
performer by persons who are themselves universally known and
admired, what have you to do with public opinion? Public
opinion must inevitably follow the opinion of the best judges.
The public after all is mainly composed of untutored minds,
that know not good from bad themselves; but when they hear
a man praised by the great authorities, they take it for granted
that he is not undeserving of praise, and praise him accordingly.
It is the same at the games: most of the spectators know

enough to clap or hiss, but the judging is done by some five or six persons.'

Harmonides had no time to put this policy into practice. The story goes that in his first public competition he worked so energetically at his flute, that he breathed his last into it, and expired then and there, before he could be crowned. His first Dionysiac performance was also his last.

3 But Timotheus's remarks need not be confined to Harmonides, nor to his profession : they seem applicable to all whose ambition prompts them to exhibit their talents and to aim at the approbation of the public. Accordingly, when I, like Harmonides, was debating within myself the speediest means of becoming known, I took Timotheus's advice : ' Who,' I asked myself, ' is the foremost man in all this city ? Whose credit is highest with his neighbours ? Who shall be my *multum in parvo* ? ' Only one name could reasonably suggest itself—your own ; which stands for the perfection of every excellence, the glass of culture and the mould of wit. To submit my works to you, to win *your* approbation—if such a thing might be !—were to reach the goal of my desire ; for your suffrage carries the rest with it. Whom, indeed, could I substitute in your place, and hope to preserve a reputation for sanity ? In a sense, no doubt, I shall be hazarding all on one cast of the die : yet with more truth I might be said to have summoned the whole population into one audience-chamber ; for your single judgement must assuredly outweigh the rest, taken individually or collectively. The Spartan kings had two votes each to the ordinary man's one : but you are a whole Privy Council and Senate in yourself. Your influence is unequalled in the Court of Literature, and, above all, yours is the casting-vote of acquittal ; an encouraging thought for me, who might well be uneasy otherwise at the extent of my hardihood. Moreover, I am not wholly without a claim on your interest, as belonging to that city which has

so often enjoyed peculiar benefits at your hand, in addition to
those which it has shared with the nation at large; and this
encourages me to hope that in the present instance, if judgement is going against me, and the votes of acquittal are in
a minority, you will use your prerogative, and make all right
with that casting-vote of yours. I may have had successes, 4
I may have made a name, my lectures may have been well
received:—all this amounts to nothing; it is visionary; it is
a mere bubble. The truth must come to light now; I am
put to a final test; there will be no room for doubt or hesitation after this. It rests with you, whether my literary rank
shall be assured, or my pretensions—but no! with such a con-
test before me, I will abstain from words of evil omen.

Ye Gods, give me approval *here*, and set the seal upon my
reputation! I may then face the world with a light heart:
he who has carried the prize at Olympia need fear no other
course.   F.

THE SCYTHIAN

ANACHARSIS was not the first Scythian who was induced by
the love of Greek culture to leave his native country and visit
Athens: he had been preceded by Toxaris, a man of high ability
and noble sentiments, and an eager student of manners and
customs; but of low origin, not like Anacharsis a member of
the royal family or of the aristocracy of his country, but what
they call 'an eight-hoof man,' a term which implies the possession of a waggon and two oxen. Toxaris never returned to
Scythia, but died at Athens, where he presently came to be
ranked among the Heroes; and sacrifice is still paid to 'the
Foreign Physician,' as he was styled after his deification. Some
account of the significance of this name, the origin of his worship, and his connexion with the sons of Asclepius, will not,

I think, be out of place: for it will be seen from this that the Scythians, in conferring immortality on mortals, and sending them to keep company with Zamolxis, do not stand alone; since the Athenians permit themselves to make Gods of Scythians upon Greek soil.

2   At the time of the great plague, the wife of Architeles the Areopagite had a vision: the Scythian Toxaris stood over her and commanded her to tell the Athenians that the plague would cease if they would sprinkle their back-streets with wine. The Athenians attended to his instructions, and after several sprinklings had been performed, the plague troubled them no more; whether it was that the perfume of the wine neutralized certain noxious vapours, or that the hero, being a medical hero, had some other motive for his advice. However that may be, he continues to this day to draw a fee for his professional services, in the shape of a white horse, which is sacrificed on his tomb. This tomb was pointed out by Dimaenete as the place from which he issued with his instructions about the wine; and beneath it Toxaris was found buried, his identity being established not merely by the inscription, of which only a part remained legible, but also by the figure engraved on the monument, which was that of a Scythian, with a bow, ready strung, in his left hand, and in the right what appeared to be a book. You may still make out more than half the figure, with the bow and book complete: but the upper portion of the stone, including the face, has suffered from the ravages of time. It is situated not far from the Dipylus, on your left as you leave the Dipylus for the Academy. The mound is of no great size, and the pillar lies prostrate: yet it never lacks a garland, and there are statements to the effect that fever-patients have been known to be cured by the hero; which indeed is not surprising, considering that he once healed an entire city.

3   However, my reason for mentioning Toxaris was this. He

was still alive, when Anacharsis landed at Piraeus and made his
way up to Athens, in no small perturbation of spirit; a foreigner
and a barbarian, everything was strange to him, and many things
caused him uneasiness; he knew not what to do with himself;
he saw that every one was laughing at his attire; he could find
no one to speak his native tongue;—in short he was heartily
sick of his travels, and made up his mind that he would just see
Athens, and then retreat to his ship without loss of time, get
on board, and so back to the Bosphorus; once there he had no
great journey to perform before he would be home again. In
this frame of mind he had already reached the Ceramicus, when
his good genius appeared to him in the guise of Toxaris. The
attention of the latter was immediately arrested by the dress
of his native country, nor was it likely that he would have any
difficulty in recognizing Anacharsis, who was of noble birth and
of the highest rank in Scythia. Anacharsis, on the other hand,
could not be expected to see a compatriot in Toxaris, who was
dressed in the Greek fashion, without sword or belt, wore no
beard, and from his fluent speech might have been an Athenian
born; so completely had time transformed him. 'You are
surely Anacharsis, the son of Daucetas?' he said, addressing
him in the Scythian language. Anacharsis wept tears of joy;
he not only heard his mother-tongue, but heard it from one
who had known him in Scythia. 'How comes it, sir, that you
know me?' he asked.

'I too am of that country; my name is Toxaris; but it is
probably not known to you, for I am a man of no family.'

'Are you that Toxaris,' exclaimed the other, 'of whom I
heard that for love of Greece he had left wife and children in
Scythia, and gone to Athens, and was there dwelling in high
honour?'

'What, is my name still remembered among you?—Yes, I
am Toxaris.'

'Then,' said Anacharsis, 'you see before you a disciple, who has caught your enthusiasm for Greece; it was with no other object than this that I set out on my travels. The hardships I have endured in the countries through which I passed on my way hither are infinite; and I had already decided, when I met you, that before the sun set I would return to my ship; so much was I disturbed at the strange and outlandish sights that I have seen. And now, Toxaris, I adjure you by Scimetar and Zamolxis, our country's Gods,—take me by the hand, be my guide, and make me acquainted with all that is best in Athens and in the rest of Greece; their great men, their wise laws, their customs, their assemblies, their constitution, their every-day life. You and I have both travelled far to see these things: you will not suffer me to depart without seeing them?'

5 'What! come to the very door, and then turn back? This is not the language of enthusiasm. However, there is no fear of that—you will not go back, Athens will not let you off so easily. She is not so much at a loss for charms wherewith to detain the stranger: she will take such a hold on you, that you will forget your own wife and children—if you have any. Now I will put you into the readiest way of seeing Athens, ay, and Greece, and the glories of Greece. There is a certain philosopher living here; he is an Athenian, but has travelled a great deal in Asia and Egypt, and held intercourse with the most eminent men. For the rest, he is none of your moneyed men: indeed, he is quite poor; be prepared for an old man, dressed as plainly as could be. Yet his virtue and wisdom are held in such esteem, that he was employed by them to draw up a constitution, and his ordinances form their rule of life. Make this man your friend, study him, and rest assured that in knowing him you know Greece; for he is an epitome of all that is excellent in the Greek character. I can do you no greater service than to introduce you to him.'

'Let us lose no time, then, Toxaris. Take me to him. But 6 perhaps that is not so easily done? He may slight your intercessions on my behalf?'

'You know not what you say. Nothing gives him greater pleasure than to have an opportunity of showing his hospitality to strangers. Only follow me, and you shall see how courteous and benevolent he is, and how devout a worshipper of the God of Hospitality. But stay: how fortunate! here he comes towards us. See, he is wrapped in thought, and mutters to himself.—Solon!' he cried; 'I bring you the best of gifts—a 7 stranger who craves your friendship. He is a Scythian of noble family; but has left all and come here to enjoy the society of Greeks, and to view the wonders of their country. I have hit upon a simple expedient which will enable him to do both, to see all that is to be seen, and to form the most desirable acquaintances: in other words, I have brought him to Solon, who, if I know anything of his character, will not refuse to take him under his protection, and to make him a Greek among Greeks.— It is as I told you, Anacharsis: having seen Solon, you have seen all; behold Athens; behold Greece. You are a stranger no longer: all men know you, all men are your friends; this it is to possess the friendship of the venerable Solon. Conversing with him, you will forget Scythia and all that is in it. Your toils are rewarded, your desire is fulfilled. In him you have the mainspring of Greek civilization, in him the ideals of Athenian philosophers are realized. Happy man—if you know your happiness—to be the friend and intimate of Solon!'

It would take too long to describe the pleasure of Solon at 8 Toxaris's 'gift,' his words on the occasion, and his subsequent intercourse with Anacharsis—how he gave him the most valuable instruction, procured him the friendship of all Athens, showed him the sights of Greece, and took every trouble to make his stay in the country a pleasant one; and how Anacharsis for his part regarded the sage with such reverence, that he was never willingly absent from his side. Suffice it to say, that the promise of Toxaris was fulfilled: thanks to Solon's good offices, Anacharsis speedily became familiar with Greece and with Greek society, in which he was treated with the consideration due to one who came thus strongly recommended; for here too Solon was a lawgiver: those whom he esteemed were loved and admired by all. Finally, if we may believe the statement of Theoxenus, Anacharsis was presented with the freedom of the city, and initiated into the mysteries; nor does it seem likely that he would ever have returned to Scythia, had not Solon died.

9   And now perhaps I had better put the moral to my tale, if it is not to wander about in a headless condition. What are Anacharsis and Toxaris doing here to-day in Macedonia, bringing Solon with them too, poor old gentleman, all the way from Athens? It is time for me to explain. The fact is, my situation is pretty much that of Anacharsis. I crave your indulgence, in venturing to compare myself with royalty. Anacharsis, after all, was a barbarian; and I should hope that we Syrians are as good as Scythians. And I am not comparing myself with Anacharsis the king, but Anacharsis the barbarian. When first I set foot in your city, I was filled with amazement at its size, its beauty, its population, its resources and splendour generally. For a time I was dumb with admiration; the sight was too much for me. I felt like the island lad Telemachus, in the palace of Menelaus; and well I might, as I viewed this city in all her pride;

A garden she, whose flowers are ev'ry blessing.

10   Thus affected, I had to bethink me what course I should adopt. For as to lecturing here, my mind had long been made up about *that*; what other audience could I have in view, that

I should pass by this great city in silence ? To make a clean breast of it, then, I set about inquiring who were your great men ; for it was my design to approach them, and secure their patronage and support in facing the public. Unlike Anacharsis, who had but one informant, and a barbarian at that, I had many ; and all told me the same tale, in almost the same words. ' Sir,' they said, ' we have many excellent and able men in this city—nowhere will you find more : but two there are who stand pre-eminent ; who in birth and in prestige are without a rival, and in learning and eloquence might be matched with the Ten Orators of Athens. They are regarded by the public with feelings of absolute devotion : their will is law ; for they will nothing but the highest interests of the city. Their courtesy, their hospitality towards strangers, their unassuming benevolence, their modesty in the midst of greatness, their gentleness, their affability,—all these you will presently experience, and will have something to say on the subject yourself. But—wonder of wonders !—these two are of one house, II father and son. For the father, conceive to yourself a Solon, a Pericles, an Aristides : as to the son, his manly comeliness and noble stature will attract you at the first glance ; and if he do but say two words, your ears will be taken captive by the charm that sits upon his tongue. When he speaks in public, the city listens like one man, open-mouthed ; 'tis Athens listening to Alcibiades ; yet the Athenians presently repented of their infatuation for the son of Clinias, but here love grows to reverence ; the welfare of this city, the happiness of her citizens, are all bound up in one man. Once let the father and son admit you to their friendship, and the city is yours ; they have but to raise a finger, to put your success beyond a doubt.'—Such, by Heaven (if Heaven must be invoked for the purpose), such was the unvarying report I heard ; and I now know from experience that it fell far short of the truth.

> Then up, nor waste thy days
> In indolent delays,

as the Cean poet cries; I must strain every nerve, work body
and soul, to gain these friends. That once achieved, fair weather
and calm seas are before me, and my haven is near at hand.

F.

THE WAY TO WRITE HISTORY

My dear Philo,

There is a story of a curious epidemic at Abdera, just after
the accession of King Lysimachus. It began with the whole
population's exhibiting feverish symptoms, strongly marked and
unintermittent from the very first attack. About the seventh
day, the fever was relieved, in some cases by a violent flow of
blood from the nose, in others by perspiration not less violent.
The mental effects, however, were most ridiculous; they were
all stage-struck, mouthing blank verse and ranting at the top
of their voices. Their favourite recitation was the *Andromeda*
of Euripides; one after another would go through the great
speech of Perseus; the whole place was full of pale ghosts, who
were our seventh-day tragedians vociferating,

> O Love, who lord'st it over Gods and men,

and the rest of it. This continued for some time, till the coming
of winter put an end to their madness with a sharp frost. I find
the explanation of the form it took in this fact: Archelaus was
then the great tragic actor, and in the middle of the summer,
during some very hot weather, he had played the *Andromeda*
there; most of them took the fever in the theatre, and con-
valescence was followed by a relapse—into tragedy, the *Andromeda* haunting their memories, and Perseus hovering, Gorgon's
head in hand, before the mind's eye.

Well, to compare like with like, the majority of our educated 2
class is now suffering from an Abderite epidemic. They are
not stage-struck, indeed; that would have been a minor infatuation—to be possessed with other people's verses, not bad
ones either; no; but from the beginning of the present excite-
ments—the barbarian war, the Armenian disaster, the succession
of victories—you cannot find a man but is writing history;
nay, every one you meet is a Thucydides, a Herodotus, a Xenophon. The old saying must be true, and war be the father of
all things [1], seeing what a litter of historians it has now teemed
forth at a birth.

Such sights and sounds, my Philo, brought into my head that 3
old anecdote about the Sinopean. A report that Philip was
marching on the town had thrown all Corinth into a bustle;
one was furbishing his arms, another wheeling stones, a third
patching the wall, a fourth strengthening a battlement, every
one making himself useful somehow or other. Diogenes having
nothing to do—of course no one thought of giving *him* a job—
was moved by the sight to gird up his philosopher's cloak and
begin rolling his tub-dwelling energetically up and down the
Craneum; an acquaintance asked, and got, the explanation:
'I do not want to be thought the only idler in such a busy
multitude; I am rolling my tub to be like the rest.'

I too am reluctant to be the only dumb man at so vociferous 4
a season; I do not like walking across the stage, like a 'super',
in gaping silence; so I decided to roll *my* cask as best I could.
I do not intend to write a history, or attempt actual narrative;
I am not courageous enough for that; have no apprehensions
on my account; I realize the danger of rolling the thing over
the rocks, especially if it is only a poor little jar of brittle earthen-
ware like mine; I should very soon knock against some pebble
and find myself picking up the pieces. Come, I will tell you

[1] See note on *Icaromenippus*, 8.

my idea for campaigning in safety, and keeping well out of range.

> Give a wide berth to all that foam and spray,

and to the anxieties which vex the historian—that I shall be wise enough to do; but I propose to give a little advice, and lay down a few principles for the benefit of those who do venture. I shall have a share in their building, if not in the dedicatory inscription; my finger-tips will at least have touched their wet mortar.

5   However, most of them see no need for advice here: *there might as well be an art of talking, seeing, or eating; history-writing is perfectly easy, comes natural, is a universal gift; all that is necessary is the faculty of translating your thoughts into words.* But the truth is—you know it without my telling, old friend—, it is *not* a task to be lightly undertaken, or carried through without effort; no, it needs as much care as any sort of composition whatever, if one means to create 'a possession for ever,' as Thucydides calls it. Well, I know I shall not get a hearing from many of them, and some will be seriously offended —especially any who have finished and produced their work; in cases where its first reception was favourable, it would be folly to expect the authors to recast or correct; has it not the stamp of finality? is it not almost a State document? Yet even they may profit by my words; *we* are not likely to be attacked again; we have disposed of all our enemies; but there might be a Celto-Gothic or an Indo-Bactrian war; then our friends' composition might be improved by the application of my measuring-rod—always supposing that they recognize its correctness; failing that, let them do their own mensuration with the old foot-rule; the doctor will not particularly mind, though all Abdera insists on spouting the *Andromeda*.

6   Advice has two provinces—one of choice, the other of avoid-

ance ; let us first decide what the historian is to avoid—of what faults he must purge himself—, and then proceed to the measures he must take for putting himself on the straight high road. This will include the manner of his beginning, the order in which he should marshal his facts, the questions of proportion, of discreet silence, of full or cursory narration, of comment and connexion. Of all that, however, later on ; for the present we deal with the vices to which bad writers are liable. As to those faults of diction, construction, meaning, and general amateurishness, which are common to every kind of composition, to discuss them is neither compatible with my space nor relevant to my purpose.

But there are mistakes peculiar to history ; your own observa- 7 tion will show you just those which a constant attendance at authors' readings [1] has impressed on me ; you have only to keep your ears open at every opportunity. It will be convenient, however, to refer by the way to a few illustrations in recent histories. Here is a serious fault to begin with. It is the fashion to neglect the examination of facts, and give the space gained to eulogies of generals and commanders ; those of their own side they exalt to the skies, the other side they disparage intemperately. They forget that between history and panegyric there is a great gulf fixed, barring communication ; in musical phrase, the two things are a couple of octaves apart. The panegyrist has only one concern—to commend and gratify his living theme some way or other ; if misrepresentation will serve his purpose, he has no objection to that. History, on the other hand, abhors the intrusion of any least scruple of false-

---

[1] These were very common in Roman Imperial times, for purposes of advertisement, of eliciting criticism, &c. ' The audience at recitations may be compared with the modern literary reviews, discharging the functions of a preventive and emendatory, not merely of a correctional tribunal. Before publication a work might thus be known to more hearers than it would now find readers.' Mayor, *Juvenal*, iii. 9.

hood ; it is like the windpipe, which the doctors tell us will not tolerate a morsel of stray food.

8   Another thing these gentlemen seem not to know is that poetry and history offer different wares, and have their separate rules. Poetry enjoys unrestricted freedom ; it has but one law—the poet's fancy. He is inspired and possessed by the Muses ; if he chooses to horse his car with winged steeds, or set others a-galloping over the sea, or standing corn, none challenges his right ; his Zeus, with a single cord, may haul up earth and sea, and hold them dangling together—there is no fear the cord may break, the load come tumbling down and be smashed to atoms. In a complimentary picture of Agamemnon, there is nothing against his having Zeus's head and eyes, his brother Posidon's chest, Ares's belt—in fact, the son of Atreus and Aërope will naturally be an epitome of all Divinity ; Zeus or Posidon or Ares could not singly or severally provide the requisite perfections. But, if history adopts such servile arts, it is nothing but poetry without the wings ; the exalted tones are missing ; and imposition of other kinds without the assistance of metre is only the more easily detected. It is surely a great, a superlative weakness, this inability to distinguish history from poetry ; what, bedizen history, like her sister, with tale and eulogy and their attendant exaggerations ? as well take some mighty athlete with muscles of steel, rig him up with purple drapery and meretricious ornament, rouge and powder his cheeks ; faugh, what an object would one make of him with such defilements !

9   I would not be understood to exclude eulogy from history altogether ; it is to be kept to its place and used with moderation, is not to tax the reader's patience ; I shall presently show, indeed, that in all such matters an eye is to be had to posterity. It is true, there is a school which makes a pretty division of history into the agreeable and the useful, and defends the intro-

duction of panegyric on the ground that it is agreeable, and pleases the general reader. But nothing could be further from the truth. In the first place the division is quite a false one; history has only one concern and aim, and that is the useful; which again has one single source, and that is truth. The agreeable is no doubt an addition, if it is present; so is beauty to an athlete; but a Nicostratus, who is a fine fellow and proves himself a better man than either of his opponents, gets his recognition as a Heracles, however ugly his face may be; and if one opponent is the handsome Alcaeus himself—handsome enough to make Nicostratus in love with him, says the story—, that does not affect the issue. History too, if it can deal incidentally in the agreeable, will attract a multitude of lovers; but so long as it does its proper business efficiently—and that is the establishment of truth—, it may be indifferent to beauty.

It is further to be remarked, that in history sheer extrava- 10 gance has not even the merit of being agreeable; and the extravagance of eulogy is doubly repulsive, as extravagance, and as eulogy; at least it is only welcome to the vulgar majority, not to that critical, that perhaps hypercritical audience, whom no slip can escape, who are all eyes like Argus, but keener than he, who test every word as a moneychanger might his coins, rejecting the false on the spot, but accepting the good and heavy and true; it is they that we should have in mind as we write history, and never heed the others, though they applaud till they crack their voices. If you neglect the critics, and indulge in the cloying sweetness of tales and eulogies and such baits, you will soon find your history a 'Heracles in Lydia.' No doubt you have seen some picture of him: he is Omphale's slave, dressed up in an absurd costume, his lion-skin and club transferred to her, as though she were the true Heracles, while he, in saffron robe and purple jacket, is combing wool and wincing under Omphale's slipper. A degrading spectacle it is—the dress loose and flapping open, and all that was man in him turned to woman.

11   The vulgar may very likely extend their favour to this; but the select (whose judgement you disregard) will get a good deal of entertainment out of your heterogeneous, disjointed, fragmentary stuff. There is nothing which has not a beauty of its own; but take it out of its proper sphere, and the misuse turns its beauty to ugliness. Eulogy, I need hardly say, may possibly please one person, the eulogized, but will disgust every one else; this is particularly so with the monstrous exaggerations which are in fashion; the authors are so intent on the patron-hunt that they cannot relinquish it without a full exhibition of servility; they have no idea of finesse, never mask their flattery, but blurt out their unconvincing bald tale anyhow.

12   The consequence is, they miss even their immediate end; the objects of their praise are more inclined (and quite right too) to dislike and discard them for toadies—if they are men of spirit, at any rate. Aristobulus inserted in his history an account of a single combat between Alexander and Porus, and selected this passage to read aloud to the former; he reckoned that his best chance of pleasing was to invent heroic deeds for the king, and heighten his achievements. Well, they were on board ship in the Hydaspes; Alexander took hold of the book, and tossed it overboard; 'the author should have been treated the same way, by rights,' he added, 'for presuming to fight duels for me like that, and shoot down elephants single-handed.' A very natural indignation in Alexander, of a piece with his treatment of the intrusive architect; this person offered to convert the whole of Mount Athos into a colossal statue of the king—who however decided that he was a toady, and actually gave him less employment in ordinary than before.

13   The fact is, there is nothing agreeable in these things, except to any one who is fool enough to enjoy commendations which

the slightest inquiry will prove to be unfounded; of course there *are* ugly persons—women more especially—who ask artists to paint them as beautiful as they can; they think they will be really better-looking if the painter heightens the rose a little and distributes a good deal of the lily. There you have the origin of the present crowd of historians, intent only upon the passing day, the selfish interest, the profit which they reckon to make out of their work; execration is their desert—in the present for their undisguised clumsy flattery, in the future for the stigma which their exaggerations bring upon history in general. If any one takes some admixture of the agreeable to be an absolute necessity, let him be content with the independent beauties of style; these are agreeable without being false; but they are usually neglected now, for the better foisting upon us of irrelevant substitutes.

Passing from that point, I wish to put on record some fresh 14 recollections of Ionian histories—supported, now I think of it, by Greek analogies also of recent date—both concerned with the war already alluded to. You may trust my report, the Graces be my witness; I would take oath to its truth, if it were polite to swear on paper. One writer started with invoking the Muses to lend a hand. What a tasteful exordium! How suited to the historic spirit! How appropriate to the style! When he had got a little way on, he compared our ruler to Achilles, and the Parthian king to Thersites; he forgot that Achilles would have done better if he had had Hector instead of Thersites to beat, if there had been a man of might fleeing in front,

> But at his heels a mightier far than he.

He next proceeded to say something handsome about himself, as a fit chronicler of such brilliant deeds. As he got near his point of departure, he threw in a word for his native town of Miletus, adding that he was thus improving on Homer, who never so much as mentioned his birthplace. And he concluded his preface with a plain express promise to advance our cause and personally wage war against the barbarians, to the best of his ability. The actual history, and recital of the causes of hostilities, began with these words :—' The detestable Vologesus (whom Heaven confound !) commenced war on the following pretext.'

15 Enough of him. Another is a keen emulator of Thucydides, and by way of close approximation to his model starts with his own name—most graceful of beginnings, redolent of Attic thyme ! Look at it : ' Crepereius Calpurnianus of Pompeio-polis wrote the history of the war between Parthia and Rome, how they warred one upon the other, beginning with the com-mencement of the war.' After that exordium, what need to describe the rest—what harangues he delivers in Armenia, re-suscitating our old friend the Corcyrean envoy—what a plague he inflicts on Nisibis (which would not espouse the Roman cause), lifting the whole thing bodily from Thucydides—except the Pelasgicum and the Long Walls, where the victims of the earlier plague found shelter ; there the difference ends ; like the other, ' it began in Ethiopia, whence it descended to Egypt,' and to most of the Parthian empire, where it very discreetly remained. I left him engaged in burying the poor Athenians in Nisibis, and knew quite well how he would continue after my exit. Indeed it is a pretty common belief at present that you are writing like Thucydides, if you just use his actual words, *mutatis mutandis* [1]. Ah, and I almost forgot to mention one thing : this same writer gives many names of weapons and mili-tary engines in Latin—*phossa* for trench, *pons* for bridge, and so forth. Just think of the dignity of history, and the Thucydidean style—the Attic embroidered with these Latin words, like a toga relieved and picked out with the purple stripe—so harmonious !

[1] Omitting, with Dindorf, the words which appear in the Teubner text, after emendation, as : μικρὰ ῥάκια, ὅπως καὶ αὐτὸς ἂν φαίης, οὐ δι' αὐτήν.

Another puts down a bald list of events, as prosy and common- 16
place as a private's or a carpenter's or a sutler's diary. However, there is more sense in this poor man's performance ; he
flies his true colours from the first ; he has cleared the ground
for some educated person who knows how to deal with history.
The only fault I have to find with him is that he inscribes his
volumes with a solemnity rather disproportioned to the rank of
their contents—' Parthian History, by Callimorphus, Surgeon of
the 6th Pikemen, volume so-and-so.' Ah, yes, and there is a
lamentable preface, which closes with the remark that, since
Asclepius is the son of Apollo, and Apollo director of the Muses
and patron of all culture, it is very proper for a doctor to write
history. Also, he starts in Ionic, but very soon, for no apparent
reason, abandons it for every-day Greek, still keeping the Ionic
*e*s and *k*s and *ou*s, but otherwise writing like ordinary people—
rather too ordinary, indeed.

Perhaps I should balance him with a philosophic historian ; 17
this gentleman's name I will conceal, and merely indicate his
attitude, as revealed in a recent publication at Corinth. Much
had been expected of him, but not enough ; starting straight
off with the first sentence of the preface, he subjects his readers
to a dialectic catechism, his thesis being the highly philosophic
one, that no one but a philosopher should write history. Very
shortly there follows a second logical process, itself followed by
a third ; in fact the whole preface is one mass of dialectic
figures. There is flattery, indeed, *ad nauseam*, eulogy vulgar
to the point of farce ; but never without the logical trimmings ;
always that dialectical catechism. I confess it strikes me as a
vulgarity also, hardly worthy of a philosopher with so long and
white a beard, when he gives it in his preface as our ruler's
special good fortune that philosophers should consent to record
his actions ; he had better have left us to reach that conclusion
for ourselves—if at all.

18 Again, it would be a sinful neglect to omit the man who begins like this :—' I devise to tell of Romans and Persians ' ; then a little later, ' For 'twas Heaven's decree that the Persians should suffer evils ' ; and again, ' One Osroes there was, whom Hellenes name Oxyroes '—and much more in that style. He corresponds, you see, to one of my previous examples ; only he is a second Herodotus, and the other a second Thucydides.

19 There is another distinguished artist in words—again rather more Thucydidean than Thucydides—, who gives, according to his own idea, the clearest, most convincing descriptions of every town, mountain, plain, or river. I wish my bitterest foe no worse fate than the reading of them. Frigid ? Caspian snows, Celtic ice, are warm in comparison. A whole book hardly suffices him for the Emperor's shield—the Gorgon on its boss, with eyes of blue and white and black, rainbow girdle, and snakes twined and knotted. Why, Vologesus's breeches or his bridle, God bless me, they take up several thousand lines apiece ; the same for the look of Osroes's hair as he swims the Tigris— or what the cave was like that sheltered him, ivy and myrtle and bay clustered all together to shut out every ray of light. You observe how indispensable it all is to the history ; without the scene, how could we have comprehended the action ?

20 It is helplessness about the real essentials, or ignorance of what should be given, that makes them take refuge in word-painting—landscapes, caves, and the like ; and when they do come upon a series of important matters, they are just like a slave whose master has left him his money and made him a rich man ; he does not know how to put on his clothes or take his food properly ; partridges or sweetbreads or hare are served ; but he rushes in, and fills himself up with peasoup or salt fish, till he is fit to burst. Well, the man I spoke of gives the most unconvincing wounds and singular deaths : some one has his big toe injured, and dies on the spot ; the general Priscus calls

out, and seven-and-twenty of the enemy fall dead at the sound. As to the numbers killed, he actually falsifies dispatches; at Europus he slaughters 70,236 of the enemy, while the Romans lose two, and have seven wounded! How any man of sense can tolerate such stuff, I do not know.

Here is another point quite worth mention. This writer has 21 such a passion for unadulterated Attic, and for refining speech to the last degree of purity, that he metamorphoses the Latin names and translates them into Greek; Saturninus figures as Cronius, Fronto must be Phrontis, Titianus Titanius, with queerer transmogrifications yet. Further, on the subject of Severian's death, he accuses all other writers of a blunder in putting him to the sword; he is really to have starved himself to death, as the most painless method; the fact, however, is that it was all over in three days, whereas seven days is the regular time for starvation; are we perhaps to conceive an Osroes waiting about for Severian to complete the process, and putting off his assault till after the seventh day?

Then, Philo, how shall we class the historians who indulge in 22 poetical phraseology? 'The catapult rocked responsive,' they say; 'Loud thundered the breach'; or, somewhere else in this delectable history, 'Thus Edessa was girdled with clash of arms, and all was din and turmoil,' or, 'The general pondered in his heart how to attack the wall.' Only he fills up the interstices with such wretched common lower-class phrases as 'The military prefect wrote His Majesty,' 'The troops were procuring the needful,' 'They got a wash [1] and put in an appearance,' and so on. It is like an actor with one foot raised on a high buskin, and the other in a slipper.

[1] It was suggested in the Introduction that Lucian's criticism is for practical purposes out of date; but Prescott writes: 'He was surrounded by a party of friends, who had *dropped in*, it seems, after mass, to inquire after the state of his health, some of whom had remained to partake of his repast.'

23   You will find others writing brilliant high-sounding prefaces of outrageous length, raising great expectations of the wonders to follow—and then comes a poor little appendix of a—history ; it is like nothing in the world but a child—say the Eros you must have seen in a picture playing in an enormous mask of Heracles or a Titan ; *parturiunt montes*, cries the audience, very naturally. That is not the way to do things ; the whole should be homogeneous and uniform, and the body in proportion to the head—not a helmet of gold, a ridiculous breastplate patched up out of rags or rotten leather, shield of wicker, and pig-skin greaves. You will find plenty of historians prepared to set the Rhodian Colossus's head on the body of a dwarf ; others on the contrary show us headless bodies, and plunge into the facts without exordium. These plead the example of Xenophon, who starts with ' Darius and Parysatis had two children' ; if they only knew it, there is such a thing as a *virtual* exordium, not realized as such by everybody ; but of that hereafter.

24   However, any mistake in mere expression or arrangement is excusable ; but when you come to fancy geography, differing from the other not by miles or leagues, but by whole days' journeys, where is the classical model for that ? One writer has taken so little trouble with his facts—never met a Syrian, I suppose, nor listened to the stray information you may pick up at the barber's—, that he thus locates Europus :—' Europus lies in Mesopotamia, two days' journey from the Euphrates, and is a colony from Edessa.' Not content with that, this enterprising person has in the same book taken up my native Samosata and shifted it, citadel, walls, and all, into Mesopotamia, giving it the two rivers for boundaries, and making them shave past it, all but touching the walls on either side. I suspect you would laugh at me, Philo, if I were to set about convincing you that I am neither Parthian nor Mesopotamian, as this whimsical colony-planter makes me.

By the way, he has also a very attractive tale of Severian, learnt, he assures us on oath, from one of the actual fugitives. According to this, he would not die by the sword, the rope, or poison, but contrived a death which should be tragic and impressive. He was the owner of some large goblets of the most precious glass; having made up his mind to die, he broke the largest of these, and used a splinter of it for the purpose, cutting his throat with the glass. A dagger or a lancet, good enough instruments for a manly and heroic death, he could not come at, forsooth!

Then, as Thucydides composed a funeral oration over the first victims of that old war, our author feels it incumbent on him to do the same for Severian; they all challenge Thucydides, you see, little as he can be held responsible for the Armenian troubles. So he buries Severian, and then solemnly ushers up to the grave, as Pericles's rival, one Afranius Silo, a centurion; the flood of rhetoric which follows is so copious and remarkable that it drew tears from me—ye Graces!—tears of laughter; most of all where the eloquent Afranius, drawing to a close, makes mention, with weeping and distressful moans, of all those costly dinners and toasts. But he is a very Ajax in his conclusion. He draws his sword, gallantly as an Afranius should, and in sight of all cuts his throat over the grave—and God knows it was high time for an execution, if oratory can be felony. The historian states that all the spectators admired and lauded Afranius; as for me, I was inclined to condemn him on general grounds—he had all but given a catalogue of sauces and dishes, and shed tears over the memory of departed cakes—, but his capital offence was that he had not cut the historian-tragedian's throat before he left this life himself.

I assure you, my friend, I could largely increase my list of such offenders; but one or two more will suffice, before proceeding to the second part of my undertaking, the suggestions for improvement. There are some, then, who leave alone, or deal very cursorily with, all that is great and memorable; amateurs and not artists, they have no selective faculty, and loiter over copious laboured descriptions of the veriest trifles; it is as if a visitor to Olympia, instead of examining, commending or describing to his stay-at-home friends the general greatness and beauty of the Zeus, were to be struck with the exact symmetry and polish of its footstool, or the proportions of its shoe, and give all his attention to these minor points.

28   For instance, I have known a man get through the battle of Europus in less than seven whole lines, and then spend twenty mortal hours on a dull and perfectly irrelevant tale about a Moorish trooper. The trooper's name was Mausacas; he wandered up the hills in search of water, and came upon some Syrian yokels getting their lunch; at first they were afraid of him, but when they found he was on the right side, they invited him to share the meal; for one of them had travelled in the Moorish country, having a brother serving in the army. Then come long stories and descriptions of how he hunted there, and saw a great herd of elephants at pasture, and was nearly eaten up by a lion, and what huge fish he had bought at Caesarea. So this quaint historian leaves the terrible carnage to go on at Europus, and lets the pursuit, the forced armistice, the settling of outposts, shift for themselves, while he lingers far into the evening watching Malchion the Syrian cheapen big mackarel at Caesarea; if night had not come all too soon, I dare say he would have dined with him when the fish was cooked. If all this had not been accurately set down in the history, what sad ignorance we should have been left in! The loss to the Romans would have been irreparable, if Mausacas the Moor had got nothing to quench his thirst, and come back fasting to camp. Yet I am wilfully omitting innumerable details of yet greater importance—the arrival of a flute-girl from the next village,

the exchange of gifts (Mausacas's was a spear, Malchion's a brooch), and other incidents most essential to the battle of Europus. It is no exaggeration to say that such writers never give the rose a glance, but devote all their curiosity to the thorns on its stem.

Another entertaining person, who has never set foot outside 29 Corinth, nor travelled as far as its harbour—not to mention seeing Syria or Armenia—, starts with words which impressed themselves on my memory :—' Seeing is believing : I therefore write what I have seen, not what I have been told.' His personal observation has been so close that he describes the Parthian ' Dragons ' (they use this ensign as a numerical formula—a thousand men to the Dragon, I believe) : they are huge live dragons, he says, breeding in Persian territory beyond Iberia ; these are first fastened to great poles and hoisted up aloft, striking terror at a distance while the advance is going on ; then, when the battle begins, they are released and set on the enemy ; numbers of our men, it seems, were actually swallowed by them, and others strangled or crushed in their coils ; of all this he was an eye-witness, taking his observations, however, from a safe perch up a tree. Thank goodness he did not come to close quarters with the brutes ! we should have lost a very remarkable historian, and one who did doughty deeds in this war with his own right hand ; for he had many adventures, and was wounded at Sura (in the course of a stroll from the Craneum to Lerna, apparently). All this he used to read to a Corinthian audience, which was perfectly aware that he had never so much as seen a battle-picture. Why, he did not know one weapon or engine from another ; the names of manœuvres and formations had no meaning for him ; flank or front, line or column, it was all one.

Then there is a splendid fellow, who has boiled down into 30 the compass of five hundred lines (or less, to be accurate) the whole business from beginning to end—campaigns in Armenia, in Syria, in Mesopotamia, on the Tigris, and in Media; and having done it, he calls it a history. His title very narrowly misses being longer than his book: 'An account of the late campaigns of the Romans in Armenia, Mesopotamia, and Media, by Antiochianus, victor at the festival of Apollo'; he had probably won some junior flat race.

31 I have known one writer compile a history of the future, including the capture of Vologesus, the execution of Osroes (he is to be thrown to the lions), and, crowning all, our long-deferred triumph. In this prophetic vein, he sweeps hastily on to the end of his work; yet he finds time for the foundation in Mesopotamia of a city, greatest of the great, and fairest of the fair; he is still debating, however, whether the most appropriate name will be Victoria, Concord, or Peacetown; that is yet unsettled; we must leave the fair city unnamed for the present; but it is already thickly populated—with empty dreams and literary drivellings. He has also pledged himself to an account of coming events in India, and a circumnavigation of the Atlantic; nay, the pledge is half redeemed; the preface to the *India* is complete; the third legion, the Celtic contingent, and a small Moorish division, have crossed the Indus in full force under Cassius; our most original historian will soon be posting us up in their doings—their method of 'receiving elephants,' for instance—in letters dated Muziris or Oxydracae.

32 These people's uneducated antics are infinite; they have no eyes for the noteworthy, nor, if they had eyes, any adequate faculty of expression; invention and fiction provide their matter, and belief in the first word that comes their style; they pride themselves on the number of books they run to, and yet more on their titles; for these again are quite absurd:
—*So-and-so's so many books of Parthian victories; The Parthis*, book I; *The Parthis*, book II—quite a rival to the

Atthis, eh ? Another does it (I have read the book) still more neatly—' *The Parthonicy of Demetrius of Sagalassus*.' I do not wish to ridicule or make a jest of these pretty histories ; I write for a practical purpose : any one who avoids these and similar errors is already well on the road to historical success ; nay, he is almost there, if the logical axiom is correct, that, with incompatibles, denial of the one amounts to affirmation of the other.

Well, I may be told, *you have now a clear field ; the thorns and brambles have all been extirpated, the débris of others' buildings has been carted off, the rough places have been made smooth ; come, do a little construction yourself, and show that you are not only good at destroying, but capable of yourself planning a model, in which criticism itself shall find nothing to criticize.* 33

Well then, my perfect historian must start with two indispensable qualifications ; the one is political insight, the other the faculty of expression ; the first is a gift of nature, which can never be learnt ; the second should have been acquired by long practice, unremitting toil, and loving study of the classics. There is nothing technical here, and no room for any advice of mine ; this essay does not profess to bestow insight and acumen on those who are not endowed with them by nature ; valuable, or invaluable rather, would it have been, if it could recast and modify like that, transmute lead into gold, tin into silver, magnify a Conon or Leotrophides into Titormus or Milo. 34

But what is the function of professional advice ? not the creation of qualities which should be already there, but the indication of their proper use. No trainer, of course,—let him be Iccus, Herodicus, Theon, or who he may—will suggest that he can take a Perdiccas [1] and make an Olympic victor of him, 35

---

[1] Omitting, with Dindorf, a note on Perdiccas which runs thus : 'if Perdiccas it was, and not rather Seleucus's son Antiochus, who was wasted to a shadow by his passion for his step-mother.'

fit to face Theagenes of Thasos or Polydamas of Scotussa; what he *will* tell you is that, given a constitution that will stand training, his system will considerably improve it. So with us—we are not to have every failure cast in our teeth, if we claim to have invented a system for so great and difficult a subject. We do not offer to take the first comer and make a historian of him—only to point out to any one who has natural insight and acquired literary skill certain straight roads (they may or may not be so in reality) which will bring him with less waste of time and effort to his goal.

36   I do not suppose you will object that the man with insight has no need of system and instruction upon the things he is ignorant of; in that case he might have played the harp or flute untaught, and in fact have been omniscient. But, as things are at present, he cannot perform in these ways untaught, though with some assistance he will learn very easily, and soon be able to get along by himself.

37   You now know what sort of a pupil I (like the trainer) insist upon. He must not be weak either at understanding or at making himself understood, but a man of penetration, a capable administrator—potentially, that is,—with a soldierly spirit (which does not however exclude the civil spirit), and some military experience; at the least he must have been in camp, seen troops drilled or manœuvred, know a little about weapons and military engines, the differences between line and column, cavalry and infantry tactics (with the reasons for them), frontal and flank attacks; in a word, none of your armchair strategists relying wholly on hearsay.

38   But first and foremost, let him be a man of independent spirit, with nothing to fear or hope from anybody; else he will be a corrupt judge open to undue influences. If Philip's eye is knocked out at Olynthus by Aster the Amphipolite archer, it is not his business to exclaim, but just to show him as he is;

he is not to think whether Alexander will be annoyed by a circumstantial account of the cruel murder of Clitus at table. If a Cleon has the ear of the assembly, and a monopoly of the tribune, he will not shrink on that account from describing him as a pestilent madman; all Athens will not stop him from dwelling on the Sicilian disaster, the capture of Demosthenes, the death of Nicias, the thirst, the foul water, and the shooting down of the drinkers. He will consider very rightly that no man of sense will blame him for recounting the effects of misfortune or folly in their entirety; he is not the author, but only the reporter of them. If a fleet is destroyed, it is not he who sinks it; if there is a rout, he is not in pursuit—unless perhaps he ought to have prayed for better things, and omitted to do so. Of course, if silence or contradiction would have put matters right, Thucydides might with a stroke of the pen have knocked down the counterwall on Epipolae, sent Hermocrates's trireme to the bottom, let daylight through the accursed Gylippus before he had done blocking the roads with wall and trench, and, finally, have cast the Syracusans into their own quarries and sent the Athenians cruising round Sicily and Italy with Alcibiades's first high hopes still on board. Alas, not Fate itself may undo the work of Fate.

The historian's one task is to tell the thing as it happened. 39 This he cannot do, if he is Artaxerxes's physician [1], trembling before him, or hoping to get a purple cloak, a golden chain, a horse of the Nisaean breed, in payment for his laudations. A fair historian, a Xenophon, a Thucydides, will not accept that position. He may nurse some private dislikes, but he will attach far more importance to the public good, and set the truth high above his hate; he may have his favourites, but he will not spare their errors. For history, I say again, has this and this only for its own; if a man will start upon it, he must

[1] See *Ctesias* in Notes.

sacrifice to no God but Truth; he must neglect all else; his sole rule and unerring guide is this—to think not of those who are listening to him now, but of the yet unborn who shall seek his converse.

40 Any one who is intent only upon the immediate effect may reasonably be classed among the flatterers; and History has long ago realized that flattery is as little congenial to her as the arts of personal adornment to an athlete's training. An anecdote of Alexander is to the point. 'Ah, Onesicritus,' said he, ' how I should like to come to life again for a little while, and see how your stuff strikes people by that time; at present they have good enough reason to praise and welcome it; that is their way of angling for a share of my favour.' On the same principle some people actually accept Homer's history of Achilles, full of exaggerations as it is; the one great guarantee which they recognize of his truth is the fact that his subject was not living; that leaves him no motive for lying.

41 There stands my model, then: fearless, incorruptible, independent, a believer in frankness and veracity; one that will call a spade a spade, make no concession to likes and dislikes, nor spare any man for pity or respect or propriety; an impartial judge, kind to all, but too kind to none; a literary cosmopolite with neither suzerain nor king, never heeding what this or that man may think, but setting down the thing that befell.

42 Thucydides is our noble legislator; he marked the admiration that met Herodotus and gave the Muses' names to his nine books; and thereupon he drew the line which parts a good historian from a bad: our work is to be a possession for ever, not a bid for present reputation; we are not to seize upon the sensational, but bequeath the truth to them that come after; he applies the test of use, and defines the end which a wise historian will set before himself: it is that, should history

ever repeat itself, the records of the past may give present guidance.

Such are to be my historian's principles. As for diction and 43 style, he is not to set about his work armed to the teeth from the rhetorician's arsenal of impetuosity and incisiveness, rolling periods, close-packed arguments, and the rest ; for him a serener mood. His matter should be homogeneous and compact, his vocabulary fit to be understanded of the people, for the clearest possible setting forth of his subject.

For to those marks which we set up for the historic spirit— 44 frankness and truth—corresponds one at which the historic style should first of all aim, namely, a lucidity which leaves nothing obscure, impartially avoiding abstruse out-of-the-way expressions, and the illiberal jargon of the market ; we wish the vulgar to comprehend, the cultivated to commend us. Ornament should be unobtrusive, and never smack of elaboration, if it is not to remind us of over-seasoned dishes.

The historian's spirit should not be without a touch of the 45 poetical ; it needs, like poetry, to employ impressive and exalted tones, especially when it finds itself in the midst of battle array and conflicts by land or sea ; it is then that the poetic gale must blow to speed the vessel on, and help her ride the waves in majesty. But the diction is to be content with *terra firma*, rising a little to assimilate itself to the beauty and grandeur of the subject, but never startling the hearer, nor forgetting a due restraint ; there is great risk at such times of its running wild and falling into poetic frenzy ; and then it is that writers should hold themselves in with bit and bridle ; with them as with horses an uncontrollable temper means disaster. At these times it is best for the spirit to go a-horseback, and the expression to run beside on foot, holding on to the saddle so as not to be outstripped.

As to the marshalling of your words, a moderate compromise 46

is desirable between the harshness which results from separating
what belongs together, and the jingling concatenations—one
may almost call them—which are so common; one extreme is
a definite vice, and the other repellent.

47   Facts are not to be collected at haphazard, but with careful,
laborious, repeated investigation; when possible, a man should
have been present and seen for himself; failing that, he should
prefer the disinterested account, selecting the informants least
likely to diminish or magnify from partiality.   And here comes
the occasion for exercising the judgement in weighing pro-
babilities.

48   The material once complete, or nearly so, an abstract should
be made of it, and a rough draught of the whole work put down,
not yet distributed into its parts; the detailed arrangement
should then be introduced, after which adornment may be
added, the diction receive its colour, the phrasing and rhythm
be perfected.

49   The historian's position should now be precisely that of Zeus
in Homer, surveying now the Mysians', now the Thracian horse-
men's land.   Even so *he* will survey now his own party (telling
us what we looked like to him from his post of vantage), now
the Persians, and yet again both at once, if they come to blows.
And when they are face to face, his eyes are not to be on one
division, nor yet on one man, mounted or afoot—unless it be
a Brasidas leading the forlorn hope, or a Demosthenes repelling
it; his attention should be for the generals first of all; their
exhortations should be recorded, the dispositions they make,
and the motives and plans that prompted them.   When the
engagement has begun, he should give us a bird's-eye view
of it, show the scales oscillating, and accompany pursuers and
pursued alike.

50   All this, however, with moderation; a subject is not to be
ridden to death; no neglect of proportion, no childish engross-

ment, but easy transitions. He should call a halt here, while
he crosses over to another set of operations which demands
attention ; that settled up, he can return to the first set, now
ripe for him ; he must pass swiftly to each in turn, keeping his
different lines of advance as nearly as possible level, fly from
Armenia to Media, thence swoop straight upon Iberia, and
then take wing for Italy, everywhere present at the nick of
time.

He has to make of his brain a mirror, unclouded, bright, and 51
true of surface ; then he will reflect events as they presented
themselves to him, neither distorted, discoloured, nor variable.
Historians are not writing fancy school essays ; what they have
to say is before them, and will get itself said somehow, being
solid fact ; their task is to arrange and put it into words ; they
have not to consider what to say, but how to say it. The historian, we may say, should be like Phidias, Praxiteles, Alcamenes,
or any great sculptor. They similarly did not create the gold,
silver, ivory, or other material they used ; it was ready to
their hands, provided by Athens, Elis, or Argos ; they only made
the model, sawed, polished, cemented, proportioned the ivory,
and plated it with gold ; that was what their art consisted in—
the right arrangement of their material. The historian's business is similar—to superinduce upon events the charm of order,
and set them forth in the most lucid fashion he can manage.
When subsequently a hearer feels as though he were looking at
what is being told him, and expresses his approval, then our
historical Phidias's work has reached perfection, and received
its appropriate reward.

When all is ready, a writer will sometimes start without 52
formal preface, if there is no pressing occasion to clear away
preliminaries by that means, though even then his explanation
of what he is to say constitutes a virtual preface.

When a formal preface is used, one of the three objects to 53 which a public speaker devotes his exordium may be neglected ; the historian, that is, has not to bespeak goodwill—only attention and an open mind. The way to secure the reader's attention is to show that the affairs to be narrated are great in themselves, throw light on Destiny, or come home to his business and bosom ; and as to the open mind, the lucidity in the body of the work, which is to secure that, will be facilitated by a preliminary view of the causes in operation and a precise summary of events.

54 Prefaces of this character have been employed by the best historians—by Herodotus, ' to the end that what befell may not grow dim by lapse of time, seeing that it was great and wondrous, and showed forth withal Greeks vanquishing and barbarians vanquished '; and by Thucydides, ' believing that that war would be great and memorable beyond any previous one ; for indeed great calamities took place during its course.'

55 After the preface, long or short in proportion to the subject, should come an easy natural transition to the narrative ; for the body of the history which remains is nothing from beginning to end but a long narrative ; it must therefore be graced with the narrative virtues—smooth, level, and consistent progress, neither soaring nor crawling, and the charm of lucidity—which is attained, as I remarked above, partly by the diction, and partly by the treatment of connected events. For, though all parts must be independently perfected, when the first is complete the second will be brought into essential connexion with it, and attached like one link of a chain to another ; there must be no possibility of separating them ; no mere bundle of parallel threads ; the first is not simply to be next to the second, but part of it, their extremities intermingling.

56 Brevity is always desirable, and especially where matter is abundant ; and the problem is less a grammatical than a substantial one ; the solution, I mean, is to deal summarily with

all immaterial details, and give adequate treatment to the
principal events ; much, indeed, is better omitted altogether.
Suppose yourself giving a dinner, and extremely well provided ;
there is pastry, game, kickshaws without end, wild boar, hare,
sweetbreads ; well, you will not produce among these a pike,
or a bowl of peasoup, just because they are there in the kitchen ;
you will dispense with such common things.

Restraint in descriptions of mountains, walls, rivers, and the 57
like, is very important ; you must not give the impression that
you are making a tasteless display of word-painting, and ex-
patiating independently while the history takes care of itself.
Just a light touch—no more than meets the need of clearness—,
and you should pass on, evading the snare, and denying yourself all such indulgences. You have the mighty Homer's example in such a case ; poet as he is, he yet hurries past Tantalus
and Ixion, Tityus and the rest of them. If Parthenius, Eu-
phorion, or Callimachus had been in his place, how many lines
do you suppose it would have taken to get the water to Tantalus's lip ; how many more to set Ixion spinning ? Better
still, mark how Thucydides—a very sparing dealer in description—leaves the subject at once, as soon as he has given an idea
(very necessary and useful, too) of an engine or a siege-opera-
tion, of the conformation of Epipolae, or the Syracusan harbour.
It may occur to you that his account of the plague is long ;
but you must allow for the subject ; then you will appreciate
his brevity ; *he* is hastening on ; it is only that the weight of
matter holds him back in spite of himself.

When it comes in your way to introduce a speech, the first 58
requirement is that it should suit the character both of the
speaker and of the occasion ; the second is (once more) lucidity ;
but in these cases you have the counsel's right of showing your
eloquence.

Not so with praise or censure ; these should be sparing, 59

cautious, avoiding hypercriticism and producing proofs, always brief, and never intrusive; historical characters are not prisoners on trial. Without these precautions you will share the ill name of Theopompus, who delights in flinging accusations broadcast, makes a business of the thing in fact, and of himself rather a public prosecutor than a historian.

60   It may occasionally happen that some extraordinary story has to be introduced; it should be simply narrated, without guarantee of its truth, thrown down for any one to make what he can of it; the writer takes no risks and shows no preference.

61   But the general principle I would have remembered—it will ever be on my lips—is this: do not write merely with an eye to the present, that those now living may commend and honour you; aim at eternity, compose for posterity, and from it ask your reward; and that reward?—that it be said of you, 'This was a man indeed, free and free-spoken; flattery and servility were not in him; he was truth all through.' It is a name which a man of judgement might well prefer to all the fleeting hopes of the present.

62   Do you know the story of the great Cnidian architect? He was the builder of that incomparable work, whether for size or beauty, the Pharus tower. Its light was to warn ships far out at sea, and save them from running on the Paraetonia, a spot so fatal to all who get among its reefs that escape is said to be hopeless. When the building was done, he inscribed on the actual masonry his own name, but covered this up with plaster, on which he then added the name of the reigning king. He knew that, as happened later, letters and plaster would fall off together, and reveal the words:

SOSTRATUS SON OF DEXIPHANES OF CNIDUS
ON BEHALF OF ALL MARINERS
TO THE SAVIOUR GODS

He looked not, it appears, to that time, nor to the space of his own little life, but to this time, and to all time, as long as his tower shall stand and his art abide.

So too should the historian write, consorting with Truth and 63 not with flattery, looking to the future hope, not to the gratification of the flattered.

There is your measuring-line for just history. If any one be found to use it, well; I have not written in vain : if none, yet have I rolled my tub on the Craneum.   H.

THE TRUE HISTORY

INTRODUCTION

ATHLETES and physical trainers do not limit their attention to the questions of perfect condition and exercise ; they say there is a time for relaxation also—which indeed they represent as the most important element in training. I hold it equally true for literary men that after severe study they should unbend the intellect, if it is to come perfectly efficient to its next task.

The rest they want will best be found in a course of literature 2 which does not offer entertainment pure and simple, depending on mere wit or felicity, but is also capable of stirring an educated curiosity—in a way which I hope will be exemplified in the following pages. They are intended to have an attraction independent of any originality of subject, any happiness of general design, any verisimilitude in the piling up of fictions. This attraction is in the veiled reference underlying all the details of my narrative ; they parody the cock-and-bull stories of ancient poets, historians, and philosophers ; I have only refrained from adding a key because I could rely upon you to recognize as you read.

Ctesias, son of Ctesiochus of Cnidus, in his work on India and 3 its characteristics, gives details for which he had neither the evidence of his eyes nor of hearsay. Iambulus's *Oceanica* is full of marvels ; the whole thing is a manifest fiction, but at the same time pleasant reading. Many other writers have adopted the same plan, professing to relate their own travels, and describing monstrous beasts, savages, and strange ways of life. The fount and inspiration of their humour is the Homeric Odysseus, entertaining Alcinous's court with his prisoned winds, his men one-eyed or wild or cannibal, his beasts with many heads, and his metamorphosed comrades ; the Phaeacians were simple folk, and he fooled them to the top of their bent.

4 When I come across a writer of this sort, I do not much mind his lying ; the practice is much too well established for that, even with professed philosophers ; I am only surprised at his expecting to escape detection. Now I am myself vain enough to cherish the hope of bequeathing something to posterity ; I see no reason for resigning my right to that inventive freedom which others enjoy ; and, as I have no truth to put on record, having lived a very humdrum life, I fall back on falsehood—but falsehood of a more consistent variety ; for I now make the only true statement you are to expect—that I am a liar. This confession is, I consider, a full defence against all imputations. My subject is, then, what I have neither seen, experienced, nor been told, what neither exists nor could conceivably do so. I humbly solicit my readers' incredulity.

BOOK I

5 Starting on a certain date from the Pillars of Heracles, I sailed with a fair wind into the Atlantic. The motives of my voyage were a certain intellectual restlessness, a passion for novelty, a curiosity about the limits of the ocean and the peoples who might dwell beyond it. This being my design, I provisioned and watered my ship on a generous scale. My crew amounted

to fifty, all men whose interests, as well as their years, corresponded with my own. I had further provided a good supply of arms, secured the best navigator to be had for money, and had the ship—a sloop—specially strengthened for a long and arduous voyage.

For a day and a night we were carried quietly along by the 6 breeze, with land still in sight. But with the next day's dawn the wind rose to a gale, with a heavy sea and a dark sky ; we found ourselves unable to take in sail. We surrendered ourselves to the elements, let her run, and were storm-driven for more than eleven weeks. On the eightieth day the sun came out quite suddenly, and we found ourselves close to a lofty wooded island, round which the waves were murmuring gently, the sea having almost fallen by this time. We brought her to land, disembarked, and after our long tossing lay a considerable time idle on shore ; we at last made a start, however, and leaving thirty of our number to guard the ship I took the other twenty on a tour of inspection.

We had advanced half a mile inland through woods, when we 7 came upon a brazen pillar, inscribed in Greek characters—which however were worn and dim—' Heracles and Dionysus reached this point.' Not far off were two footprints on rock ; one might have been an acre in area, the other being smaller ; and I conjecture that the latter was Dionysus's, and the other Heracles's ; we did obeisance, and proceeded. Before we had gone far, we found ourselves on a river which ran wine ; it was very like Chian ; the stream full and copious, even navigable in parts. This evidence of Dionysus's sojourn was enough to convince us that the inscription on the pillar was authentic. Resolving to find the source, I followed the river up, and discovered, instead of a fountain, a number of huge vines covered with grapes ; from the root of each there issued a trickle of perfectly clear wine, the joining of which made the river. It was well stocked with great fish, resembling wine both in colour and taste; catching and eating some, we at once found ourselves intoxicated; and indeed when opened the fish were full of wine-lees; presently it occurred to us to mix them with ordinary water fish, thus diluting the strength of our spirituous food.

8   We now crossed the river by a ford, and came to some vines of a most extraordinary kind. Out of the ground came a thick well-grown stem; but the upper part was a woman, complete from the loins upward. They were like our painters' representations of Daphne in the act of turning into a tree just as Apollo overtakes her. From the finger-tips sprang vine twigs, all loaded with grapes; the hair of their heads was tendrils, leaves, and grape-clusters. They greeted us and welcomed our approach, talking Lydian, Indian, and Greek, most of them the last. They went so far as to kiss us on the mouth; and whoever was kissed staggered like a drunken man. But they would not permit us to pluck their fruit, meeting the attempt with cries of pain. Some of them made further amorous advances; and two of my comrades who yielded to these solicitations found it impossible to extricate themselves again from their embraces; the man became one plant with the vine, striking root beside it; his fingers turned to vine twigs, the tendrils were all round him, and embryo grape-clusters were already visible on him.

9   We left them there and hurried back to the ship, where we told our tale, including our friends' experiment in viticulture. Then after taking some casks ashore and filling them with wine and water we bivouacked near the beach, and next morning set sail before a gentle breeze. But about midday, when we were out of sight of the island, a waterspout suddenly came upon us, which swept the ship round and up to a height of some three hundred and fifty miles above the earth. She did not fall back into the sea, but was suspended aloft, and at the same time carried along by a wind which struck and filled the sails.

For a whole week we pursued our airy course, and on the 10 eighth day descried land; it was an island with air for sea, glistening, spherical, and bathed in light. We reached it, cast anchor, and landed; inspection soon showed that it was inhabited and cultivated. In the daytime nothing could be discerned outside of it; but night revealed many neighbouring islands, some larger and some smaller than ours; there was also another land below us containing cities, rivers, seas, forests, and mountains; and this we concluded to be our Earth.

We were intending to continue our voyage, when we were 11 discovered and detained by the Horse-vultures, as they are called. These are men mounted on huge vultures, which they ride like horses; the great birds have ordinarily three heads. It will give you some idea of their size if I state that each of their quill-feathers is longer and thicker than the mast of a large merchantman. This corps is charged with the duty of patrolling the land, and bringing any strangers it may find to the king; this was what was now done with us. The king surveyed us, and, forming his conclusions from our dress, 'Strangers,' said he, 'you are Greeks, are you not?' we assented. 'And how did you traverse this vast space of air?' In answer we gave a full account of ourselves, to which he at once replied with his own history. It seemed he too was a mortal, named Endymion, who had been conveyed up from our Earth in his sleep, and after his arrival had become king of the country; this was, he told us, what we knew on our Earth as the moon. He bade us be of good cheer and entertain no apprehensions; all our needs should be supplied.

'And if I am victorious,' he added, 'in the campaign which 12 I am now commencing against the inhabitants of the Sun, I promise you an extremely pleasant life at my court.' We asked about the enemy, and the quarrel. 'Phaethon,' he replied, 'king of the Sun (which is inhabited, like the Moon), has long been at war with us. The occasion was this : I wished at one time to collect the poorest of my subjects and send them as a colony to Lucifer, which is uninhabited. Phaethon took umbrage at this, met the emigrants half way with a troop of Horse-ants, and forbade them to proceed. On that occasion, being in inferior force, we were worsted and had to retreat ; but I now intend to take the offensive and send my colony. I shall be glad if you will participate ; I will provide your equipment and mount you on vultures from the royal coops ; the expedition starts to-morrow.' I expressed our readiness to do his pleasure.

13   That day we were entertained by the king ; in the morning we took our place in the ranks as soon as we were up, our scouts having announced the approach of the enemy. Our army numbered 100,000 (exclusive of camp-followers, engineers, infantry, and allies), the Horse-vultures amounting to 80,000, and the remaining 20,000 being mounted on Salad-wings. These latter are also enormous birds, fledged with various herbs, and with quill-feathers resembling lettuce leaves. Next these were the Millet-throwers and the Garlic-men. Endymion had also a contingent from the North of 30,000 Flea-archers and 50,000 Wind-coursers. The former have their name from the great fleas, each of the bulk of a dozen elephants, which they ride. The Wind-coursers are infantry, moving through the air without wings ; they effect this by so girding their shirts, which reach to the ankle, that they hold the wind like a sail and propel their wearers ship-fashion. These troops are usually employed as skirmishers. 70,000 Ostrich-slingers and 50,000 Horse-cranes were said to be on their way from the stars over Cappadocia. But as they failed to arrive I did not actually see them ; and a description from hearsay I am not prepared to give, as the marvels related of them put some strain on belief.

14   Such was Endymion's force. They were all armed alike ;

their helmets were made of beans, which grow there of great size and hardness; the breastplates were of overlapping lupine-husks sewn together, these husks being as tough as horn; as to shields and swords, they were of the Greek type.

When the time came, the array was as follows: on the right 15 were the Horse-vultures, and the King with the *élite* of his forces, including ourselves. The Salad-wings held the left, and in the centre were the various allies. The infantry were in round numbers 60,000,000; they were enabled to fall in thus: there are in the Moon great numbers of gigantic spiders, considerably larger than an average Aegean island; these were instructed to stretch webs across from the Moon to Lucifer; as soon as the work was done, the King drew up his infantry on this artificial plain, entrusting the command to Nightbat, son of Fairweather, with two lieutenants.

On the enemy's side, Phaethon occupied the left with his 16 Horse-ants; they are great winged animals resembling our ants except in size; but the largest of them would measure a couple of acres. The fighting was done not only by their riders; they used their horns also; their numbers were stated at 50,000. On their right was about an equal force of Sky-gnats—archers mounted on great gnats; and next them the Sky-pirouetters, light-armed infantry only, but of some military value; they slung monstrous radishes at long range, a wound from which was almost immediately fatal, turning to gangrene at once; they were supposed to anoint their missiles with mallow juice. Next came the Stalk-fungi, 10,000 heavy-armed troops for close quarters; the explanation of their name is that their shields are mushrooms, and their spears asparagus stalks. Their neighbours were the Dog-acorns, Phaethon's contingent from Sirius. These were 5,000 in number, dog-faced men fighting on winged acorns. It was reported that Phaethon too was disappointed of the slingers whom he had summoned from the

Milky Way, and of the Cloud-centaurs. These latter, however, arrived, most unfortunately for us, after the battle was decided ; the slingers failed altogether, and are said to have felt the resentment of Phaethon, who wasted their territory with fire. Such was the force brought by the enemy.

17   As soon as the standards were raised and the asses on both sides (their trumpeters) had brayed, the engagement commenced. The Sunite left at once broke without awaiting the onset of the Horse-vultures, and we pursued, slaying them. On the other hand, their right had the better of our left, the Sky-gnats pressing on right up to our infantry. When these joined in, however, they turned and fled, chiefly owing to the moral effect of our success on the other flank. The rout became decisive, great numbers were taken and slain, and blood flowed in great quantities on to the clouds, staining them as red as we see them at sunset ; much of it also dropped earthwards, and suggested to me that it was possibly some ancient event of the same kind which persuaded Homer that Zeus had rained blood at the death of Sarpedon.

18   Relinquishing the pursuit, we set up two trophies, one for the infantry engagement on the spiders' webs, and one on the clouds for the air-battle. It was while we were thus engaged that our scouts announced the approach of the Cloud-centaurs, whom Phaethon had expected in time for the battle. They were indeed close upon us, and a strange sight, being compounded of winged horses and men ; the human part, from the middle upwards, was as tall as the Colossus of Rhodes, and the equine the size of a large merchantman. Their number I cannot bring myself to write down, for fear of exciting incredulity. They were commanded by Sagittarius. Finding their friends defeated, they sent a messenger after Phaethon to bring him back, and, themselves in perfect order, charged the disarrayed Moonites, who had left their ranks and were scattered in pursuit or pillage ;

they routed the whole of them, chased the King home, and killed the greater part of his birds ; they tore up the trophies, and overran the woven plain ; I myself was taken, with two of my comrades. Phaethon now arrived, and trophies were erected on the enemy's part. We were taken off to the Sun the same day, our hands tied behind with a piece of the cobweb.

They decided not to lay siege to the city ; but after their 19 return they constructed a wall across the intervening space, cutting off the Sun's rays from the Moon. This wall was double, and built of clouds ; the consequence was total eclipse of the Moon, which experienced a continuous night. This severity forced Endymion to negotiate. He entreated that the wall might be taken down, and his kingdom released from this life of darkness ; he offered to pay tribute, conclude an alliance, abstain from hostilities in future, and give hostages for these engagements. The Sunites held two assemblies on the question, in the first of which they refused all concessions ; on the second day, however, they relented, and peace was concluded on the following terms.

Articles of peace between the Sunites and their allies of the 20 one part, and the Moonites and their allies of the other part.

1. The Sunites shall demolish the party-wall, shall make no further incursion into the Moon, and shall hold their captives to ransom at a fixed rate.

2. The Moonites shall restore to the other stars their autonomy, shall not bear arms against the Sunites, and shall conclude with them a mutual defensive alliance.

3. The King of the Moonites shall pay to the King of the Sunites, annually, a tribute of ten thousand jars of dew, and give ten thousand hostages of his subjects.

4. The high contracting parties shall found the colony of Lucifer in common, and shall permit persons of any other nationality to join the same.

5. These articles shall be engraved on a pillar of electrum, which shall be set up on the border in mid-air.

Sworn to on behalf of the Sun by Firebrace, Heaton, and Flashman; and on behalf of the Moon by Nightwell, Monday, and Shimmer.

21 Peace concluded, the removal of the wall and restoration of captives at once followed. As we reached the Moon, we were met and welcomed by our comrades and King Endymion, all weeping for joy. The King wished us to remain and take part in founding the colony, and, women not existing in the Moon, offered me his son in marriage. I refused, asking that we might be sent down to the sea again; and finding that he could not prevail, he entertained us for a week, and then sent us on our way.

22 I am now to put on record the novelties and singularities which attracted my notice during our stay in the Moon.

23 When a man becomes old, he does not die, but dissolves in smoke into the air. There is one universal diet; they light a fire, and in the embers roast frogs, great numbers of which are always flying in the air; they then sit round as at table, snuffing up the fumes which rise and serve them for food; their drink is air compressed in a cup till it gives off a moisture resembling dew. Beauty with them consists in a bald head and hairless body; a good crop of hair is an abomination. On the comets, as I was told by some of their inhabitants who were there on a visit, this is reversed. They have beards, however, just above the knee; no toe-nails, and but one toe on each foot. They are all tailed, the tail being a large cabbage of an evergreen kind, which does not break if they fall upon it.

24 Their mucus is a pungent honey; and after hard work or exercise they sweat milk all over, which a drop or two of the honey curdles into cheese. The oil which they make from onions is very rich, and as fragrant as balsam. They have an

abundance of water-producing vines, the stones of which resemble hailstones; and my own belief is that it is the shaking
of these vines by hurricanes, and the consequent bursting of the
grapes, that results in our hailstorms. They use the belly as a
pouch in which to keep necessaries, being able to open and shut
it. It contains no intestines or liver, only a soft hairy lining;
their young, indeed, creep into it for protection from cold.

The clothing of the wealthy is soft glass, and of the poor, 25
woven brass; the land is very rich in brass, which they work
like wool after steeping it in water. It is with some hesitation
that I describe their eyes, the thing being incredible enough to
bring doubt upon my veracity. But the fact is that these
organs are removable; any one can take out his eyes and do
without till he wants them; then he has merely to put them
in; I have known many cases of people losing their own and
borrowing at need; and some—the rich, naturally—keep a
large stock. Their ears are plane-leaves, except with the breed
raised from acorns; theirs being of wood.

Another marvel I saw in the palace. There is a large mirror 26
suspended over a well of no great depth; any one going down
the well can hear every word spoken on our Earth; and if he
looks at the mirror, he sees every city and nation as plainly as
though he were standing close above each. The time I was
there, I surveyed my own people and the whole of my native
country; whether they saw me also, I cannot say for certain.
Any one who doubts the truth of this statement has only to go
there himself, to be assured of my veracity.

When the time came, we took our leave of King and court, 27
got on board, and weighed anchor. Endymion's parting gifts
to me were two glass shirts, five of brass, and a suit of lupine
armour, all of which, however, I afterwards left in the whale's
belly; he also sent, as our escort for the first fifty miles, a
thousand of his Horse-vultures.

28 We passed on our way many countries, and actually landed on Lucifer, now in process of settlement, to water. We then entered the Zodiac and passed the Sun on the left, coasting close by it. My crew were very desirous of landing, but the wind would not allow of this. We had a good view of the country, however, and found it covered with vegetation, rich, well-watered, and full of all good things. The Cloud-centaurs, now in Phaethon's pay, espied us and pounced upon the ship, but left us alone when they learned that we were parties to the treaty.

29 By this time our escort had gone home. We now took a downward course, and twenty-four hours' sailing brought us to Lampton. This lies between the atmospheres of the Pleiads and the Hyads, though in point of altitude it is considerably lower than the Zodiac. When we landed, we found no human beings, but numberless lamps bustling about or spending their time in the market-place and harbour; some were small, and might represent the lower classes, while a few, the great and powerful, were exceedingly bright and conspicuous. They all had their own homes or lodgings, and their individual names, like us; we heard them speak, and they did us no harm, offering us entertainment, on the contrary; but we were under some apprehension, and none of us accepted either food or bed. There is a Government House in the middle of the city, where the Governor sits all night long calling the roll-call; any one not answering to his name is capitally punished as a deserter; that is to say, he is extinguished. We were present and witnessed the proceedings, and heard lamps defending their conduct and advancing reasons for their lateness. I there recognized our own house lamp, accosted him, and asked for news of my friends, in which he satisfied me. We stayed there that night, set sail next morning, and found ourselves sailing, now, nearly as low as the clouds. Here we were surprised to find

Cloud-cuckoo-land; we were prevented from landing by the direction of the wind, but learned that the King's name was Crookbeak, son of Fitz-Ousel. I bethought me of Aristophanes, the learned and veracious poet whose statements had met with unmerited incredulity. Three days more, and we had a distinct view of the Ocean, though there was no land visible except the islands suspended in air; and these had now assumed a brilliant fiery hue. About noon on the fourth day the wind slackened and fell, and we were deposited upon the sea.

The joy and delight with which the touch of water affected 30 us is indescribable; transported at our good fortune, we flung ourselves overboard and swam, the weather being calm and the sea smooth. Alas, how often is a change for the better no more than the beginning of disaster! We had but two days' delightful sail, and by the rising sun of the third we beheld a crowd of whales and marine monsters, and among them one far larger than the rest—some two hundred miles in length. It came on open-mouthed, agitating the sea far in front, bathed in foam, and exhibiting teeth whose length much surpassed the height of our great phallic images, all pointed like sharp stakes and white as elephants' tusks. We gave each other a last greeting, took a last embrace, and so awaited our doom. The monster was upon us; it sucked us in; it swallowed ship and crew entire. We escaped being ground by its teeth, the ship gliding in through the interstices.

Inside, all was darkness at first, in which we could dis- 31 tinguish nothing; but when it next opened its mouth, an enormous cavern was revealed, of great extent and height; a city of ten thousand inhabitants might have had room in it. Strewn about were small fish, the *disjecta membra* of many kinds of animal, ships' masts and anchors, human bones, and merchandise; in the centre was land with hillocks upon it, the alluvial deposit, I supposed, from what the whale swallowed. This was wooded with trees of all kinds, and vegetables were growing with all the appearance of cultivation. The coast might have measured thirty miles round. Sea-birds, such as gulls and halcyons, nested on the trees.

32 We spent some time weeping, but at last got our men up and had the ship made fast, while we rubbed wood to get a fire and prepared a meal out of the plentiful materials around us; there were fragments of various fish, and the water we had taken in at Lucifer was unexhausted. Upon getting up next day, we caught glimpses, as often as the whale opened his mouth, of land, of mountains, it might be of the sky alone, or often of islands; we realized that he was dashing at a great rate to every part of the sea. We grew accustomed to our condition in time, and I then took seven of my comrades and entered the wood in search of information. I had scarcely gone half a mile when I came upon a shrine, which its inscription showed to have been raised to Posidon; a little further were a number of graves with pillars upon them, and close by a spring of clear water; we also heard a dog bark, saw some distant smoke, and conjectured that there must be a habitation.

33 We accordingly pressed on, and found ourselves in presence of an old man and a younger one, who were working hard at a plot of ground and watering it by a channel from the spring. We stood still, divided between fear and delight. They were standing speechless, no doubt with much the same feelings. At length the old man spoke :—' What are you, strangers; are you spirits of the sea, or unfortunate mortals like ourselves? As for us, we are men, bred on land; but now we have suffered a sea change, and swim about in this containing monster, scarce knowing how to describe our state; reason tells us we are dead, but instinct that we live.' This loosed my tongue in turn. ' We too, father,' I said, ' are men, just arrived; it is but a day or two since we were swallowed with our ship. And now we have

come forth to explore the forest; for we saw that it was vast
and dense. Methinks some heavenly guide has brought us to
the sight of you, to the knowledge that we are not prisoned all
alone in this monster. I pray you, let us know your tale, who
you are and how you entered.' Then he said that, before he
asked or answered questions, he must give us such entertainment as he could; so saying, he brought us to his house—a
sufficient dwelling furnished with beds and what else he might
need—, and set before us green-stuff and nuts and fish, with
wine for drink. When we had eaten our fill, he asked for our
story. I told him all as it had passed, the storm, the island,
the airy voyage, the war, and so to our descent into the
whale.

It was very strange, he said, and then gave us his history in 34
return. 'I am a Cyprian, gentlemen. I left my native land
on a trading voyage with my son here and a number of servants.
We had a fine ship, with a mixed cargo for Italy; you may
have seen the wreckage in the whale's mouth. We had a fair
voyage to Sicily, but on leaving it were caught in a gale, and
carried in three days out to the Atlantic, where we fell in with
the whale and were swallowed, ship and crew; of the latter we
two alone survived. We buried our men, built a temple to
Posidon, and now live this life, cultivating our garden, and
feeding on fish and nuts. It is a great wood, as you see, and in
it are vines in plenty, from which we get delicious wine; our
spring you may have noticed; its water is of the purest and
coldest. We use leaves for bedding, keep a good fire, snare the
birds that fly in, and catch living fish by going out on the
monster's gills; it is there also that we take our bath when we
are disposed. There is moreover at no great distance a salt
lake two or three miles round, producing all sorts of fish; in
this we swim and sail, in a little boat of my building. It is
now seven and twenty years since we were swallowed.

35 'Our lot might have been endurable enough, but we have bad and troublesome neighbours, unfriendly savages all.' 'What,' said I, 'are there other inhabitants?' 'A great many,' he replied, 'inhospitable and abhorrent to the sight. The western part of the wood (so to name the caudal region) is occupied by the Stockfish tribe; they have eels' eyes and lobster faces, are bold warriors, and eat their meat raw. Of the sides of the cavern, the right belongs to the Tritonomendetes, who from the waist upwards are human, and weazels below; their notions of justice are slightly less rudimentary than the others'. The left is in possession of the Crabhands and the Tunnyheads, two tribes in close alliance. The central part is inhabited by the Crays and the Flounderfoots, the latter warlike and extremely swift. As to this district near the mouth, the East, as it were, it is in great part desert, owing to the frequent inundations. I hold it of the Flounderfoots, paying an annual tribute of five hundred oysters.

36 'Such is the land; and now it is for you to consider how we may make head against all these tribes, and what shall be our manner of life.' 'What may their numbers be, all told?' I asked. 'More than a thousand.' 'And how armed?' 'They have no arms but fishbones.' 'Why then,' I said, 'let us fight them by all means; we are armed, and they are not; and, if we win, we shall live secure.' We agreed on this course, and returned to the ship to make our preparations. The pretext for war was to be non-payment of the tribute, which was on the point of falling due. Messengers, in fact, shortly came to demand it, but the old man sent them about their business with an insolent answer. The Flounderfoots and Crays were enraged, and commenced operations with a tumultuous inroad upon Scintharus—this was our old man's name.

37 Expecting this, we were awaiting the attack in full armour. We had put five and twenty men in ambush, with directions to

fall on the enemy's rear as soon as they had passed; they executed their orders, and came on from behind cutting them down, while the rest of us—five and twenty also, including Scintharus and his son—met them face to face with a spirited and resolute attack. It was risky work, but in the end we routed and chased them to their dens. They left one hundred and seventy dead, while we lost only our navigating officer, stabbed in the back with a mullet rib, and one other.

We held the battlefield for the rest of that day and the night 38 following, and erected a trophy consisting of a dolphin's backbone upright. Next day the news brought the other tribes out, with the Stockfish under a general called Slimer on the right, the Tunnyheads on the left, and the Crabhands in the centre; the Tritonomendetes stayed at home, preferring neutrality. We did not wait to be attacked, but charged them near Posidon's temple with loud shouts, which echoed as in a subterranean cave. Their want of armour gave us the victory; we pursued them to the wood, and were henceforth masters.

Soon after, they sent heralds to treat for recovery of their 39 dead, and for peace. But we decided to make no terms with them, and marching out next day exterminated the whole, with the exception of the Tritonomendetes. These too, when they saw what was going on, made a rush for the gills, and cast themselves into the sea. We went over the country, now clear of enemies, and occupied it from that time in security. Our usual employments were exercise, hunting, vine-dressing, and fruit-gathering; we were in the position of men in a vast prison from which escape is out of the question, but within which they have luxury and freedom of movement. This manner of life lasted for a year and eight months.

It was on the fifth of the next month, about the second gape 40 (the whale, I should say, gaped regularly once an hour, and we reckoned time that way)—about the second gape, then, a sudden shouting and tumult became audible; it sounded like boat-swains giving the time and oars beating. Much excited, we crept right out into our monster's mouth, stood inside the teeth, and beheld the most extraordinary spectacle I ever looked upon—giants of a hundred yards in height rowing great islands as we do triremes. I am aware that what I am to relate must sound improbable; but I cannot help it. Very long islands they were, but of no great height; the circumference of each would be about eleven miles; and its complement of giants was some hundred and twenty. Of these some sat along each side of the island, rowing with big cypresses, from which the branches and leaves were not stripped; in the stern, so to speak, was a considerable hillock, on which stood the helmsman with his hand on a brazen steering-oar of half a mile in length; and on the deck forward were forty in armour, the combatants; they resembled men except in their hair, which was flaming fire, so that they could dispense with helmets. The work of sails was done by the abundant forest on all the islands, which so caught and held the wind that it drove them where the steers-man wished; there was a boatswain timing the stroke, and the islands jumped to it like great galleys.

41 We had seen only two or three at first; but there appeared afterwards as many as six hundred, which formed in two lines and commenced an action. Many crashed into each other stem to stem, many were rammed and sunk, others grappled, fought an obstinate duel, and could hardly get clear after it. Great courage was shown by the troops on deck, who boarded and dealt destruction, giving no quarter. Instead of grappling-irons, they used huge captive squids, which they swung out on to the hostile island; these grappled the wood and so held the island fast. Their missiles, effective enough, were oysters the size of waggons, and sponges which might cover an acre.

Aeolocentaur and Thalassopot were the names of the rival 42
chiefs; and the question between them was one of plunder;
Thalassopot was supposed to have driven off several herds of
dolphins, the other's property; we could hear them vociferating the charge and calling out their Kings' names. Aeolocentaur's fleet finally won, sinking one hundred and fifty of the
enemy's islands and capturing three with their crews; the re-
mainder backed away, turned and fled. The victors pursued
some way, but, as it was now evening, returned to the disabled
ones, secured most of the enemy's, and recovered their own, of
which as many as eighty had been sunk. As a trophy of victory
they slung one of the enemy's islands to a stake which they
planted in our whale's head. They lay moored round him that
night, attaching cables to him or anchoring hard by; they had
vast glass anchors, very strong. Next morning they sacrificed
on the whale's back, buried their dead there, and sailed off
rejoicing, with something corresponding to our paean. So
ended the battle of the islands.

Book II

I now began to find life in the whale unendurable; I was 1
tired to death of it, and concentrated my thoughts on plans of
escape. Our first idea was to excavate a passage through the
beast's right side, and go out through it. We actually began
boring, but gave it up when we had penetrated half a mile
without getting through. We then determined to set fire to
the forest, our object being the death of the whale, which would
remove all difficulties. We started burning from the tail end;
but for a whole week he made no sign; on the eighth and ninth
days it was apparent that he was unwell; his jaws opened only
languidly, and each time closed again very soon. On the tenth
and eleventh days mortification had set in, evidenced by a
horrible stench; on the twelfth, it occurred to us, just in time,

that we must take the next occasion of the mouth's being open to insert props between the upper and lower molars, and so prevent his closing it; else we should be imprisoned and perish in the dead body. We successfully used great beams for the purpose, and then got the ship ready with all the water and provisions we could manage. Scintharus was to navigate her. Next day the whale was dead.

2　We hauled the vessel up, brought her through one of the gaps, slung her to the teeth, and so let her gently down to the water. We then ascended the back, where we sacrificed to Posidon by the side of the trophy, and, as there was no wind, encamped there for three days. On the fourth day we were able to start. We found and came into contact with many corpses, the relics of the sea-fight, and our wonder was heightened when we measured them. For some days we enjoyed a moderate breeze, after which a violent north wind rose, bringing hard frost; the whole sea was frozen—not merely crusted over, but solidified to four hundred fathoms' depth; we got out and walked about. The continuance of the wind making life intolerable, we adopted the plan, suggested by Scintharus, of hewing an extensive cavern in the ice, in which we stayed a month, lighting fires and feeding on fish; we had only to dig these out. In the end, however, provisions ran short, and we came out; the ship was frozen in, but we got her free; we then hoisted sail, and were carried along as well as if we had been afloat, gliding smoothly and easily over the ice. After five days more the temperature rose, a thaw set in, and all was water again.

3　A stretch of five and thirty miles brought us to a small desert isle, where we got water—of which we were now in want—, and shot two wild bulls before we departed. These animals had their horns not on the top of the head, but, as Momus recommended, below the eyes. Not long after this, we entered a sea of milk, in which we observed an island, white in colour, and full of vines. The island was one great cheese, quite firm, as we afterwards ascertained by eating it, and three miles round. The vines were covered with fruit, but the drink we squeezed from it was milk instead of wine. In the centre of the island was a temple to Galatea the Nereid, as the inscription informed us. During our stay there, the ground itself served us for bread and meat, and the vine-milk for drink. We learned that the queen of these regions was Tyro, daughter of Salmoneus, on whom Posidon had conferred this dignity at her decease.

After spending five days there we started again with a gentle 4 breeze and a rippling sea. A few days later, when we had emerged from the milk into blue salt water, we saw numbers of men walking on the sea; they were like ourselves in shape and stature, with the one exception of the feet, which were of cork; whence, no doubt, their name of Corksoles. It struck us as curious that they did not sink in, but travelled quite comfortably clear of the water. Some of them came up and hailed us in Greek, saying that they were making their way to their native land of Cork. They ran alongside for some distance, and then turned off and went their own way, wishing us a pleasant voyage. A little further we saw several islands; close to us on the left was Cork, our friends' destination, consisting of a city founded on a vast round cork; at a greater distance, and a little to the right, were five others of considerable size and high out of the water, with great flames rising from them.

There was also a broad low one, as much as sixty miles in 5 length, straight in our course. As we drew near it, a marvellous air was wafted to us, exquisitely fragrant, like the scent which Herodotus describes as coming from Arabia Felix. Its sweetness seemed compounded of rose, narcissus, hyacinth, lilies and violets, myrtle and bay and flowering vine. Ravished with the perfume, and hoping for reward of our long toils, we drew slowly near. Then were unfolded to us haven after haven, spacious and sheltered, and crystal rivers flowing placidly to the sea. There were meadows and groves and sweet birds, some singing on the shore, some on the branches ; the whole bathed in limpid balmy air. Sweet zephyrs just stirred the woods with their breath, and brought whispering melody, delicious, incessant, from the swaying branches ; it was like Pan-pipes heard in a desert place. And with it all there mingled a volume of human sound, a sound not of tumult, but rather of revels where some flute, and some praise the fluting, and some clap their hands commending flute or harp.

6 Drawn by the spell of it we came to land, moored the ship, and left her, in charge of Scintharus and two others. Taking our way through flowery meadows we came upon the guardians of the peace, who bound us with rose-garlands—their strongest fetters—and brought us to the governor. As we went they told us this was the island called of the Blest, and its governor the Cretan Rhadamanthus. When we reached the court, we found there were three cases to be taken before our turn would come.

7 The first was that of Ajax, son of Telamon, and the question was whether he was to be admitted to the company of Heroes ; it was objected that he had been mad and taken his own life. After long pleadings Rhadamanthus gave his decision : he was to be put under the charge of Hippocrates the physician of Cos for the hellebore treatment, and, when he had recovered his wits, to be made free of the table.

8 The second was a matrimonial case, the parties Theseus and Menelaus, and the issue possession of Helen. Rhadamanthus gave it in favour of Menelaus, on the ground of the great toils and dangers the match had cost him—added to the fact that Theseus was provided with other wives in the Amazon queen and the daughters of Minos.

The third was a dispute for precedence between Alexander 9
son of Philip and Hannibal the Carthaginian; it was won by
the former, who had a seat assigned him next to Cyrus the
elder.

It was now our turn. The judge asked by what right we set 10
foot on this holy ground while yet alive. In answer we related
our story. He then had us removed while he held a long con-
sultation with his numerous assessors, among whom was the
Athenian Aristides the Just. He finally reached a conclusion
and gave judgement: on the charges of curiosity and travelling
we were remanded till the date of our deaths; for the present
we were to stay in the island, with admission to the Heroic
society, for a fixed term, after which we must depart. The
limit he appointed for our stay was seven months.

Our rose-chains now fell off of their own accord, we were 11
released and taken into the city, and to the Table of the Blest.
The whole of this city is built of gold, and the enclosing wall
of emerald. It has seven gates, each made of a single cinnamon
plank. The foundations of the houses, and all ground inside
the wall, are ivory; temples are built of beryl, and each contains an altar of one amethyst block, on which they offer hecatombs. Round the city flows a river of the finest perfume,
a hundred royal cubits in breadth, and fifty deep, so that there
is good swimming. The baths, supplied with warm dew instead
of ordinary water, are in great crystal domes heated with cinnamon wood.

Their raiment is fine cobweb, purple in colour. They have no 12
bodies, but are intangible and unsubstantial—mere form without
matter; but, though incorporeal, they stand and move, think
and speak; in short, each is a naked soul, but carries about the
semblance of body; one who did not touch them would never
know that what he looked at was not substantial; they are
shadows, but upright, and coloured. A man there does not

grow old, but stays at whatever age he brought with him. There is no night, nor yet bright day; the morning twilight, just before sunrise, gives the best idea of the light that prevails. They have also but one season, perpetual spring, and the wind is always in the west.

13 The country abounds in every kind of flower, in shrubs and garden herbs. There are twelve vintages in the year, the grapes ripening every month; and they told us that pomegranates, apples, and other fruits were gathered thirteen times, the trees producing twice in their month Minous. Instead of grain, the corn develops loaves, shaped like mushrooms, at the top of the stalks. Round the city are 365 springs of water, the same of honey, and 500, less in volume however, of perfume. There are also seven rivers of milk and eight of wine.

14 The banqueting-place is arranged outside the city in the Elysian Plain. It is a fair lawn closed in with thick-grown trees of every kind, in the shadow of which the guests recline, on cushions of flowers. The waiting and handing is done by the winds, except only the filling of the wine-cup. That is a service not required; for all round stand great trees of pellucid crystal, whose fruit is drinking-cups of every shape and size. A guest arriving plucks a cup or two and sets them at his place, where they at once fill with wine. So for their drink; and instead of garlands, the nightingales and other singing birds pick flowers with their beaks from the meadows round, and fly over snowing the petals down and singing the while. Nor is perfume forgotten; thick clouds draw it up from the springs and river, and hanging overhead are gently squeezed by the winds till they spray it down in fine dew.

15 During the meal there is music and song. In the latter kind, Homer's verse is the favourite; he is himself a member of the festal company, reclining next above Odysseus. The choirs are of boys and girls, conducted and led by Eunomus the Locrian,

Arion of Lesbos, Anacreon and Stesichorus; this last had made his peace with Helen, and I saw him there. When these have finished, a second choir succeeds, of swans and swallows and nightingales; and when their turn is done, all the trees begin to pipe, conducted by the winds.

I have still to add the most important element in their good 16 cheer: there are two springs hard by, called the Fountain of Laughter, and the Fountain of Delight. They all take a draught of both these before the banquet begins, after which the time goes merrily and sweetly.

I should now like to name the famous persons I saw. To 17 begin with, all the demi-gods, and the besiegers of Troy, with the exception of Ajax the Locrian; he, they said, was undergoing punishment in the place of the wicked. Of barbarians there were the two Cyruses, Anacharsis the Scythian, Zamolxis the Thracian, and the Latin Numa; and then Lycurgus the Spartan, Phocion and Tellus of Athens, and the Wise Men, but without Periander. And I saw Socrates son of Sophroniscus in converse with Nestor and Palamedes; clustered round him were Hyacinth the Spartan, Narcissus of Thespiae, Hylas, and many another comely boy. With Hyacinth I suspected that he was in love; at least he was for ever poking questions at him. I heard that Rhadamanthus was dissatisfied with Socrates, and had several times threatened him with expulsion, if he insisted on talking nonsense, and would not drop his irony and enjoy himself. Plato was the only one I missed, but I was told that he was living in his own Utopia, working the constitution and laws which he had drawn up.

For popularity, Aristippus and Epicurus bore the palm, in 18 virtue of their kindliness, sociability, and good-fellowship. Aesop the Phrygian was there, and held the office of jester. Diogenes of Sinope was much changed; he had married Lais the courtesan, and often in his cups would oblige the company with

a dance, or other mad pranks. The Stoics were not represented
at all; they were supposed to be still climbing the steep hill of
Virtue; and as to Chrysippus himself, we were told that he was
not to set foot on the island till he had taken a fourth course
of hellebore. The Academics contemplated coming, but were
taking time for consideration; they could not yet regard it as
a certainty that any such island existed. There was probably
the added difficulty that they were not comfortable about the
judgement of Rhadamanthus, having themselves disputed the
possibility of judgement. It was stated that many of them
had started to follow persons travelling to the island, but,
their energy failing, had abandoned the journey half-way and
gone back.

19 I have mentioned the most noteworthy of the company, and
add that the most highly respected among them are, first Achilles,
and second Theseus.

20 Before many days had passed, I accosted the poet Homer,
when we were both disengaged, and asked him, among other
things, where he came from; it was still a burning question
with us, I explained. He said he was aware that some brought
him from Chios, others from Smyrna, and others again from
Colophon; the fact was, he was a Babylonian, generally known
not as Homer, but as Tigranes; but when later in life he was
given as a *homer* or hostage to the Greeks, that name clung to
him. Another of my questions was about the so-called spurious
lines; had he written them, or not? He said they were all
genuine; so I now knew what to think of the critics Zenodotus
and Aristarchus, and all their lucubrations. Having got a
categorical answer on that point, I tried him next on his reason
for starting the Iliad at the wrath of Achilles; he said he had
no exquisite reason; it had just come into his head that way.
Another thing I wanted to know was whether he had composed
the Odyssey before the Iliad, as generally believed. He said

this was not so. As to his reported blindness, I did not need to ask; he had his sight, so there was an end of that. It became a habit of mine, whenever I saw him at leisure, to go up and ask him things, and he answered quite readily—especially after his acquittal; a libel suit had been brought against him by Thersites, on the ground of the ridicule to which he is subjected in the poem; Homer had briefed Odysseus, and been acquitted.

It was during our sojourn that Pythagoras arrived; he had **21** undergone seven transmigrations, lived the lives of that number of animals, and completed his psychic travels. It was the entire right half of him that was gold. He was at once given the franchise, but the question was still pending whether he was to be known as Pythagoras or Euphorbus. Empedocles also came, scorched all over and baked right through; but not all his entreaties could gain him admittance.

The progress of time brought round the Games of the Dead. **22** The umpires were Achilles, holding that office for the fifth, and Theseus for the seventh time. A full report would take too long; but I will summarize the events. The wrestling went to Carus the Heraclid, who won the garland from Odysseus. The boxing resulted in a tie, the pair being the Egyptian Areus, whose grave is in Corinth, and Epeus. For mixed boxing and wrestling they have no prize. Who won the flat race, I have forgotten. In poetry, Homer really did much the best, but the award was for Hesiod. All prizes were plaited wreaths of peacock feathers.

Just after the Games were over, news came that the Damned **23** had broken their fetters, overpowered their guard, and were on the point of invading the island, the ringleaders being Phalaris of Agrigentum, Busiris the Egyptian, Diomedes the Thracian, Sciron, and Pityocamptes. Rhadamanthus at once drew up the Heroes on the beach, giving the command to Theseus, Achilles, and Ajax Telamonius, now in his right senses. The battle was fought, and won by the Heroes, thanks especially to Achilles. Socrates, who was in the right wing, distinguished himself still more than in his lifetime at Delium, standing firm and showing no sign of trepidation as the enemy came on; he was afterwards given as a reward of valour a large and beautiful park in the outskirts, to which he invited his friends for conversation, naming it the Post-mortem Academy.

24 The defeated party were seized, re-fettered, and sent back for severer torments. Homer added to his poems a description of this battle, and at my departure handed me the MS. to bring back to the living world; but it was unfortunately lost with our other property. It began with the line:

> Tell now, my Muse, how fought the mighty Dead.

According to their custom after successful war, they boiled beans, held the feast of victory, and kept high holiday. From this Pythagoras alone held aloof, fasting and sitting far off, in sign of his abhorrence of bean-eating.

25 We were in the middle of our seventh month, when an incident happened. Scintharus's son, Cinyras, a fine figure of a man, had fallen in love with Helen some time before, and it was obvious that she was very much taken with the young fellow; there used to be nods and becks and takings of wine between them at table, and they would go off by themselves for strolls in the wood. At last love and despair inspired Cinyras with the idea of an elopement. Helen consented, and they were to fly to one of the neighbouring islands, Cork or Cheese Island. They had taken three of the boldest of my crew into their confidence; Cinyras said not a word to his father, knowing that he would put a stop to it. The plan was carried out; under cover of night, and in my absence—I had fallen asleep at table—, they got Helen away unobserved and rowed off as hard as they could.

About midnight Menelaus woke up, and finding his wife's
place empty raised an alarm, and got his brother to go with
him to King Rhadamanthus. Just before dawn the look-outs
announced that they could make out the boat, far out at sea.
So Rhadamanthus sent fifty of the Heroes on board a boat
hollowed out of an asphodel trunk, with orders to give chase.
Pulling their best, they overtook the fugitives at noon, as they
were entering the milky sea near the Isle of Cheese; so nearly
was the escape effected. The boat was towed back with a
chain of roses. Helen shed tears, and so felt her situation as
to draw a veil over her face. As to Cinyras and his associates,
Rhadamanthus interrogated them to find whether they had more
accomplices, and, being assured to the contrary, had them
whipped with mallow twigs, bound, and dismissed to the place
of the wicked.

It was further determined that we should be expelled pre-
maturely from the island; we were allowed only one day's
grace. This drew from me loud laments and tears for the bliss
that I was now to exchange for renewed wanderings. They
consoled me for their sentence, however, by telling me that it
would not be many years before I should return to them, and
assigning me my chair and my place at table—a distinguished
one—in anticipation. I then went to Rhadamanthus, and was
urgent with him to reveal the future to me, and give me directions for our voyage. He told me that I should come to my
native land after many wanderings and perils, but as to the
time of my return he would give me no certainty. He pointed,
however, to the neighbouring islands, of which five were visible,
besides one more distant, and informed me that the wicked
inhabited these, the near ones, that is, 'from which you see the
great flames rising; the sixth yonder is the City of Dreams;
and beyond that again, but not visible at this distance, is Calypso's
isle. When you have passed these, you will come to the great

continent which is opposite your own; there you will have many adventures, traverse divers tribes, sojourn among inhospitable men, and at last reach your own continent.' That was all he would say.

28   But he pulled up a mallow root and handed it to me, bidding me invoke it at times of greatest danger. When I arrived in this world, he charged me to abstain from stirring fire with a knife, from lupines, and from the society of boys over eighteen; these things if I kept in mind, I might look for return to the island. That day I made ready for our voyage, and when the banquet hour came, I shared it. On the morrow I went to the poet Homer and besought him to write me a couplet for inscription; when he had done it, I carved it on a beryl pillar which I had set up close to the harbour; it ran thus:

> This island, ere he took his homeward way,
> The blissful Gods gave Lucian to survey.

29   I stayed out that day too, and next morning started, the Heroes attending to see me off. Odysseus took the opportunity to come unobserved by Penelope and give me a letter for Calypso in the isle Ogygia. Rhadamanthus sent on board with me the ferryman Nauplius, who, in case we were driven on to the islands, might secure us from seizure by guaranteeing that our destination was different. As soon as our progress brought us out of the scented air, it was succeeded by a horrible smell as of bitumen, brimstone, and pitch all burning together; mingled with this were the disgusting and intolerable fumes of roasting human flesh; the air was dark and thick, distilling a pitchy dew upon us; we could also hear the crack of whips and the yelling of many voices.

30   We only touched at one island, on which we also landed. It was completely surrounded by precipitous cliffs, arid, stony, rugged, treeless, unwatered. We contrived to clamber up the

rocks, and advanced along a track beset with thorns and snags—
a hideous scene. When we reached the prison and the place of
punishment, what first drew our wonder was the character
of the whole. The very ground stood thick with a crop of knife-
blades and pointed stakes ; and it was ringed round with rivers,
one of slime, a second of blood, and the innermost of flame. This
last was very broad and quite impassable ; the flame flowed
like water, swelled like the sea, and teemed with fish, some resembling firebrands, and others, the small ones, live coals ; these
were called lamplets.

One narrow way led across all three ; its gate was kept by 31
Timon of Athens. Nauplius secured us admission, however,
and then we saw the chastisement of many kings, and many
common men ; some were known to us ; indeed there hung
Cinyras, swinging in eddies of smoke. Our guides described
the life and guilt of each culprit ; the severest torments were
reserved for those who in life had been liars and written false
history ; the class was numerous, and included Ctesias of Cnidus,
and Herodotus. The fact was an encouragement to me, knowing that I had never told a lie.

I soon found the sight more than I could bear, and returning 32
to the ship bade farewell to Nauplius and resumed the voyage.
Very soon we seemed quite close to the Isle of Dreams, though
there was a certain dimness and vagueness about its outline ;
but it had something dreamlike in its very nature ; for as we
approached it receded, and seemed to get further and further
off. At last we reached it and sailed into Slumber, the port,
close to the ivory gates where stands the temple of the Cock.
It was evening when we landed, and upon proceeding to the
city we saw many strange dreams. But I intend first to describe
the city, as it has not been done before ; Homer indeed mentions
it, but gives no detailed description.

The whole place is embowered in wood, of which the trees 33

are poppy and mandragora, all thronged with bats; this is the only winged thing that exists there. A river, called the Somnambule, flows close by, and there are two springs at the gates, one called Wakenot, and the other Nightlong. The rampart is lofty and of many colours, in the rainbow style. The gates are not two, as Homer says, but four, of which two look on to the plain Stupor; one of them is of iron, the other of pottery, and we were told that these are used by the grim, the murderous, and the cruel. The other pair face the sea and port, and are of horn—it was by this that we had entered—and of ivory. On the right as you enter the city stands the temple of Night, which deity divides with the Cock their chief allegiance; the temple of the latter is close to the port. On the left is the palace of Sleep. He is the governor, with two lieutenants, Nightmare, son of Whimsy, and Flittergold, son of Fantasy. A well in the middle of the market-place goes by the name of Heavyhead; beside which are the temples of Deceit and Truth. In the market also is the shrine in which oracles are given, the priest and prophet, by special appointment from Sleep, being Antiphon the dream-interpreter.

34 The dreams themselves differed widely in character and appearance. Some were well-grown, smooth-skinned, shapely, handsome fellows, others rough, short, and ugly; some apparently made of gold, others of common cheap stuff. Among them some were found with wings, and other strange variations; others again were like the mummers in a pageant, tricked out as kings or Gods or what not. Many of them we felt that we had seen in our world, and sure enough these came up and claimed us as old acquaintance; they took us under their charge, found us lodgings, entertained us with lavish kindness, and, not content with the magnificence of this present reception, promised us royalties and provinces. Some of them also took us to see our friends, doing the return trip all in the day.

For thirty days and nights we abode there—a very feast of 35 sleep. Then on a sudden came a mighty clap of thunder : we woke ; jumped up ; provisioned ; put off. In three days we were at the Isle of Ogygia, where we landed. Before delivering the letter, I opened and read it ; here are the contents : *ODYS-SEUS TO CALYPSO, GREETING. Know that in the far-away days when I built my raft and sailed away from you, I suffered shipwreck ; I was hard put to it, but Leucothea brought me safe to the land of the Phaeacians ; they gave me passage home, and there I found a great company suing for my wife's hand and living riotously upon our goods. All them I slew, and in after years was slain by Telegonus, the son that Circe bare me. And now I am in the Island of the Blest, ruing the day when I left the life I had with you, and the everlasting life you proffered. I watch for opportunity, and meditate escape and return.* Some words were added, commending us to her hospitality.

A little way from the sea I found the cave just as it is in 36 Homer, and herself therein at her spinning. She took and read the letter, wept for a space, and then offered us entertainment ; royally she feasted us, putting questions the while about Odysseus and Penelope ; what were her looks ? and was she as discreet as Odysseus had been used to vaunt her ? To which we made such answers as we thought she would like.

Leaving her, we went on board, and spent the night at anchor 37 just off shore ; in the morning we started with a stiff breeze, which grew to a gale lasting two days ; on the third day we fell in with the Pumpkin-pirates. These are savages of the neighbouring islands who prey upon passing ships. They use large boats made of pumpkins ninety feet long. The pumpkin is dried and hollowed out by removal of the pulp, and the boat is completed by the addition of cane masts and pumpkin-leaf sails. Two boatfuls of them engaged us, and we had many casualties from their pumpkin-seed missiles. The fight was long and well matched ; but about noon we saw a squadron of Nuttars coming up in rear of the enemy. It turned out that the two parties were at war ; for as soon as our assailants observed the others, they left us alone and turned to engage them.

38 Meanwhile we hoisted sail and made the best of our way off, leaving them to fight it out. It was clear that the Nut-tars must win, as they had both superior numbers—there were five sail of them—and stronger vessels. These were made of nutshells, halved and emptied, measuring ninety feet from stem to stern. As soon as they were hull down, we attended to our wounded ; and from that time we made a practice of keeping on our armour, to be in instant readiness for an attack—no vain precaution either.

39 Before sunset, for instance, there assailed us from a bare island some twenty men mounted on large dolphins—pirates again. Their dolphins carried them quite well, curvetting and neighing. When they got near, they divided, and subjected us to a cross fire of dry cuttlefish and crabs' eyes. But our arrows and javelins were too much for them, and they fled back to the island, few of them unwounded.

40 At midnight, in calm weather, we found ourselves colliding with an enormous halcyon's nest ; it was full seven miles round. The halcyon was brooding, not much smaller herself than the nest. She got up, and very nearly capsized us with the fanning of her wings ; however, she went off with a melancholy cry. When it was getting light, we got on to the nest, and found on examination that it was composed like a vast raft of large trees. There were five hundred eggs, larger in girth than a tun of Chian. We could make out the chicks inside and hear them croaking ; we hewed open one egg with hatchets, and dug out an unfledged chick bulkier than twenty vultures.

41 Sailing on, we had left the nest some five and twenty miles behind, when a miracle happened. The wooden goose of our

stern-post suddenly clapped its wings and started cackling; Scintharus, who was bald, recovered his hair; most striking of all, the ship's mast came to life, putting forth branches sideways, and fruit at the top; this fruit was figs, and a bunch of black grapes, not yet ripe. These sights naturally disturbed us, and we fell to praying the Gods to avert any disaster they might portend.

We had proceeded something less than fifty miles when we 42 saw a great forest, thick with pines and cypresses. This we took for the mainland; but it was in fact deep sea, set with trees; they had no roots, but yet remained in their places, floating upright, as it were. When we came near and realized the state of the case, we could not tell what to do; it was impossible to sail between the trees, which were so close as to touch one another, and we did not like the thought of turning back. I climbed the tallest tree to get a good view, and found that the wood was five or six miles across, and was succeeded by open water. So we determined to hoist the ship on to the top of the foliage, which was very dense, and get her across to the other sea, if possible. It proved to be so. We attached a strong cable, got up on the tree-tops, and hauled her after us with some difficulty; then we laid her on the branches, hoisted sail, and floating thus were propelled by the wind. A line of Antimachus came into my head:

And as they voyaged thus the woodland through—

Well, we made our way over and reached the water, into 43 which we let her down in the same way. We then sailed through clear transparent sea, till we found ourselves on the edge of a great gorge which divided water from water, like the land fissures which are often produced by earthquakes. We got the sails down and brought her to just in time to escape making the plunge. We could bend over and see an awful mysterious gulf perhaps a hundred miles deep, the water standing wall against wall. A glance round showed us not far off to the right a water bridge which spanned the chasm, and gave a moving surface crossing from one sea to the other. We got out the sweeps, pulled her to the bridge, and with great exertions effected that astonishing passage.

44   There followed a sail through smooth water, and then a small island, easy of approach, and inhabited; its occupants were the Ox-heads, savage men with horns, after the fashion of our poets' Minotaur. We landed and went in search of water and provisions, of which we were now in want. The water we found easily, but nothing else; we heard, however, not far off, a numerous lowing; supposing it to indicate a herd of cows, we went a little way towards it, and came upon these men. They gave chase as soon as they saw us, and seized three of my comrades, the rest of us getting off to sea. We then armed—for we would not leave our friends unavenged—and in full force fell on the Ox-heads as they were dividing our slaughtered men's flesh. Our combined shout put them to flight, and in the pursuit we killed about fifty, took two alive, and returned with our captives. We had found nothing to eat; the general opinion was for slaughtering the prisoners; but I refused to accede to this, and kept them in bonds till an embassy came from the Ox-heads to ransom them; so we understood the motions they made, and their tearful supplicatory lowings. The ransom consisted of a quantity of cheese, dried fish, onions, and four deer; these were three-footed, the two forefeet being joined into one. In exchange for all this we restored the prisoners, and after one day's further stay departed.

45   By this time we were beginning to observe fish, birds on the wing, and other signs of land not far off; and we shortly saw men, practising a mode of navigation new to us; for they were boat and crew in one. The method was this: they float on their backs, erect a sail, and then, holding the sheets with their

hands, catch the wind. These were succeeded by others who sat on corks, to which were harnessed pairs of dolphins, driven with reins. They neither attacked nor avoided us, but drove along in all confidence and peace, admiring the shape of our craft and examining it all round.

That evening we touched at an island of no great size. It was occupied by what we took for women, talking Greek. They came and greeted us with kisses, were attired like courtesans, all young and fair, and with long robes sweeping the ground. Cabbalusa was the name of the island, and Hydramardia the city's. These women paired off with us and led the way to their separate homes. I myself tarried a little, under the influence of some presentiment, and looking more closely observed quantities of human bones and skulls lying about. I did not care to raise an alarm, gather my men, and resort to arms; instead, I drew out my mallow, and prayed earnestly to it for escape from our perilous position. Shortly after, as my hostess was serving me, I saw that in place of human feet she had ass's hoofs; whereupon I drew my sword, seized, bound, and closely questioned her. Reluctantly enough she had to confess; they were sea-women called Ass-shanks, and their food was travellers. 'When we have made them drunk,' she said, 'and gone to rest with them, we overpower them in their sleep.' After this confession I left her there bound, went up on to the roof, and shouted for my comrades. When they appeared, I repeated it all to them, showed them the bones, and brought them in to see my prisoner; she at once vanished, turning to water; however, I thrust my sword into this experimentally, upon which the water became blood.

Then we marched hurriedly down to our ship and sailed away. With the first glimmering of dawn we made out a mainland, which we took for the continent that faces our own. We reverently saluted it, made prayer, and held counsel upon our

best course. Some were for merely landing and turning back
at once, others for leaving the ship, and going into the interior
to make trial of the inhabitants. But while we were deliberat-
ing, a great storm arose, which dashed us, a complete wreck, on
the shore. We managed to swim to land, each snatching up his
arms and anything else he could.

Such are the adventures that befell me up to our arrival at
that other continent: our sea-voyage; our cruise among the
islands and in the air; then our experiences in and after the
whale; with the Heroes; with the dreams; and finally with
the Ox-heads and the Ass-shanks. Our fortunes on the continent will be the subject of the following books.   H.

THE TYRANNICIDE

*A man forces his way into the stronghold of a tyrant, with the
intention of killing him. Not finding the tyrant himself, he kills
his son, and leaves the sword sticking in his body. The tyrant,
coming, and finding his son dead, slays himself with the same
sword.—The assailant now claims that the killing of the son
entitles him to the reward of tyrannicide.*

Two tyrants—a father advanced in years, a son in the prime
of life, waiting only to step into his nefarious heritage—have
fallen by my hand on a single day: I come before this court,
claiming but one reward for my twofold service. My case is
unique. With one blow I have rid you of two monsters: with
my sword I slew the son; grief for the son slew the father.
The misdeeds of the tyrant are sufficiently punished: he has
lived to see his son perish untimely; and—wondrous sequel!—
the tyrant's own hand has freed us from tyranny. I slew the
son, and used his death to slay another: in his life he shared the
iniquities of his father; in his death, so far as in him lay, he was

a parricide. Mine is the hand that freed you, mine the sword 2 that accomplished all : as to the order and manner of procedure, there, indeed, I have deviated from the common practice of tyrannicides : I slew the son, who had strength to resist me, and left my sword to deal with the aged father. In acting 3 thus, I had thought to increase your obligation to me ; a two-fold deliverance—I had supposed—would entitle me to a two-fold reward ; for I have freed you not from tyranny alone, but from the fear of tyranny, and by removing the heir of iniquity have made your salvation sure. And now it seems that my services are to go for nothing ; I, the preserver of the constitution, am to forgo the recompense prescribed by its laws. It is surely from no patriotic motive, as he asserts, that my adversary disputes my claim ; rather it is from grief at the loss of the tyrants, and a desire to avenge their death.

Bear with me, gentlemen, for a little, while I dwell in some 4 detail upon those evils of tyranny with which you are only too familiar ; I shall thus enable you to realize the extent of my services, and to enjoy the contemplation of sufferings from which you have escaped. Ours was not the common experience : we had not *one* tyranny, *one* servitude to endure, we were not subjected to the caprice of a single master. Other cities have had their tyrant : it was reserved for us to have two tyrants at once, to groan beneath a double oppression. That of the old man was light by comparison, his anger mildness, his resentment long-suffering ; age had blunted his passions, checked their head-long impetus, and curbed the lust of pleasure. His crimes, so it is said, were involuntary ; resulting from no tyrannical disposition in himself, but from the instigations of his son. For in him paternal affection had too clearly become a mania ; his son was all in all to him ; he did his bidding, committed every crime at his pleasure, dealt out punishment at his command, was subservient to him in all things ; the minister of a tyrant's

5 caprice, and that tyrant his son. The young man left him in possession of the name and semblance of rule ; so much he conceded to his years : but in all essentials *he* was the real tyrant. By him the power of the tyrant was upheld ; by him and by him alone the fruits of tyranny were gathered. He it was who maintained the garrison, intimidated the victims of oppression, and butchered those who meditated resistance ; who laid violent hands on boys and maidens, and trampled on the sanctity of marriage. Murder, banishment, confiscation, torture, brutality; all bespeak the wantonness of youth. The father followed his son's lead, and had no word of blame for the crimes in which he participated. Our situation became unbearable : for when the promptings of passion draw support from the authority of rule, then iniquity knows no further bounds.

6 We knew moreover (and here was the bitterest thought of all) that our servitude must endure—ay, endure for ever ; that our city was doomed to pass in unending succession from master to master, to be the heritage of the oppressor. To others it is no small consolation that they may count the days, and say in their hearts : ' The end will be soon ; he will die, and we shall be free.' We had no such hope : there stood the heir of tyranny before our eyes. There were others—men of spirit—who cherished like designs with myself ; yet all lacked resolution to strike the blow ; freedom was despaired of ; to contend against a succession of tyrants seemed a hopeless task.

7 Yet I was not deterred. I had reckoned the difficulties of my undertaking, and shrank not back, but faced the danger. Alone, I issued forth to cope with tyranny in all its might. Alone, did I say ? nay, not alone ; I had my sword for company, my ally and partner in tyrannicide. I saw what the end was like to be : and, seeing it, resolved to purchase your freedom with my blood. I grappled with the outer watch, with difficulty routed the guards, slew all I met, broke down all

resistance,—and so to the fountain-head, the well-spring of tyranny, the source of all our calamities; within his stronghold I found him, and there slew him with many wounds, fighting valiantly for his life.

From that moment, my end was gained: tyranny was de- 8 stroyed; we were free men. There remained the aged father, alone, unarmed, desolate; his guards scattered, his strong protector slain; no adversary this for a brave man. And now I debated within myself: ' My work is done, my aim achieved, all is as I would have it. And how shall this remnant of tyranny be punished? He is unworthy of the hand that shed that other blood: the glory of a noble enterprise shall not be so defiled. No, let some other executioner be found. It were too much happiness for him to die, and never know the worst; let him see all, for his punishment, and let the sword be ready to his hand; to that sword I leave the rest.' In this design I withdrew; and the sword—as I had foreseen—did its office, slew the tyrant, and put the finishing touch to my work.

And now I come to you, bringing democracy with me, and 9 call upon all men to take heart, and hear the glad tidings of liberty. Enjoy the work of my hands! You see the citadel cleared of the oppressors; you are under no man's orders; the law holds its course; honours are awarded, judgements given, pleadings heard. And all springs from one bold stroke, from the slaying of that son whom his father might not survive. I claim from you the recompense that is my due; and that in no paltry, grasping spirit; it was not for a wage's sake that I sought to serve my country; but I would have my deed confirmed by your award; I would not be disparaged by slanderous tongues, as one who attempted and failed, and was deemed unworthy of honour.

My adversary tells me that I am unreasonable in asking for 10 reward and distinction. I did not slay the tyrant; I have not fulfilled the requirements of the statute; there is a flaw in my claim.—And what more does he want of me? Say: did I flinch? did I not ascend into the citadel? did I not slay? are we not free men? have we a master? do we hear a tyrant's threats? did any of the evil-doers escape me?—No; all is peace; the laws are in force; freedom is assured; democracy is established; our wives, our daughters are unmolested, our sons are safe; the city keeps festival in the general joy. And who is the cause of it all? who has wrought the change? Has any man a prior claim? Then I withdraw; be his the honour and the reward. But if not—if mine was the deed, mine the risk, mine the courage to ascend and smite and punish, dealing vengeance on the father through the son—then why depreciate my services? why seek to deprive me of a people's gratitude?

11 'But you did not kill the *tyrant*; the law assigns the reward to him who kills the tyrant.' And pray what is the difference between killing him and causing his death? I see none. The law-giver had but one end in view,—freedom, equality, deliverance from oppression. This was the signal service that he deemed worthy of recompense; and this service you cannot deny that I have rendered. In slaying one whom the tyrant could not survive, I myself wrought the tyrant's death. His was the hand: the deed was mine. Let us not chop logic as to the manner and circumstances of his death, but rather ask: has he ceased to exist, and am I the cause? Your scruples might go further, and object to some future deliverer of his country, that he struck not with the sword, but with a stick or a stone or the like. Had I blockaded the tyrant, and brought about his death by starvation, you would still, I suppose, have objected that it was not the work of my own hand? Again there would have been a flaw in my claim? The increased bitterness of such a death would have counted for nothing with you? Confine your attention to this one question: does any

of our oppressors survive ? is there any ground for anxiety, any vestige of our past misery ? If not, if all is peace, then none but an envious detractor would attempt to deprive me of the reward of my labours by inquiring into the means employed.

Moreover, it is laid down in our laws (unless after all these 12 years of servitude my memory plays me false) that blood-guiltiness is of two kinds. A man may slay another with his own hand, or, without slaying him, he may put death unavoidably in his way ; in the latter case the penalty is the same as in the former ; and rightly, it being the intention of the law that the cause should rank with the act itself ; the manner in which death is brought about is not the question. You would not acquit a man who in this sense had slain another ; you would punish him as a murderer : how then can you refuse to reward as a benefactor the man who, by parity of reasoning, has shown himself to be the liberator of his country ?

Nor again can it be objected that all I did was to strike the 13 blow, and that the resulting benefits were accidental, and formed no part of my design. What had I to fear, when once the stronger of our oppressors was slain ? And why did I leave my sword in the wound, if not because I foresaw the very thing that would happen ? Are you prepared to deny that the death so occasioned was that of a tyrant both in name and in fact, or that his death was an event for which the state would gladly pay an abundant reward ? I think not. If then the tyrant is slain, how can you withhold the reward from him who occasioned his death ? What scrupulousness is this—to concern yourself with the manner of his end, while you are enjoying the freedom that results from it ? Democracy is restored : what more can you demand from him who restored it ? You refer us to the terms of the law : well, the law looks only at the end ; of the means it says nothing ; it has no concern with them. Has not the reward of tyrannicide been paid before now to him who merely expelled a tyrant? And rightly so: for he too has made free men of slaves. But I have done more: banishment may be followed by restitution: but here the family of tyrants is utterly annihilated and destroyed; the evil thing is exterminated, root and branch.

14 I implore you, gentlemen, to review my conduct from beginning to end, and see whether there has been any such omission on my part as to make my act appear less than tyrannicide in the eye of the law. The high patriotic resolve which prompts a man to face danger for the common good, and to purchase the salvation of his country at the price of his own life; this is the first requirement. Have I been wanting here? Have I lacked courage? Have I shrunk back at the prospect of the dangers through which I must pass? My enemy cannot say it of me. Now at this stage let us pause. Consider only the intention, the design, apart from its success; and suppose that I come before you to claim the reward of patriotism merely on the ground of my resolve. I have failed, and another, following in my footsteps, has slain the tyrant. Say, is it unreasonable in such a case to allow my claim? 'Gentlemen,' I might say, 'the will, the intention, was mine; I made the attempt, I did what I could; my resolve entitles me of itself to your reward.' What would my enemy say to that?

15 But in fact my case stands far otherwise. I mounted into the stronghold, I faced danger, I had innumerable difficulties to contend with, before I slew the son. Think not that it was a light or easy matter, to make my way past the watch, and single-handed to overcome one body of guards after another and put them to flight: herein is perhaps the greatest difficulty with which the tyrannicide has to contend. It is no such great matter to bring the tyrant to bay, and dispatch him. Once overcome the guards that surround him, and success is ensured;

little remains to be done. I could not make my way to the tyrants till I had mastered every one of their satellites and body-guards : each of those preliminary victories had to be won. Once more I pause, and consider my situation. I have got the better of the guards ; I am master of the garrison ; I present you the tyrant stripped, unarmed, defenceless. May I claim some credit for this, or do you still require his blood ? Well, 16 if blood you must have, that too is not wanting ; my hands are not unstained ; the glorious deed is accomplished ; the youthful tyrant, the terror of all men, his father's sole security and pro-tection, the equivalent of many bodyguards, is slain in the prime of his strength. Have I not earned my reward ? Am I to have no credit for all that is done ? What if I had killed one of his guards, some underling, some favourite domestic ? Would it not have been thought a great thing, to go up and dispatch the tyrant's friend within his own walls, in the midst of his armed attendants ? But who *was* my victim ? The tyrant's son, himself a more grievous tyrant than his father, more cruel in his punishments, more violent in his excesses ; a pitiless master ; one, above all, whose succession to the supreme power promised a long continuance of our miseries. Shall I concede 17 that this is the sum of my achievements ? Shall we put it, that the tyrant has escaped, and lives ? Still I claim my recom-pense. What say you, gentlemen ? do you withhold it ? The son, perhaps, caused you no uneasiness ; he was no despot, no grievous oppressor ?

And now for the final stroke. All that my adversary demands of me, I have performed ; and that in the most effectual manner. I slew the tyrant when I slew his son ; slew him not with a single blow—he could have asked no easier expiation of his guilt than that—but with prolonged torment. I showed him his beloved lying in the dust, in pitiable case, weltering in blood. And what if he were a villain ? he was still his son, still the old man's likeness in the pride of youth. These are the wounds that fathers feel; this the tyrannicide's sword of justice; this the death, the vengeance, that befits cruelty and oppression. The tyrant who dies in a moment, and knows not his loss, and sees not such 18 sights as these, dies unpunished. I knew—we all knew—his affection for his son; knew that not for one day would he survive his loss. Other fathers may be devoted to their sons: his devotion was something more than theirs. How should it be otherwise? In him, and in him alone, the father saw the zealous guardian of his lawless rule, the champion of his old age, the sole prop of tyranny. If grief did not kill him on the spot, despair, I knew, must do so; there could be no further joy in life for him when his protector was slain. Nature, grief, despair, foreboding, terror,—these were my allies; with these I hemmed him in, and drove him to his last desperate resolve. Know that your oppressor died childless, heartbroken, weeping, groaning in spirit; the time of his mourning was short, but it was a father mourning for his son; he died by his own hand, bitterest, most awful of deaths; that death comes lightly, by comparison, which is dealt by another.

19 Where is my sword?

Does any one else know anything of this sword? Does any one claim it? Who took it up into the citadel? The tyrant used this sword. Who had it before him? Who put it in his way?—Sword, fellow labourer, partner of my enterprise,—we have faced danger and shed blood to no purpose. We are slighted. Men say that we have not earned our reward.

Suppose that I had advanced a claim solely on my sword's behalf: suppose that I had said to you: 'Gentlemen, the tyrant had resolved to slay himself, but was without a weapon at the moment, when this sword of mine supplied his need, and thereby played its part in our deliverance.' Should you not have considered that the owner of a weapon so public-spirited was entitled to honour and reward? Should you not have recompensed him, and inscribed his name among those of your benefactors; consecrated his sword, and worshipped it as a God?

Now consider how the tyrant may be supposed to have acted 20 and spoken as his end approached.—His son lies mortally wounded at my hand; the wounds are many, and are exposed to view, that so the father's heart may be torn asunder at the very first sight of him. He cries out piteously to his father, not for help —he knows the old man's feebleness—, but for sympathy in his sufferings. I meanwhile am making my way home: I have written in the last line of my tragedy, and now I leave the stage clear for the actor; there is the body, the sword, all that is necessary to complete the scene. The father enters. He beholds his son, his only son, gasping, blood-stained, weltering in gore; he sees the wounds—mortal wound upon wound—and exclaims: 'Son, we are slain, we are destroyed, we are stricken in the midst of our power. Where is the assassin? For what fate does he reserve me, who am dead already in thy death, O my son? Because I am old he fears me not, he withholds his vengeance, and would prolong my torment.' Then he looks 21 for a sword; he has always gone unarmed himself, trusting all to his son. The sword is not wanting; it has been waiting for him all this time; I left it ready for the deed that was to follow. He draws it from the wound and speaks: 'Sword, that but a moment past hast slain me, complete thy work: comfort the stricken father, aid his aged hand; dispatch, slay, make an end of the tyrant and his grief. Would that I had met thee first, that my blood had been shed before his! I could but have died a tyrant's death, and should have left an avenger behind me. And now I die childless: I have not so much as a murderer at my need.' Even as he speaks, with trembling hand he plunges the sword into his breast: he is in haste to die; but that feeble hand lacks strength to do its dread office.

22 Is he punished? Are these wounds? Is this death? A
tyrant's death? Is there reward for this?

The closing scene you have all witnessed : the son—no mean
antagonist—prostrate in death; the father fallen upon him;
blood mingling with blood, the drink-offering of Victory and
Freedom ; and in the midst my sword, that wrought all ; judge
by its presence there, whether the weapon was unworthy of its
master, whether it did him faithful service. Had all been done
by my hand, it had been little ; the strangeness of the deed is
its glory. The tyranny was overthrown by me, and no other ;
but many actors had their part to play in the drama. The first
part was mine ; the second was the son's ; the third the tyrant's ;
and my sword was never absent from the stage.   F.

THE DISINHERITED

*A disinherited son adopts the medical profession. His father
going mad, and being given up by the other physicians, he treats
him successfully, and is then reinstated in his rights. Subsequently
his step-mother also goes mad; he is bidden to cure her, and,
declaring his inability to do so, is once more disinherited.*

THERE is neither novelty nor strangeness, gentlemen of the
jury, in my father's present proceedings. It is not the first
time his passions have taken this direction ; it has become an
instinctive habit with him to pay a visit to this familiar court.
Still, my unfortunate position has this much of novelty about
it : the charge I have to meet is not personal, but professional ;
I am to be punished for the inability of Medicine to do my
father's bidding. A curious demand, surely, that healing should
be done to order, and depend not on the limits of one's art, but
on the wishes of one's father. For my part, I should be only

too glad to find drugs in the pharmacopoeia which could relieve not only disordered wits, but disordered tempers; then I might be serviceable to my father. As it is, he is completely cured of madness, but is worse-tempered than ever. The bitterest part of it is, he is sane enough in all other relations, and mad only where his healer is concerned. You see what my medical fee amounts to; I am again disinherited, cut off from my family once more, as though the sole purpose of my brief reinstatement had been the accentuation of my disgrace by repetition.

When a thing is within the limits of possibility, I require no 2 bidding; I came before I was summoned, to see what I could do in this case. But when there is absolutely no hope, I will not meddle. With this particular patient, such caution is especially incumbent upon me; how my father would treat me, if I tried and failed, I can judge by his disinheriting me when I refused to try. Gentlemen, I am sorry for my step-mother's illness—for she was an excellent woman; I am sorry for my father's distress thereat; I am most sorry of all that I should seem rebellious, and be unable to give the required service; but the disease is incurable, and my art is not omni-potent. I do not see the justice of disinheriting one who, when he cannot do a thing, refuses to undertake it.

The present case throws a clear light upon the reasons for my 3 first disinheriting. The allegations of those days I consider to have been disposed of by my subsequent life; and the present charges I shall do my best to clear away with a short account of my proceedings. Wilful and disobedient son that I am, a dis-grace to my father, unworthy of my family, I thought proper to say very little indeed in answer to his long and vehement denunciations. Banished from my home, I reflected that I should find my most convincing plea, my best acquittal, in the life I then led, in practically illustrating the difference between my father's picture and the reality, in devotion to the worthiest pursuits and association with the most reputable company. But I had also a presentiment of what actually happened; it occurred to me even then that a perfectly sane father does not rage causelessly at his son, nor trump up false accusations against him. Persons were not wanting who detected incipient madness; it was the warning and precursor of a stroke which would fall before long—this unreasoning dislike, this harsh conduct, this fluent abuse, this malignant prosecution, all this violence, passion, and general ill temper. Yes, gentlemen, I saw that the time might come when Medicine would serve me well.

4   I went abroad, attended lectures by the most famous foreign physicians, and by hard work and perseverance mastered my craft. Upon my return, I found that my father's madness had developed, and that he had been given up by the local doctors, who are not distinguished for insight, and are much to seek in accurate diagnosis. I did no more than a son's duty when I forgot and forgave the disinheritance, and visited him without waiting to be called in; I had in fact nothing to complain of that was properly his act; his errors were not his, but, as I have implied, those of his illness. I came unsummoned, then. But I did not treat him at once; that is not our custom, nor what our art enjoins upon us. What we are taught to do is first of all to ascertain whether the disease is curable or incurable— has it passed beyond our control? After that, if it is susceptible of treatment, we treat it, and do our very best to relieve the sufferer. But if we realize that the complaint has got the entire mastery, we have nothing to do with it at all. That is the tradition that has come down to us from the fathers of our art, who direct us not to attempt hopeless cases. Well, I found that there was yet hope for my father; the complaint had not gone too far; I watched him for a long time; formed my conclusions with scrupulous care; then, I commenced operations and exhibited my drugs without hesitation—though many of his

friends were suspicious of my prescription, impugned the treatment, and took notes to be used against me.

My step-mother was present, distressed and doubtful—the result not of any dislike to me, but of pure anxiety, based on her full knowledge of his sad condition; no one but her, who had lived with and nursed him, knew the worst. However, I never faltered; the symptoms would not lie to me, nor my art fail me; when the right moment came, I applied the treatment, in spite of the timidity of some of my friends, who were afraid of the scandal that might result from a failure; it would be said that the medicine was my vengeful retort to the disinheritance. To make a long story short, it was at once apparent that he had taken no harm; he was in his senses again, and aware of all that went on. The company were amazed; my step-mother thanked me, and every one could see that she was delighted both at my triumph and at her husband's recovery. He himself— to give credit where it is due—did not take time to consider, nor to ask advice, but, as soon as he heard the story, undid what he had done, made me his son again, hailed me as his preserver and benefactor, confessed that I had now given my proofs, and withdrew his previous charges. All this was delightful to the better, who were many, among his friends, but distasteful to the persons who enjoy a quarrel more than a reconciliation. I observed at the time that all were not equally pleased; there were changes of colour, uneasy glances, signs of mortification, in one quarter at least, which told of envy and hatred. With us, who had recovered each other, all was naturally affection and rejoicing.

Quite a short time after, my step-mother's disorder commenced —a very terrible and unaccountable one, gentlemen of the jury. I observed it from its very beginning; it was no slight superficial case, this; it was a long-established but hitherto latent mental disease, which now burst out and forced its way into notice. There are many signs by which we know that madness is incurable—among them a strange one which I noticed in this case. Ordinary society has a soothing, alleviating effect; the patient forgets to be mad; but if he sees a doctor, or even hears one mentioned, he at once displays acute irritation—an infallible sign that he is far gone, incurable in fact. I was distressed to notice this symptom; my step-mother was a worthy person who deserved a better fate, and I was all compassion for her.

7 But my father in his simplicity, knowing neither when nor how the trouble began, and quite unable to gauge its gravity, bade me cure her by the drugs that had cured him. His idea was that madness was to be nothing else but mad; the disease was the same, its effects the same, and it must admit of the same treatment. When I told him, as was perfectly true, that his wife was incurable, and confessed that the case was beyond me, he thought it an outrage, said I was refusing because I chose to, and treating the poor woman shamefully—in short, visited upon me the limitations of my art. Such ebullitions are common enough in distress; we all lose our tempers then with the people who tell us the truth. I must nevertheless defend myself and my profession, as well as I can, against his strictures.

8 I will begin with some remarks upon the law under which I am to be disinherited; my father will please to observe that it is not quite so much now as before a matter for his absolute discretion. You will find, sir, that the author of the law has not conferred the right of disherison upon *any* father against *any* son upon *any* pretext. It is true he has armed fathers with this weapon; but he has also protected sons against its illegitimate use. That is the meaning of his insisting that the procedure shall not be irresponsible and uncontrolled, but come under the legal cognizance of inspectors whose decision will be uninfluenced by passion or misrepresentation. He knew how

often irritation is unreasonable, and what can be effected by a lying tale, a trusted slave, or a spiteful woman. He would not have the deed done without form of law ; sons were not to be condemned unheard and out of hand ; they are to have the ear of the court for so long by the clock, and there is to be adequate inquiry into the facts.

My father's competence, then, being confined to preferring 9 his complaints, and the decision whether they are reasonable or not resting with you, I shall be within my rights in requesting you to defer consideration of the grievance on which he bases the present suit, until you have determined whether a second disinheritance is admissible in the abstract. He has cast me off, has exercised his legal rights, enforced his parental powers to the full, and then restored me to my position as his son. Now it is iniquitous, I maintain, that fathers should have these un-limited penal powers, that disgrace should be multiplied, appre-hension made perpetual, the law now chastize, now relent, now resume its severity, and justice be the shuttlecock of our fathers' caprices It is quite proper for the law to humour, encourage, give effect to, *one* punitive impulse on the part of him who has begotten us ; but if, after shooting his bolt, insisting on his right, indulging his wrath, he discovers our merits and takes us back, then he should be held to his decision, and not allowed to oscillate, waver, do and undo any more. Originally, he had no means of knowing whether his offspring would turn out well or ill ; that is why parents who have decided to bring up children before they knew their nature are permitted to reject such as are found unworthy of their family.

But when a man has taken his son back, not upon compulsion, 10 but of his own motion and after inquiry, how can further chop-ping and changing be justified ? What further occasion for the law ? Its author might fairly say to you, sir : *If your son was vicious and deserved to be disinherited, what were you about*

to recall him? Why have him home again? Why suspend the
law's operation? You were a free agent; you need not have
done it. The laws are not your play-ground; you are not to put
the courts in motion every time your mood varies; the laws are not
to be suspended to-day and enforced to-morrow, with juries to look
on at the proceedings, or rather to be the ministers of your whims,
executioners or peace-makers according to your taste and fancy.
The boy cost you one begetting, and one rearing; in return for
which you may disinherit him, once, always provided you have
reason to show for it. Disinheriting as a regular habit, a promiscuous pastime, is not included in the patria potestas.

Gentlemen of the jury, I entreat you in Heaven's name not
to permit him, after voluntarily reinstating me, reversing the
previous decision, and renouncing his anger, to revive the old
sentence and have recourse to the same paternal rights; the
period of their validity is past and gone; his own act suffices
to annul and exhaust their power. You know the general rule
of the courts, that a party dissatisfied with the verdict of a
ballot-provided jury is allowed an appeal to another court;
but that is not so when the parties have agreed upon arbitrators,
and, after such selection, put the matter in their hands. They
had the choice, there, of not recognizing the court *ab initio*;
if they nevertheless did so, they may fairly be expected to
abide by its award. Similarly you, sir, had the choice of never
taking back your son, if you thought him unworthy; having
decided that he was worthy, and taken him back, you cannot
be permitted to disinherit him anew; the evidence of his not
deserving it is your own admission of his worth. It is only
right that the reinstatement and reconciliation should be
definitive, after such abundant investigation; there have been
two trials, observe: the first, that in which you rejected me;
the second, that in your own conscience, which reversed the
decision of the other; the fact of reversal only adds force to

the later result. Abide, then, by your second thoughts, and uphold your own verdict. You are to be my father; such was your determination, approved and ratified.

Suppose I were not your begotten, but only your adopted son, I hold that you could not then have disinherited me; for what it is originally open to us not to do, we have no right, having done, to undo. But where there is both the natural tie, and that of deliberate choice, how can a second rejection, a re-peated deprivation of the one relationship, be justified ? Or again, suppose I had been a slave, and you had seen reason to put me in irons, and afterwards, convinced of my innocence, made me a free man ; could you, upon an angry impulse, have enslaved me again ? Assuredly not ; the law makes these acts binding and irrevocable. Upon this contention, that the volun-tary annulment of a disinheritance precludes a repetition of the act, I could enlarge further, but will not labour the point.

You have next to consider the character of the man now to be disinherited. I lay no stress upon the fact that I was then nothing, and am now a physician ; my art will not help me here. As little do I insist that I was then young, and am now middle-aged, with my years as a guarantee against misconduct ; perhaps there is not much in that either. But, gentlemen, at the time of my previous expulsion, if I had never done my father any harm (as I should maintain), neither had I done him any good ; whereas now I have recently been his preserver and benefactor ; could there be worse ingratitude than so, and so soon, to requite me for saving him from that terrible fate ? My care of him goes for nothing ; it is lightly forgotten, and I am driven forth desolate—I, whose wrongs might have ex-cused my rejoicing at his troubles, but who, so far from bearing malice, saved him and restored him to his senses.

For, gentlemen, it is no ordinary slight kindness that he is choosing this way of repaying. You all know (though he may not realize) what he was capable of doing, what he had to endure, what his state was, in fact, during those bad days. The doctors had given him up, his relations had cleared away and dared not come near him; but I undertook his case and restored him to the power of—accusing me and going to law. Let me help your imagination, sir. You were very nearly in the state in which your wife now is, when I gave you back your understanding. It is surely not right that my reward for that should be this—that your understanding should be used against me alone. That it is no trifling kindness I have done you is apparent from the very nature of your accusation. The ground of your hatred is that she whom I do not cure is in extremities, is terribly afflicted; then, seeing that I relieved you of just such an affliction, there is surely better reason for you to love and be grateful to me for your own release from such horrors. But you are unconscionable enough to make the first employment of your restored faculties an indictment of me; you smite your healer, the ancient hate revives, and we have you reciting the same old law again. My art's handsome fee, the worthy payment for my drugs, is—your present manifestation of vigour!

15   But you, gentlemen of the jury, will you allow him to punish his benefactor, drive away his preserver, pay for his wits with hatred, and for his recovery with chastisement? I hope better things of your justice. However flagrantly I had now been misconducting myself, I had a large balance of gratitude to draw upon. With that consideration in his memory, he need not have been extreme to mark what is now done amiss; it might have inspired him with ready indulgence, the more if the antecedent service was great enough to throw anything that might follow into the shade. That fairly states my relation to him; I preserved him; he owes his life absolutely to me; his existence, his sanity, his understanding, are my gifts, given,

moreover, when all others despaired and confessed that the case was beyond their skill.

The service that I did was the more meritorious, it seems to 16 me, in that I was not at the time my father's son, nor under any obligation to undertake the case; I was independent of him, a mere stranger; the natural bond had been snapped. Yet I was not indifferent; I came as a volunteer, uninvited, at my own instance. I brought help, I persevered, I effected the cure, I restored him, thereby securing myself at once a father and an acquittal; I conquered anger with kindness, disarmed law with affection, purchased readmission to my family with important service, proved my filial loyalty at that critical moment, was adopted (or adopted myself, rather) on the recommendation of my art, while my conduct in trying circumstances proved me a son by blood also. For I had anxiety and fatigue enough in being always on the spot, ministering to my patient, watching for my opportunities, now humouring the disease when it gathered strength, now availing myself of a remission to combat it. Of all a physician's tasks the most hazardous is the care of patients like this, with the personal attendance it involves; for in their moments of exasperation they are apt to direct their fury upon any one they can come at. Yet I never shrank or hesitated; I was always there; I had a life-and-death struggle with the malady, and the final victory was with me and my drugs.

Now I can fancy a person who hears all this objecting hastily, 17 'What a fuss about giving a man a dose of medicine!' But the fact is, there are many preliminaries to be gone through; the ground has to be prepared; the body must first be made susceptible to treatment; the patient's whole condition has to be studied; he must be purged, reduced, dieted, properly exercised, enabled to sleep, coaxed into tranquillity. Now other invalids will submit to all this; but mania robs its victims of self-control;

they are restive and jib ; their physicians are in danger, and treatment at a disadvantage. Constantly, when we are on the very point of success and full of hope, some slight hitch occurs, and a relapse takes place which undoes all in a moment, neutralizing our care and tripping up our art.

18 Now, after my going through all this, after my wrestle with this formidable disease and my triumph over so elusive an ailment, is it still your intention to support him in disinheriting me ? Shall he interpret the laws as he will against his benefactor ? Will you look on while he makes war upon nature ? I obey nature, gentlemen of the jury, in saving my father from death, and myself from the loss of him, unjust as he had been. He on the contrary defers to law (he calls it law) in ruining and cutting off from his kin the son who has obliged him. He is a cruel father, I a loving son. I own the authority of nature : he spurns and flings it from him. How misplaced is this paternal hate ! How worse misplaced this filial love ! For I must reproach myself—my father will have it so. And the reproach ? That where I should hate (for I am hated), I love, and where I should love little, I love much. Yet surely nature requires of parents that they love their children more than of children that they love their parents. But he deliberately disregards both the law, which secures children their family rights during good behaviour, and nature, which inspires parents with fervent love for their offspring. Having greater incentives to affection, you might suppose that he would confer the fruits of it upon me in larger measure, or at the least reciprocate and emulate my love. Alas, far from it ! he returns hate for love, persecution for devotion, wrong for service, disinheritance for respect ; the laws which guard, he converts into means of assailing, the rights of children. Ah, my father, how do you force law into your service in this battle against nature !

19 The facts, believe me, are not as you would have them. You

are a bad exponent, sir, of good laws. In this matter of affection there is no war between law and nature; they hunt in
couples, they work together for the remedying of wrongs.
When you evil entreat your benefactor, you are wronging nature;
now I ask, do you wrong the laws as well as nature? You do;
it is their intention to be fair and just and give sons their rights;
but you will not allow it; you hound them on again and again
upon one child as though he were many; you keep them ever
busy punishing, when their own desire is peace and goodwill
between father and son. I need hardly add that, as against
the innocent, they may be said to have no existence. But let
me tell you, ingratitude also is an offence known to the law;
an action will lie against a person who fails to recompense his
benefactor. If he adds to such failure an attempt to punish,
he has surely reached the uttermost limits of wrong in
this sort. And now I think I have sufficiently established
two points: first, my father has not the right, after once exert-
ing his parental privilege and availing himself of the law, to
disinherit me again; and secondly, it is on general grounds
inadmissible to cast off and expel from his family one who has
rendered service so invaluable.

Let us next proceed to the actual reasons given for the dis- 20
inheritance; let us inquire into the nature of the charge. We
must first go back for a moment to the intention of the legislator. We will grant you for the sake of argument, sir, that it
is open to you to disinherit as often as you please; we will
further concede you this right against your benefactor; but
I presume that disinheritance is not to be the beginning and
the ending in itself; you will not resort to it, that is, without
sufficient cause. The legislator's meaning is not that the
father can disinherit, whatever his grievance may be, that
nothing is required beyond the wish and a complaint; in that
case, what is the court's function? No, gentlemen, it is your

business to inquire whether the parental anger rests upon good and sufficient grounds. That is the question which I am now to put before you; and I will take up the story from the moment when sanity was restored.

21   The first-fruits of this was the withdrawal of the disinheritance; I was preserver, benefactor, everything. So far my conduct is not open to exception, I take it. Well, and later on what fault has my father to find? What attention or filial duty did I omit? Did I stay out o' nights, sir? Do you charge me with untimely drinkings and revellings? Was I extravagant? Did I get into some disreputable brawl? Did any such complaint reach you? None whatever. Yet these are just the offences for which the law contemplates disherison. Ah, but my step-mother fell ill. Indeed, and do you make that a charge against me? Do you prefer a suit for ill health? I understand you to say no.

22   What *is* the grievance, then?—*That you refuse to treat her at my bidding, and for such disobedience to your father deserve to be disinherited.*—Gentlemen, I will explain presently how the nature of this demand results in a seeming disobedience, but a real inability. Meanwhile, I simply remark that neither the authority which the law confers on him, nor the obedience to which I am bound, is indiscriminate. Among orders, some have no sanction, while the disregard of others justifies anger and punishment. My father may be ill, and I neglect him; he may charge me with the management of his house, and I take no notice; he may tell me to look after his country estate, and I evade the task. In all these and similar cases, the parental censure will be well deserved. But other things again are for the sons to decide, as questions of professional skill or policy—especially if the father's interests are not touched. If a painter's father says to him, ' Paint this, my boy, and do not paint that ' ; or a musician's, ' Strike this note, and not the other ' ; or a bronze-

founder's, 'Cast so-and-so'; would it be tolerable that the son should be disinherited for not taking such advice? Of course not.

But the medical profession should be left still more to their 23 own discretion than other artists, in proportion to the greater nobility of their aims and usefulness of their work; this art should have a special right of choosing its objects; this sacred occupation, taught straight from Heaven, and pursued by the wisest of men, should be secured against all compulsion, enslaved to no law, intimidated and penalized by no court, exposed to no votes or paternal threats or uninstructed passions. If I had told my father directly and expressly, 'I will not do it, I refuse the case, though I could treat it, I hold my art at no man's service but my own and yours, as far as others are concerned I am a layman'—if I had taken that position, where is the masterful despot who would have applied force and compelled me to practise against my will? The appropriate inducements are request and entreaty, not laws and browbeating and tribunals; the physician is to be persuaded, not commanded; he is to choose, not be terrorized; he is not to be haled to his patient, but to come with his consent and at his pleasure. Governments are wont to give physicians the public recognition of honours, precedence, immunities and privileges; and shall the art which has State immunities not be exempt from the *patria potestas*?

All this I was entitled to say simply as a professional man, 24 even on the assumption that you had had me taught, and devoted much care and expense to my training, that this particular case had been within my competence, and I had yet declined it. But in fact you have to consider also how utterly unreasonable it is that you should not let me use at my own discretion my own acquisition. It was not as your son nor under your authority that I acquired this art; and yet it was for your advantage that I acquired it—you were the first to profit by it—, though you had contributed nothing to my training. Will you mention the fees you paid? How much did the stock of my surgery cost you? Not one penny. I was a pauper, I knew not where to turn for necessaries, and I owed my instruction to my teachers' charity. The provision my father made for my education was sorrow, desolation, distress, estrangement from my friends and banishment from my family. And do you then claim to have the use of my skill, the absolute control of what was acquired independently? You should be content with the previous service rendered to yourself, not under obligation, but of free will; for even on that occasion nothing could have been demanded of me on the score of gratitude.

25 My kindness of the past is not to be my duty of the future; a voluntary favour is not to be turned into an obligation to take unwelcome orders; the principle is not to be established that he who once cures a man is bound to cure any number of others at his bidding ever after. That would be to appoint the patients we cure our absolute masters; *we* should be paying *them*, and the fee would be slavish submission to their commands. Could anything be more absurd? Because you were ill, and I was at such pains to restore you, does that make you the owner of my art?

26 All this I could have said, if the tasks he imposed upon me had been within my powers, and I had declined to accept all of them, or, on compulsion, any of them. But I now wish you to look further into their nature. 'You cured me of madness (says he); my wife is now mad and in the condition I was in (that of course is his idea); she has been given up as I was by the other doctors, but you have shown that nothing is too hard for you; very well, then, cure her too, and make an end of her illness.' Now, put like that, it sounds very reasonable, especially in the ears of a layman innocent of medical knowledge. But

if you will listen to what I have to say for my art, you will find that there *are* things too hard for us, that all ailments are not alike, that the same treatment and the same drugs will not always answer ; and then you will understand what a difference there is between refusing and being unable. Pray bear with me while I generalize a little, without condemning my disquisition as pedantic, irrelevant, or ill-timed.

To begin with, human bodies differ in nature and temperament ; compounded as they admittedly are of the same elements, they are yet compounded in different proportions. I am not referring at present to sexual differences ; the *male* body is not the same or alike in different individuals ; it differs in temperament and constitution ; and from this it results that in different men diseases also differ both in character and in intensity ; one man's body has recuperative power and is susceptible to treatment ; another's is utterly crazy, open to every infection, and without vigour to resist disease. To suppose, then, that all fever, all consumption, lung-disease, or mania, being generically the same, will affect every subject in the same way, is what no sensible, thoughtful, or well-informed person would do ; the same disease is easily curable in one man, and not in another. Why, sow the same wheat in various soils, and the results will vary. Let the soil be level, deep, well watered, well sunned, well aired, well ploughed, and the crop will be rich, fat, plentiful. Elevated stony ground will make a difference, no sun another difference, foothills another, and so on. Just so with disease ; its soil makes it thrive and spread, or starves it. Now all this quite escapes my father ; he makes no inquiries of this sort, but assumes that all mania in every body is the same, and to be treated accordingly.

Besides such differences between males, it is obvious that the **28** female body differs widely from the male both in the diseases it is subject to and in its capacity or non-capacity of recovery.

The bracing effect of toil, exercise, and open air gives firmness and tone to the male; the female is soft and unstrung from its sheltered existence, and pale with anaemia, deficient caloric and excess of moisture. It is consequently, as compared with the male, open to infection, exposed to disease, unequal to vigorous treatment, and, in particular, liable to mania. With their emotional, mobile, excitable tendencies on the one hand, and their defective bodily strength on the other, women fall an easy prey to this affliction.

29 It is quite unfair, then, to expect the physician to cure both sexes indifferently; we must recognize how far apart they are, their whole lives, pursuits, and habits, having been distinct from infancy. Do not talk of a mad person, then, but specify the sex; do not confound distinctions and force all cases under the supposed identical title of madness; keep separate what nature separates, and then examine the respective possibilities. I began this exposition with stating that the first thing we doctors look to is the nature and temperament of our patient's body: which of the humours predominates in it; is it full-blooded or the reverse; at, or past, its prime; big or little; fat or lean? When a man has satisfied himself upon these and other such points, his opinion, favourable or adverse, upon the prospects of recovery may be implicitly relied upon.

30 It must be remembered too that madness itself has a thousand forms, numberless causes, and even some distinct names. Delusion, infatuation, frenzy, lunacy—these are not the same; they all express different degrees of the affection. Again, the causes are not only different in men and women, but, in men, they are different for the old and for the young; for instance, in young men some redundant humour is the usual cause; whereas with the old a shrewdly timed slander, or very likely a fancied domestic slight, will get hold of them, first cloud their understanding, and finally drive them distracted. As for women,

all sorts of things effect a lodgement and make easy prey of them, especially bitter dislike, envy of a prosperous rival, pain or anger. These feelings smoulder on, gaining strength with time, till at last they burst out in madness.

Such, sir, has been your wife's case, perhaps with the addition 31 of some recent trouble; for she used to have no strong dislikes, yet she is now in the grasp of the malady—and that beyond hope of medical relief. For if any physician undertakes and cures the case, you have my permission to hate me for the wrong I have done you. Yet I must go so far as to say that, even had the case not been so desperate—had there been a glimmer of hope—even then I should not have lightly intervened, nor been very ready to administer drugs; I should have been afraid of what might happen, and of the sort of stories that might get about. You know the universal belief that every step-mother, whatever her general merits, hates her step-sons; it is supposed to be a feminine mania from which none of them is exempt. If the disease had taken a wrong turn, and the medicine failed of its effect, there would very likely have been suspicions of intentional malpractice.

Your wife's condition, sir—and I describe it to you after close 32 observation—, is this: she will never mend, though she take ten thousand doses of medicine. It is therefore undesirable to make the experiment, unless your object is merely to compel me to fail and cover me with disgrace. Pray do not enable my professional brethren to triumph over me; their jealousy is enough. If you disinherit me again, I shall be left desolate, but I shall pray for no evil upon your head. But suppose— though God forbid!—suppose your malady should return; relapses are common enough in such cases, under irritation; what is my course then to be? Doubt not, I shall restore you once more; I shall not desert the post which nature assigns to children; I for my part shall not forget my descent. And then if you recover, must I look for another restitution ? You understand me ? your present proceedings are calculated to awake your disease and stir it to renewed malignancy. It is but the other day that you emerged from your sad condition, and you are vehement and loud—worst of all, you are full of anger, indulging your hatred and appealing once more to the law. Alas, father, even such was the prelude to your first madness. H.

PHALARIS, I

WE are sent to you, Priests of Delphi, by Phalaris our master, with instructions to present this bull to the God, and to speak the necessary words on behalf of the offering and its donor. Such being our errand, it remains for us to deliver his message, which is as follows :

‘ It is my desire above all things, men of Delphi, to appear to the Greeks as I really am, and not in that character in which Envy and Malice, availing themselves of the ignorance of their hearers, have represented me : and if to the Greeks in general, then most of all to you, who are holy men, associates of the God, sharers (I had almost said) of his hearth and home. If I can clear myself before you, if I can convince you that I am not the cruel tyrant I am supposed to be, then I may consider myself cleared in the eyes of all the world. For the truth of my statements, I appeal to the testimony of the God himself. Methinks *he* is not likely to be deceived by lying words. It may be an easy matter to mislead men : but to escape the penetration of a God—and that God Apollo—is impossible.

2 ‘ I was a man of no mean family ; in birth, in breeding, in education, the equal of any man in Agrigentum. In my political conduct I was ever public-spirited, in my private life mild and unassuming ; no unseemly act, no deed of violence, oppression,

or headstrong insolence was ever laid to my charge in those early days. But our city at that time was divided into factions : I saw myself exposed to the plots of my political opponents, who sought to destroy me by every means : if I would live in security, if I would preserve the city from destruction, there was but one course open to me—to seize upon the government, and thereby baffle my opponents, put an end to their machinations, and bring my countrymen to their senses. There were not a few who approved my design : patriots and men of cool judgement, they understood my sentiments, and saw that I had no alternative. With their help, I succeeded without difficulty in my enterprise.

' From that moment, the disturbances ceased. My opponents became my subjects, I their ruler ; and the city was freed from dissension. From executions and banishments and confiscations I abstained, even in the case of those who had plotted against my life. Such strong measures are indeed never more necessary than at the commencement of a new rule : but I was sanguine ; I proposed to treat them as my equals, and to win their allegiance by clemency, mildness, and humanity. My first act was to reconcile myself with my enemies, most of whom I invited to my table and took into my confidence.

' I found the city in a ruinous condition, owing to the neglect of the magistrates, who had commonly been guilty of embezzlement, if not of wholesale plunder. I repaired the evil by means of aqueducts, beautified the city with noble buildings, and surrounded it with walls. The public revenues were easily increased by proper attention on the part of the fiscal authorities. I provided for the education of the young and the maintenance of the old ; and for the general public I had games and spectacles, banquets and doles. As for rape and seduction, tyrannical violence or intimidation, I abhorred the very name of such things.

4 ' I now began to think of laying down my power ; and how to do so with safety was my only concern. The cares of government and public business had begun to weigh upon me ; I found my position as burdensome as it was invidious. But it was still a question, how to render the city independent of such assistance for the future. And whilst I—honest man !—was busied with such thoughts, my enemies were even then combining against me, and debating the ways and means of rebellion ; conspiracies were forming, arms and money were being collected, neighbour states were invited to assist, embassies were on their way to Sparta and Athens. The torments that were in store for me, had I fallen into their hands, I afterwards learnt from their public confession under torture, from which it appeared that they had vowed to tear me limb from limb with their own hands. For my escape from such a fate, I have to thank the Gods, who unmasked the conspiracy ; and, in particular, the God of Delphi, who sent dreams to warn me, and dispatched messengers with detailed information.

5 ' And now, men of Delphi, I would ask your advice. Imagine yourselves to-day in the perilous situation in which I then stood ; and tell me what was my proper course. I had almost fallen unawares into the hands of my enemies, and was casting about for means of safety. Leave Delphi for a while, and transport yourselves in spirit to Agrigentum : behold the preparations of my enemies : listen to their threats ; and say, what is your counsel ? Shall I sit quietly on the brink of destruction, exercising clemency and long-suffering as heretofore ? bare my throat to the sword ? see my nearest and dearest slaughtered before my eyes ? What would this be but sheer imbecility ? Shall I not rather bear myself like a man of spirit, give the rein to my rational indignation, avenge my injuries upon the conspirators, and use my present power with a view to my future security ? This, I know, would have been your advice.

'Now observe my procedure. I sent for the guilty persons, 6 heard their defence, produced my evidence, established every point beyond a doubt; and when they themselves admitted the truth of the accusation, I punished them; for I took it ill, not that they had plotted against my life, but that on their account I was compelled to abandon my original policy. From that day to this, I have consulted my own safety by punishing conspiracy as often as it has shown itself.

'And men call me cruel! They do not stop to ask who was the aggressor; they condemn what they think the cruelty of my vengeance, but pass lightly over the provocation, and the nature of the crime. It is as if a man were to see a temple-robber hurled from the rock at Delphi, and, without reflecting how the transgressor had stolen into your temple by night, torn down the votive-offerings, and laid hands upon the graven image of the God, were to exclaim against the inhumanity of persons who, calling themselves Greeks and holy men, could yet find it in them to inflict this awful punishment upon their fellow Greek, and that within sight of the holy place;—for the rock, as I am told, is not far from the city. Surely you would laugh to scorn such an accusation as this; and your *cruel* treatment of the impious would be universally applauded.

'But so it is: the public does not inquire into the character 7 of a ruler, into the justice or injustice of his conduct; the mere name of tyranny ensures men's hatred; the tyrant might be an Aeacus, a Minos, a Rhadamanthus,—they would be none the less eager for his destruction; their thoughts ever run on those tyrants who have been bad rulers, and the good, because they bear the same name, are held in the like detestation. I have heard that many of your tyrants in Greece have been wise men, who, labouring under that opprobrious title, have yet given proofs of benevolence and humanity, and whose pithy maxims are even now stored up in your temple among the treasures of the God.

8   ' Observe, moreover, the prominence given to punishment by all constitutional legislators ; they know that when the fear of punishment is wanting, nothing else is of avail. And this is doubly so with us who are tyrants ; whose power is based upon compulsion ; who live in the midst of enmity and treachery. The bugbear terrors of the law would never serve our turn. Rebellion is a many-headed Hydra : we cut off one guilty head, two others grow in its place. Yet we must harden our hearts, smite them off as they grow, and—like Iolaus—sear the wounds ; thus only shall we hold our own. The man who has once become involved in such a strife as this must play the part that he has undertaken ; to show mercy would be fatal. Do you suppose that any man was ever so brutal, so inhuman, as to rejoice in torture and groans and bloodshed for their own sake, when there was no occasion for punishment ? Many is the time that I have wept while others suffered beneath the lash, and groaned in spirit over the hard fate that subjected me to a torment more fierce and more abiding than theirs. For to the man who is benevolent by nature, and harsh only by compulsion, it is more painful to inflict punishment than it would be to undergo it.

9   ' Now I will speak my mind frankly. If I had to choose between punishing innocent men, and facing death myself, believe me, I should have no hesitation in accepting the latter alternative   But if I am asked, whether I had rather die an undeserved death than give their deserts to those who plotted against my life, I answer no ; and once more, Delphians, I appeal to you : which is better—to die when I deserve not death, or to spare my enemies who deserve not mercy [1] ?   No

---

[1] Apparently the speaker intended to repeat the last pair of alternatives in different words : instead of which, he gives us one of those alternatives twice over. Lucian's tautologic genius fails him for once.

man surely can be such a fool that he would not rather live than preserve his enemies by his death. Yet in spite of this how many have I spared who were palpably convicted of conspiring against me; such were Acanthus, Timocrates, and his brother Leogoras, all of whom I saved out of regard for our former intercourse.

'If you would learn more of me, apply to any of the strangers who have visited Agrigentum; and see what account they give of the treatment they received, and of my hospitality to all who land on my coasts. My messengers are waiting for them in every port, to inquire after their names and cities, that they may not go away without receiving due honour at my hands. Some—the wisest of the Greeks—have come expressly to visit me, so far are they from avoiding intercourse with me. It was but lately that I received a visit from the sage Pythagoras. The account that he had heard of me was belied by his experience; and on taking his departure he expressed admiration of my justice, and deplored the circumstances which made severity a duty. Now is it likely that one who is so benevolent to strangers should deal unjustly with his fellow citizens? is it not to be supposed that the provocation has been unusually great?

'So much then in defence of my own conduct; I have spoken the words of truth and justice, and would persuade myself that I have merited your approbation rather than your resentment. And now I must explain to you the origin of my present offering, and the manner in which it came into my hands. For it was by no instructions of mine that the statuary made this bull: far be it from me to aspire to the possession of such works of art! A countryman of my own, one Perilaus, an admirable artist, but a man of evil disposition, had so far mistaken my character as to think that he could win my regard by the invention of a new form of torture; the love of torture, he thought, was my ruling passion. He it was who made the bull and brought it to me. I no sooner set eyes on this beautiful and exquisite piece of workmanship, which lacked only movement and sound to complete the illusion, than I exclaimed : " Here is an offer-ing fit for the God of Delphi : to him I must send it." " And what will you say," rejoined Perilaus, who stood by, " when you see the ingenious mechanism within it, and learn the purpose it is designed to serve ? " He opened the back of the animal, and continued : " When you are minded to punish any one, shut him up in this receptacle, apply these pipes to the nostrils of the bull, and order a fire to be kindled beneath. The occu-pant will shriek and roar in unremitting agony ; and his cries will come to you through the pipes as the tenderest, most pathetic, most melodious of bellowings. Your victim will be punished, and you will enjoy the music."

12 ' His words revolted me. I loathed the thought of such ingenious cruelty, and resolved to punish the artificer in kind. " If this is anything more than an empty boast, Perilaus," I said to him, " if your art can really produce this effect, get inside yourself, and pretend to roar ; and we will see whether the pipes will make such music as you describe." He consented ; and when he was inside I closed the aperture, and ordered a fire to be kindled. " Receive," I cried, " the due reward of your wondrous art : let the music-master be the first to play." Thus did his ingenuity meet with its deserts. But lest the offering should be polluted by his death, I caused him to be removed while he was yet alive, and his body to be flung dishonoured from the cliffs. The bull, after due purification, I sent as an offering to your God, with an inscription upon it, setting forth all the circumstances ; the names of the donor and of the artist, the evil design of the latter, and the righteous sentence which condemned him to illustrate by his own agonized shrieks the efficacy of his musical device.

'And now, men of Delphi, you will be doing me no more than justice, if you join my ambassadors in making sacrifice on my behalf, and set up the bull in a conspicuous part of the temple; that all men may know what is my attitude towards evil-doers, and in what manner I chastise their inordinate craving after wickedness. Herein is a sufficient indication of my character: Perilaus punished, the bull consecrated, not reserved for the bellowings of other victims. The first and last melody that issued from those pipes was wrung from their artificer; that one experiment made, the harsh, inhuman notes are silenced for ever. So much for the present offering, which will be followed by many others, so soon as the God vouchsafes me a respite from my work of chastisement.'

Such was the message of Phalaris; and his statement is in strict accordance with the facts. You may safely accept our testimony, as we are acquainted with the circumstances, and can have no object in deceiving you on the present occasion. Must entreaty be added? Then on behalf of one whose character has been misrepresented, and whose severities were forced upon him against his will, we implore you,—we who are Agrigentines, Greeks like yourselves and of Dorian origin—to accept his offer of friendship, and not to thwart his benevolent intentions towards your community and the individuals of which it is composed. Take the bull into your keeping; consecrate it; and offer up your prayers on behalf of Agrigentum and of Phalaris. Suffer us not to have come hither in vain: repulse not our master with scorn: nor deprive the God of an offering whose intrinsic beauty is only equalled by its righteous associations.

F

PHALARIS, II

MEN of Delphi : I stand in no public relation to the city of Agrigentum, in no private relation to its ruler ; I am bound to him neither by gratitude for past favours, nor by the prospect of future friendship : but I have heard the just and temperate plea advanced by his emissaries, and I rise to advocate the claims of religion, the interests of our community, the duties of the priesthood ; I charge you, thwart not the pious intention of a mighty prince, nor deprive the God of an offering which in the intention of the donor is already his, and which is destined to serve as an eternal threefold record,—of the sculptor's art,

2 of inventive cruelty, and of righteous retribution. To me it seems that only to have raised this question, only to have halted between acceptance and rejection, is in itself an offence against Heaven ; nay, a glaring impiety. For what is this but a sacrilege more heinous than that of the temple-robber, who does but plunder those sacred things to which you would even deny

3 consecration ? I implore you,—your fellow priest, your partner in good report (if so it may be), or in evil (should that now befall us), implores you : close not the temple-doors upon the devout worshipper ; suffer us not to be known to the world as men who examine jealously into the offerings that are brought, and subject the donor to the narrow scrutiny of a court, and to the hazard of a vote. For who would not be deterred at the thought that the God accepts no offering without the previous sanction of his priests ?

4 Already Apollo has declared his true opinion. Had he hated Phalaris, or scorned his gift, it had been easy for him to sink the gift and the ship that bore it in mid-ocean ; instead, we learn that he vouchsafed them a calm passage and a safe arrival at

Cirrha. Clearly the monarch's piety is acceptable in his sight. 5
It behoves you to confirm his decision, and to add this bull to
the glories of the temple. Strange indeed, if the sender of so
magnificent a gift is to meet with rejection at the temple-door,
and his piety to be rewarded with the judgement that his offering
is unclean.

My opponent tells a harrowing tale of butchery and violence, 6
of plunder and abduction; it is much that he does not call himself an eyewitness thereof; we might suppose that he was but
newly arrived from Agrigentum, did we not know that his
travels have never carried him on board ship. In matters of
this kind, it is not advisable to place much reliance even on the
assertions of the supposed victims; there is no knowing how
far they are speaking the truth;—as to bringing allegations ourselves, when we know nothing of the facts, that is out of the
question. Granting even that something of the kind *did* 7
happen, it happened in Sicily: we are at Delphi; we are not
called upon to interfere. Do we propose to abandon the temple
for the law-court? Are we, whose office it is to sacrifice, and
minister to the God, and receive his offerings,—are we to sit
here debating whether certain cities on the other side of the
Ionian sea are well or ill governed? Let other men's affairs be 8
as they may, it is our business, as I take it, to know our own:
our past history, our present situation, our best interests. We
need not wait for Homer to inform us that we inhabit a land of
crags, and are tillers of a rocky soil; our eyes tell us that; if we
depended on our soil, we must go hungry all our days. Apollo;
his temple; his oracle; his worshippers; his sacrifices;—these
are the fields of the Delphians, these their revenues, their wealth,
their maintenance. I can speak the truth here. It is as the poets
say: we sow not, we plough not, yet all things grow for our
use; for a God is our husbandman, and gives us not the good
things of Greece only; all that Phrygia, all that Lydia, all that

Persia, Assyria, Phoenicia, Italy, and the far North can yield,—
all comes to Delphi. We live in prosperity and plenty ; in the
esteem of mankind we are second to none but the God himself.
So it was in the beginning : so it is now : and so may it ever be !

9   But who has ever heard before of our putting an offering to
the vote, or hindering men from paying sacrifice ? No one ;
and herein, as I maintain, is the secret of our temple's greatness, and of the abundant wealth of its offerings. Then let us
have no innovations now, no new-fangled institutions, no inquiries into the origin and nature and nationality and pedigree
of a gift ; let us take what is brought to us, and set it in the
store-chamber without more ado. In this way we shall best
10 serve both the God and his worshippers. I think it would be well
if, before you deliberate further on the question before you,
you would consider how great and how various are the issues
involved. There is the God, his temple, his sacrifices and
offerings, the ancient customs and ordinances, the reputation
of the oracle ; again, our city as a whole, our common interests,
and those of every individual Delphian among us ; lastly—and
I know not what consideration could seem of more vital importance to a well-judging mind—, our own credit or discredit with
the world at large.

11   I say, then, we have to deal not with Phalaris, not with a
single tyrant, not with this bull, not with so much weight of
bronze,—but with every king and prince who frequents our
temple at this day ; with gold and silver and all the precious
offerings that should pour in upon the God ; that God whose
12 interests claim our first attention. Say, why should we change
the old-established usage in regard to offerings ? What fault
have we to find with the ancient custom, that we should propose innovations ? Never yet, from the day when Delphi was
first inhabited, and Apollo prophesied, and the tripod gave
utterance, and the priestess was inspired, never yet have the

bringers of gifts been subjected to scrutiny. And shall they now ? Consider how the ancient custom, which granted free access to all men, has filled the temple with treasures ; how all men have brought their offerings, and how some have impoverished themselves to enrich the God. My mind misgives me that, 13 when you have assumed the censorship of offerings, you will lack employment : men may refuse to submit themselves to your court ; they may think it is enough to spend their money, without having to undergo the risk of a rejection for their pains. Would life be worth living, to the man who should be judged unworthy to offer sacrifice ? F.

ALEXANDER THE ORACLE-MONGER

You, my dear Celsus, possibly suppose yourself to be laying upon me quite a trifling task : *Write me down in a book and send me the life and adventures, the tricks and frauds, of the impostor Alexander of Abonutichus.* In fact, however, it would take as long to do this in full detail as to reduce to writing the achievements of Alexander of Macedon ; the one is among villains what the other is among heroes. Nevertheless, if you will promise to read with indulgence, and fill up the gaps in my tale from your imagination, I will essay the task. I may not cleanse that Augean stable completely, but I will do my best, and fetch you out a few loads as samples of the unspeakable filth that three thousand oxen could produce in many years.

I confess to being a little ashamed both on your account and 2 my own. There are you asking that the memory of an arch-scoundrel should be perpetuated in writing ; here am I going seriously into an investigation of this sort—the doings of a person whose deserts entitled him not to be read about by the cultivated, but to be torn to pieces in the amphitheatre by apes or foxes, with a vast audience looking on. Well, well, if any one does cast reflections of that sort upon us, we shall at least have a precedent to plead. Arrian himself, disciple of Epictetus, distinguished Roman, and product of lifelong culture as he was, had just our experience, and shall make our defence. He condescended, that is, to put on record the life of the robber Tilliborus. The robber we propose to immortalize was of a far more pestilent kind, following his profession not in the forests and mountains, but in cities ; *he* was not content to overrun a Mysia or an Ida ; *his* booty came not from a few scantily populated districts of Asia ; one may say that the scene of his depredations was the whole Roman Empire.

3   I will begin with a picture of the man himself, as lifelike (though I am not great at description) as I can make it with nothing better than words. In person—not to forget that part of him—he was a fine handsome man with a real touch of divinity about him, white-skinned, moderately bearded ; he wore besides his own hair artificial additions which matched it so cunningly that they were not generally detected. His eyes were piercing, and suggested inspiration, his voice at once sweet and sonorous. In fact there was no fault to be found with him in these respects.

4   So much for externals. As for his mind and spirit—well, if all the kind Gods who avert disaster will grant a prayer, it shall be that they bring me not within reach of such a one as he ; sooner will I face my bitterest enemies, my country's foes. In understanding, resource, acuteness, he was far above other men ; curiosity, receptiveness, memory, scientific ability—all these were his in overflowing measure. But he used them for the worst purposes. Endowed with all these instruments of good, he very soon reached a proud pre-eminence among all who have been famous for evil ; the Cercopes, Eurybatus, Phrynondas, Aristodemus, Sostratus—all thrown into the shade. In a letter to his father-in-law Rutilianus, which puts his own pretensions

in a truly modest light, he compares himself to Pythagoras. Well, I should not like to offend the wise, the divine Pythagoras; but if he had been Alexander's contemporary, I am quite sure he would have been a mere child to him. Now by all that is admirable, do not take that for an insult to Pythagoras, nor suppose I would draw a parallel between their achievements. What I mean is : if any one would make a collection of all the vilest and most damaging slanders ever vented against Pythagoras—things whose truth I would not accept for a moment—, the sum of them would not come within measurable distance of Alexander's cleverness. You are to set your imagination to work and conceive a temperament curiously compounded of falsehood, trickery, perjury, cunning; it is versatile, audacious, adventurous, yet dogged in execution; it is plausible enough to inspire confidence; it can assume the mask of virtue, and seem to eschew what it most desires. I suppose no one ever left him after a first interview without the impression that this was the best and kindest of men, ay, and the simplest and most unsophisticated. Add to all this a certain greatness in his objects; he never made a small plan; his ideas were always large.

While in the bloom of his youthful beauty, which we may 5 assume to have been great both from its later remains and from the report of those who saw it, he traded quite shamelessly upon it. Among his other patrons was one of the charlatans who deal in magic and mystic incantations; they will smooth your course of love, confound your enemies, find you treasure, or secure you an inheritance. This person was struck with the lad's natural qualifications for apprenticeship to his trade, and finding him as much attracted by rascality as attractive in appearance, gave him a regular training as accomplice, satellite, and attendant. His own ostensible profession was medicine, and his knowledge included, like that of Thoon the Egyptian's wife,

Many a virtuous herb, and many a bane;

to all which inheritance our friend succeeded. This teacher and lover of his was a native of Tyana, an associate of the great Apollonius, and acquainted with all his heroics. And now you know the atmosphere in which Alexander lived.

6 By the time his beard had come, the Tyanean was dead, and he found himself in straits; for the personal attractions which might once have been a resource were diminished. He now formed great designs, which he imparted to a Byzantine chronicler of the strolling competitive order, a man of still worse character than himself, called, I believe, Cocconas. The pair went about living on occult pretensions, shearing 'fat-heads,' as they describe ordinary people in the native Magian lingo. Among these they got hold of a rich Macedonian woman; her youth was past, but not her desire for admiration; they got sufficient supplies out of her, and accompanied her from Bithynia to Macedonia. She came from Pella, which had been a flourishing place under the Macedonian kingdom, but has now a poor and much reduced population.

7 There is here a breed of large serpents, so tame and gentle that women make pets of them, children take them to bed, they will let you tread on them, have no objection to being squeezed, and will draw milk from the breast like infants. To these facts is probably to be referred the common story about Olympias when she was with child of Alexander; it was doubtless one of these that was her bed-fellow. Well, the two saw these creatures, and bought the finest they could get for a few pence.

8 And from this point, as Thucydides might say, the war takes its beginning. These ambitious scoundrels were quite devoid of scruples, and they had now joined forces; it could not escape their penetration that human life is under the absolute dominion of two mighty principles, fear and hope, and that any one who can make these serve his ends may be sure of a rapid fortune.

They realized that, whether a man is most swayed by the one or by the other, what he must most depend upon and desire is a knowledge of futurity. So were to be explained the ancient wealth and fame of Delphi, Delos, Clarus, Branchidae; it was at the bidding of the two tyrants aforesaid that men thronged the temples, longed for fore-knowledge, and to attain it sacrificed their hecatombs or dedicated their golden ingots. All this they turned over and debated, and it issued in the resolve to establish an oracle. If it were successful, they looked for immediate wealth and prosperity; the result surpassed their most sanguine expectations.

The next things to be settled were, first the theatre of opera- 9 tions, and secondly the plan of campaign. Cocconas favoured Chalcedon, as a mercantile centre convenient both for Thrace and Bithynia, and accessible enough for the province of Asia, Galatia, and tribes still further east. Alexander, on the other hand, preferred his native place, urging very truly that an enterprise like theirs required congenial soil to give it a start, in the shape of 'fat-heads' and simpletons; that was a fair description, he said, of the Paphlagonians beyond Abonutichus; they were mostly superstitious and well-to-do; one had only to go there with some one to play the flute, the tambourine, or the cymbals, set the proverbial mantic sieve [1] a-spinning, and there they would all be gaping as if he were a God from heaven.

This difference of opinion did not last long, and Alexander 10 prevailed. Discovering, however, that a use might after all be made of Chalcedon, they went there first, and in the temple

[1] I have no information on Coscinomancy or sieve-divination. 'This kind of divination was generally practised to discover thieves. . . They tied a thread to the sieve, by which it was upheld, then prayed to the Gods to direct and assist them. After which they repeated the names of the person suspected, and he at whose name the sieve whirled round or moved was thought to have committed the fact.' *Francklin's Lucian.*

of Apollo, the oldest in the place, they buried some brazen
tablets, on which was the statement that very shortly Asclepius,
with his father Apollo, would pay a visit to Pontus, and take up
his abode at Abonutichus. The discovery of the tablets took
place as arranged, and the news flew through Bithynia and
Pontus, first of all, naturally, to Abonutichus. The people of
that place at once resolved to raise a temple, and lost no time
in digging the foundations. Cocconas was now left at Chalcedon, engaged in composing certain ambiguous crabbed oracles.
He shortly afterwards died, I believe, of a viper's bite.

11   Alexander meanwhile went on in advance; he had now
grown his hair and wore it in long curls; his doublet was white
and purple striped, his cloak pure white; he carried a scimetar
in imitation of Perseus, from whom he now claimed descent
through his mother. The wretched Paphlagonians, who knew
perfectly well that his parentage was obscure and mean on
both sides, nevertheless gave credence to the oracle, which
ran :

> Lo, sprung from Perseus, and to Phoebus dear,
> High Alexander, Podalirius' son !

Podalirius, it seems, was of so highly amorous a complexion that
the distance between Tricca and Paphlagonia was no bar to his
union with Alexander's mother. A Sibylline prophecy had also
been found :

> Hard by Sinope on the Euxine shore
> Th' Italic age a fortress prophet sees.
> To the first monad let thrice ten be added,
> Five monads yet, and then a triple score :
> Such the quaternion of th' alexic name [1].

---

[1] In l. 2 of the oracle, the Italic age is the Roman Empire; the fortress
prophet is one who belongs to a place ending in -tichus (fort). ll. 3–5 mean :
Take 1, 30, 5, 60 (the Greek symbols for which are the letters of the
alphabet A, L, E, X), and you will have four letters of the name of your
coming protector (alexic).

This heroic entry into his long-left home placed Alexander 12 conspicuously before the public; he affected madness, and frequently foamed at the mouth—a manifestation easily produced by chewing the herb soap-wort, used by dyers; but it brought him reverence and awe. The two had long ago manufactured and fitted up a serpent's head of linen; they had given it a more or less human expression, and painted it very like the real article; by a contrivance of horsehair, the mouth could be opened and shut, and a forked black serpent tongue protruded, working on the same system. The serpent from Pella was also kept ready in the house, to be produced at the right moment and take its part in the drama—the leading part, indeed.

In the fullness of time, his plan took shape. He went one 13 night to the temple foundations, still in process of digging, and with standing water in them which had collected from the rainfall or otherwise; here he deposited a goose egg, into which, after blowing it, he had inserted some new-born reptile. He made a resting-place deep down in the mud for this, and departed. Early next morning he rushed into the market-place, naked except for a gold-spangled loin-cloth; with nothing but this and his scimetar, and shaking his long loose hair, like the fanatics who collect money in the name of Cybele, he climbed on to a lofty altar and delivered a harangue, felicitating the city upon the advent of the God now to bless them with his presence. In a few minutes nearly the whole population was on the spot, women, old men, and children included; all was awe, prayer, and adoration. He uttered some unintelligible sounds, which might have been Hebrew or Phoenician, but completed his victory over his audience, who could make nothing of what he said, beyond the constant repetition of the names Apollo and Asclepius.

He then set off at a run for the future temple. Arrived at 14 the excavation and the already completed sacred fount, he got down into the water, chanted in a loud voice hymns to Asclepius and Apollo, and invited the God to come, a welcome guest, to the city. He next demanded a bowl, and when this was handed to him, had no difficulty in putting it down at the right place and scooping up, besides water and mud, the egg in which the God had been enclosed; the edges of the aperture had been joined with wax and white lead. He took the egg in his hand and announced that here he held Asclepius. The people, who had been sufficiently astonished by the discovery of the egg in the water, were now all eyes for what was to come. He broke it, and received in his hollowed palm the hardly developed reptile; the crowd could see it stirring and winding about his fingers; they raised a shout, hailed the God, blessed the city, and every mouth was full of prayers—for treasure and wealth and health and all the other good things that he might give. Our hero now departed homewards, still running, with the new-born Asclepius in his hands—the twice-born, too, whereas ordinary men can be born but once, and born moreover not of Coronis [1], nor even of her namesake the crow, but of a goose! After him streamed the whole people, in all the madness of fanatic hopes.

15   He now kept the house for some days, in hopes that the Paphlagonians would soon be drawn in crowds by the news. He was not disappointed; the city was filled to overflowing with persons who had neither brains nor individuality, who bore no resemblance to men that live by bread, and had only their outward shape to distinguish them from sheep. In a small room he took his seat, very imposingly attired, upon a couch. He took into his bosom our Asclepius of Pella (a very fine and large one, as I observed), wound its body round his neck, and let its tail hang down; there was enough of this not

[1] Coronis was the mother of Asclepius; ' corone ' is Greek for a crow.

only to fill his lap, but to trail on the ground also ; the patient creature's head he kept hidden in his armpit, showing the linen head on one side of his beard exactly as if it belonged to the visible body.

Picture to yourself a little chamber into which no very 16 brilliant light was admitted, with a crowd of people from all quarters, excited, carefully worked up, all a-flutter with expectation. As they came in, they might naturally find a miracle in the development of that little crawling thing of a few days ago into this great, tame, human-looking serpent. Then they had to get on at once towards the exit, being pressed forward by the new arrivals before they could have a good look. An exit had been specially made just opposite the entrance, for all the world like the Macedonian device at Babylon when Alexander was ill ; he was *in extremis*, you remember, and the crowd round the palace were eager to take their last look and give their last greeting. Our scoundrel's exhibition, though, is said to have been given not once, but many times, especially for the benefit of any wealthy new-comers.

And at this point, my dear Celsus, we may, if we will be 17 candid, make some allowance for these Paphlagonians and Pontics ; the poor uneducated ' fat-heads ' might well be taken in when they handled the serpent—a privilege conceded to all who choose—and saw in that dim light *its* head with the mouth that opened and shut. It was an occasion for a Democritus, nay, for an Epicurus or a Metrodorus, perhaps, a man whose intelligence was steeled against such assaults by scepticism and insight, one who, if he could not detect the precise imposture, would at any rate have been perfectly certain that, though this escaped him, the whole thing was a lie and an impossibility.

By degrees Bithynia, Galatia, Thrace, came flocking in, every 18 one who had been present doubtless reporting that he had beheld the birth of the God, and had touched him after his marvellous development in size and in expression. Next came pictures and models, bronze or silver images, and the God acquired a name. By divine command, metrically expressed, he was to be known as Glycon. For Alexander had delivered the line :

> Glycon my name, man's light, son's son to Zeus.

19 And now at last the object to which all this had led up, the giving of oracular answers to all applicants, could be attained. The cue was taken from Amphilochus in Cilicia. After the death and disappearance at Thebes of his father Amphiaraus, Amphilochus, driven from his home, made his way to Cilicia, and there did not at all badly by prophesying to the Cilicians at the rate of threepence an oracle. After this precedent, Alexander proclaimed that on a stated day the God would give answers to all comers. Each person was to write down his wish and the object of his curiosity, fasten the packet with thread, and seal it with wax, clay, or other such substance. He would receive these, and enter the holy place (by this time the temple was complete, and the scene all ready), whither the givers should be summoned in order by a herald and an acolyte ; he would learn the God's mind upon each, and return the packets with their seals intact and the answers attached, the God being ready to give a definite answer to any question that might be put.

20 The trick here was one which would be seen through easily enough by a person of your intelligence (or, if I may say so without violating modesty, of my own), but which to the ordinary imbecile would have the persuasiveness of what is marvellous and incredible. He contrived various methods of undoing the seals, read the questions, answered them as seemed good, and then folded, sealed, and returned them, to the great astonish-

ment of the recipients. And then it was, 'How could he possibly know what I gave him carefully secured under a seal that defies imitation, unless he were a true God, with a God's omniscience ?'

Perhaps you will ask what these contrivances were; well, 21 then—the information may be useful another time. One of them was this. He would heat a needle, melt with it the under part of the wax, lift the seal off, and after reading warm the wax once more with the needle—both that below the thread and that which formed the actual seal—and re-unite the two without difficulty. Another method employed the substance called collyrium ; this is a preparation of Bruttian pitch, bitumen, pounded glass, wax, and mastich. He kneaded the whole into collyrium, heated it, placed it on the seal, previously moistened with his tongue, and so took a mould. This soon hardened ; he simply opened, read, replaced the wax, and reproduced an excellent imitation of the original seal as from an engraved stone. One more I will give you. Adding some gypsum to the glue used in book-binding he produced a sort of wax, which was applied still wet to the seal, and on being taken off solidified at once and provided a matrix harder than horn, or even iron. There are plenty of other devices for the purpose, to rehearse which would seem like airing one's knowledge. Moreover, in your excellent pamphlets against the magians (most useful and instructive reading they are) you have yourself collected enough of them—many more than those I have mentioned.

So oracles and divine utterances were the order of the day, 22 and much shrewdness he displayed, eking out mechanical ingenuity with obscurity, his answers to some being crabbed and ambiguous, and to others absolutely unintelligible. He did however distribute warning and encouragement according to his lights, and recommend treatments and diets ; for he had, as I originally stated, a wide and serviceable acquaintance with drugs; he was particularly given to prescribing 'cytmides,' which were a salve prepared from goat's fat, the name being of his own invention. For the realization of ambitions, advancement, or successions, he took care never to assign early dates; the formula was, 'All this shall come to pass when it is my will, and when my prophet Alexander shall make prayer and entreaty on your behalf.'

23 There was a fixed charge of a shilling the oracle. And, my friend, do not suppose that this would not come to much; he made something like £3,000 *per annum*; people were insatiable —would take from ten to fifteen oracles at a time. What he got he did not keep to himself, nor put it by for the future; what with accomplices, attendants, inquiry agents, oracle writers and keepers, amanuenses, seal-forgers, and interpreters, he had now a host of claimants to satisfy.

24 He had begun sending emissaries abroad to make the shrine known in foreign lands; his prophecies, discovery of runaways, conviction of thieves and robbers, revelations of hidden treasure, cures of the sick, restoration of the dead to life—all these were to be advertised. This brought them running and crowding from all points of the compass; victims bled, gifts were presented, and the prophet and disciple came off better than the God; for had not the oracle spoken?—

> Give what ye give to my attendant priest;
> My care is not for gifts, but for my priest.

25 A time came when a number of sensible people began to shake off their intoxication and combine against him, chief among them the numerous Epicureans; in the cities, the imposture with all its theatrical accessories began to be seen through. It was now that he resorted to a measure of intimidation; he proclaimed that Pontus was overrun with

atheists and Christians, who presumed to spread the most scandalous reports concerning him; he exhorted Pontus, as it valued the God's favour, to stone these men. Touching Epicurus, he gave the following response. An inquirer had asked how Epicurus fared in Hades, and was told:

> Of slime is his bed,
> And his fetters of lead.

The prosperity of the oracle is perhaps not so wonderful, when one learns what sensible, intelligent questions were in fashion with its votaries. Well, it was war to the knife between him and Epicurus, and no wonder. What fitter enemy for a charlatan who patronized miracles and hated truth, than the thinker who had grasped the nature of things and was in solitary possession of that truth? As for the Platonists, Stoics, Pythagoreans, they were his good friends; he had no quarrel with them. But the unmitigated Epicurus, as he used to call him, could not but be hateful to him, treating all such pretensions as absurd and puerile. Alexander consequently loathed Amastris beyond all the cities of Pontus, knowing what a number of Lepidus's friends and others like-minded it contained. He would not give oracles to Amastrians; when he once did, to a senator's brother, he made himself ridiculous, neither hitting upon a presentable oracle for himself, nor finding a deputy equal to the occasion. The man had complained of colic, and what he meant to prescribe was pig's foot dressed with mallow. The shape it took was:

> In basin hallowed
> Be pigments mallowed.

I have mentioned that the serpent was often exhibited by 26 request; he was not completely visible, but the tail and body were exposed, while the head was concealed under the prophet's dress. By way of impressing the people still more, he announced that he would induce the God to speak, and give his responses without an intermediary. His simple device to this end was a tube of cranes' windpipes, which he passed, with due regard to its matching, through the artificial head, and, having an assistant speaking into the end outside, whose voice issued through the linen Asclepius, thus answered questions. These oracles were called *autophones*, and were not vouchsafed casually to any one, but reserved for officials, the rich, and the lavish.

27   It was an autophone which was given to Severian regarding the invasion of Armenia. He encouraged him with these lines :

> Armenia, Parthia, cowed by thy fierce spear,
> To Rome, and Tiber's shining waves, thou com'st,
> Thy brow with leaves and radiant gold encircled.

Then when the foolish Gaul took his advice and invaded, to the total destruction of himself and his army by Othryades, the adviser expunged that oracle from his archives and substituted the following :

> Vex not th' Armenian land ; it shall not thrive ;
> One in soft raiment clad shall from his bow
> Launch death, and cut thee off from life and light.

28   For it was one of his happy thoughts to issue prophecies after the event as antidotes to those premature utterances which had not gone right. Frequently he promised recovery to a sick man before his death, and after it was at no loss for second thoughts :

> No longer seek to arrest thy fell disease ;
> Thy fate is manifest, inevitable.

29   Knowing the fame of Clarus, Didymus, and Mallus for sooth-

saying much like his own, he struck up an alliance with them, sending on many of his clients to those places.   So

> Hie thee to Clarus now, and hear my sire.

And again,

> Draw near to Branchidae and counsel take.

Or

> Seek Mallus ; be Amphilochus thy counsellor.

So things went within the borders of Ionia, Cilicia, Paphla- 30 gonia, and Galatia.   When the fame of the oracle travelled to Italy and entered Rome, the only question was, who should be first ; those who did not come in person sent messages, the powerful and respected being the keenest of all.   First and foremost among these was Rutilianus ; he was in most respects an excellent person, and had filled many high offices in Rome ; but he suffered from religious mania, holding the most extra-ordinary beliefs on that matter ; show him a bit of stone smeared with unguents or crowned with flowers, and he would incontinently fall down and worship, and linger about it praying and asking for blessings.   The reports about our oracle nearly induced him to throw up the appointment he then held, and fly to Abonutichus ; he actually did send messenger upon messenger.   His envoys were ignorant servants, easily taken in.   They came back having really seen certain things, relating others which they probably thought they had seen and heard, and yet others which they deliberately invented to curry favour with their master.   So they inflamed the poor old man and drove him into confirmed madness.

He had a wide circle of influential friends, to whom he com- 31 municated the news brought by his successive messengers, not without additional touches of his own.   All Rome was full of his tales ; there was quite a commotion, the gentlemen of the Court being much fluttered, and at once taking measures to learn something of their own fate. The prophet gave all who came a hearty welcome, gained their goodwill by hospitality and costly gifts, and sent them off ready not merely to report his answers, but to sing the praises of the God and invent miraculous tales of the shrine and its guardian.

32   This triple rogue now hit upon an idea which would have been too clever for the ordinary robber. Opening and reading the packets which reached him, whenever he came upon an equivocal, compromising question, he omitted to return the packet; the sender was to be under his thumb, bound to his service by the terrifying recollection of the question he had written down. You know the sort of things that wealthy and powerful personages would be likely to ask. This blackmail brought him in a good income.

33   I should like to quote you one or two of the answers given to Rutilianus. He had a son by a former wife, just old enough for advanced teaching. The father asked who should be his tutor, and was told,

> Pythagoras, and the mighty battle-bard.

When the child died a few days after, the prophet was abashed, and quite unable to account for this summary confutation. However, dear good Rutilianus very soon restored the oracle's credit by discovering that this was the very thing the God had foreshown; he had not directed him to choose a living teacher; Pythagoras and Homer were long dead, and doubtless the boy was now enjoying their instructions in Hades. Small blame to Alexander if he had a taste for dealings with such specimens of humanity as this.

34   Another of Rutilianus's questions was, Whose soul he had succeeded to, and the answer:

> First thou wast Peleus' son, and next Menander;
> Then thine own self; next, a sunbeam shalt be;
> And nine score annual rounds thy life shall measure.

At seventy, he died of melancholy, not waiting for the God to pay in full.

That was an autophone too. Another time Rutilianus con- 35 sulted the oracle on the choice of a wife. The answer was express :

> Wed Alexander's daughter and Selene's.

He had long ago spread the report that the daughter he had had was by Selene : she had once seen him asleep, and fallen in love, as is her way with handsome sleepers. The sensible Rutilianus lost no time, but sent for the maiden at once, celebrated the nuptials, a sexagenarian bridegroom, and lived with her, propitiating his divine mother-in-law with whole hecatombs, and reckoning himself now one of the heavenly company.

His finger once in the Italian pie, Alexander devoted himself 36 to getting further. Sacred envoys were sent all over the Roman Empire, warning the various cities to be on their guard against pestilence and conflagrations, with the prophet's offers of security against them. One oracle in particular, an autophone again, he distributed broadcast at a time of pestilence. It was a single line :

> Phoebus long-tressed the plague-cloud shall dispel.

This was everywhere to be seen written up on doors as a prophylactic. Its effect was generally disappointing ; for it somehow happened that the protected houses were just the ones to be desolated. Not that I would suggest for a moment that the line was their destruction ; but, accidentally no doubt, it did so fall out. Possibly common people put too much confidence in the verse, and lived carelessly without troubling to help the oracle against its foe ; were there not the words fighting their battle, and long-tressed Phoebus discharging his arrows at the pestilence ?

37 In Rome itself he established an intelligence bureau well manned with his accomplices. They sent him people's characters, forecasts of their questions, and hints of their ambitions, so that he had his answers ready before the messengers reached him.

38 It was with his eye on this Italian propaganda, too, that he took a further step. This was the institution of mysteries, with hierophants and torch-bearers complete. The ceremonies occupied three successive days. On the first, proclamation was made on the Athenian model to this effect: 'If there be any atheist or Christian or Epicurean here spying upon our rites, let him depart in haste; and let all such as have faith in the God be initiated and all blessing attend them.' He led the litany with, 'Christians, avaunt!' and the crowd responded, 'Epicureans, avaunt!' Then was presented the child-bed of Leto and birth of Apollo, the bridal of Coronis, Asclepius born. The second day, the epiphany and nativity of the God Glycon.

39 On the third came the wedding of Podalirius and Alexander's mother; this was called Torch-day, and torches were used. The finale was the loves of Selene and Alexander, and the birth of Rutilianus's wife. The torch-bearer and hierophant was Endymion-Alexander. He was discovered lying asleep; to him from heaven, represented by the ceiling, enter as Selene one Rutilia, a great beauty, and wife of one of the Imperial procurators. She and Alexander were lovers off the stage too, and the wretched husband had to look on at their public kissing and embracing; if there had not been a good supply of torches, things might possibly have gone even further. Shortly after, he reappeared amidst a profound hush, attired as hierophant; in a loud voice he called, 'Hail, Glycon!', whereto the Eumolpidae and Ceryces of Paphlagonia, with their clod-hopping shoes and their garlic breath, made sonorous response, 'Hail, Alexander!'

40 The torch ceremony with its ritual skippings often enabled

him to bestow a glimpse of his thigh, which was thus discovered to be of gold; it was presumably enveloped in cloth of gold, which glittered in the lamp-light. This gave rise to a debate between two wiseacres, whether the golden thigh meant that he had inherited Pythagoras's soul, or merely that their two souls were alike; the question was referred to Alexander himself, and King Glycon relieved their perplexity with an oracle:

> Waxes and wanes Pythagoras' soul: the seer's
> Is from the mind of Zeus an emanation.
> His Father sent him, virtuous men to aid,
> And with his bolt one day shall call him home.

I will now give you a conversation between Glycon and one 43 Sacerdos of Tius; the intelligence of the latter you may gauge from his questions. I read it inscribed in golden letters in Sacerdos's house at Tius. 'Tell me, lord Glycon,' said he, 'who you are.' 'The new Asclepius.' 'Another, different from the former one? Is that the meaning?' 'That it is not lawful for you to learn.' 'And how many years will you sojourn and prophesy among us?' 'A thousand and three.' 'And after that, whither will you go?' 'To Bactria; for the barbarians too must be blessed with my presence.' 'The other oracles, at Didymus and Clarus and Delphi, have they still the spirit of your grandsire Apollo, or are the answers that now come from them forgeries?' 'That, too, desire not to know; it is not lawful.' 'What shall I be after this life?' 'A camel; then a horse; then a wise man, no less a prophet than Alexander.' Such was the conversation. There was added to it an oracle in verse, inspired by the fact that Sacerdos was an associate of Lepidus:

> Shun Lepidus; an evil fate awaits him.

As I have said, Alexander was much afraid of Epicurus, and the solvent action of his logic on imposture.

On one occasion, indeed, an Epicurean got himself into great 44 trouble by daring to expose him before a great gathering. He came up and addressed him in a loud voice. ' Alexander, it was you who induced So-and-so the Paphlagonian to bring his slaves before the governor of Galatia, charged with the murder of his son who was being educated in Alexandria. Well, the young man is alive, and has come back, to find that the slaves had been cast to the beasts by your machinations.' What had happened was this. The lad had sailed up the Nile, gone on to a Red Sea port, found a vessel starting for India, and been persuaded to make the voyage. He being long overdue, the unfortunate slaves supposed that he had either perished in the Nile or fallen a victim to some of the pirates who infested it at that time; so they came home to report his disappearance. Then followed the oracle, the sentence, and finally the young man's return with the story of his absence.

45   All this the Epicurean recounted. Alexander was much annoyed by the exposure, and could not stomach so well deserved an affront; he directed the company to stone the man, on pain of being involved in his impiety and called Epicureans. However, when they set to work, a distinguished Pontic called Demostratus, who was staying there, rescued him by interposing his own body; the man had the narrowest possible escape from being stoned to death—as he richly deserved to be; what business had he to be the only sane man in a crowd of madmen, and needlessly make himself the butt of Paphlagonian infatuation?

46   This was a special case; but it was the practice for the names of applicants to be read out the day before answers were given; the herald asked whether each was to receive his oracle; and sometimes the reply came from within, To perdition! One so repulsed could get shelter, fire or water, from no man; he must be driven from land to land as a blasphemer, an atheist, and— lowest depth of all—an Epicurean.

In this connexion Alexander once made himself supremely 47 ridiculous. Coming across Epicurus's *Accepted Maxims*, the most admirable of his books, as you know, with its terse present- ment of his wise conclusions, he brought it into the middle of the market-place, there burned it on a fig-wood fire for the sins of its author, and cast its ashes into the sea. He issued an oracle on the occasion :

> The dotard's maxims to the flames be given.

The fellow had no conception of the blessings conferred by that book upon its readers, of the peace, tranquillity, and indepen- dence of mind it produces, of the protection it gives against terrors, phantoms, and marvels, vain hopes and inordinate desires, of the judgement and candour that it fosters, or of its true purging of the spirit, not with torches and squills and such rubbish, but with right reason, truth, and frankness.

Perhaps the greatest example of our rogue's audacity is what 48 I now come to. Having easy access to Palace and Court by Rutilianus's influence, he sent an oracle just at the crisis of the German war, when M. Aurelius was on the point of engaging the Marcomanni and Quadi. The oracle required that two lions should be flung alive into the Danube, with quantities of sacred herbs and magnificent sacrifices. I had better give the words :

> To rolling Ister, swoln with Heaven's rain,
> Of Cybelean thralls, those mountain beasts,
> Fling ye a pair ; therewith all flowers and herbs
> Of savour sweet that Indian air doth breed.
> Hence victory, and fame, and lovely peace.

These directions were precisely followed ; the lions swam across to the enemy's bank, where they were clubbed to death by the barbarians, who took them for dogs or a new kind of wolves ; and our forces immediately after met with a severe defeat, losing some twenty thousand men in one engagement. This was followed by the Aquileian incident, in the course of which that city was nearly lost. In view of these results, Alexander warmed up that stale Delphian defence of the Croesus oracle : the God had foretold a victory, forsooth, but had not stated whether Romans or barbarians should have it.

49 The constant increase in the number of visitors, the inadequacy of accommodation in the city, and the difficulty of finding provisions for consultants, led to his introducing what he called *night oracles*. He received the packets, slept upon them, in his own phrase, and gave answers which the God was supposed to send him in dreams. These were generally not lucid, but ambiguous and confused, especially when he came to packets sealed with exceptional care. He did not risk tampering with these, but wrote down any words that came into his head, the results obtained corresponding well enough to his conception of the oracular. There were regular interpreters in attendance, who made considerable sums out of the recipients by expounding and unriddling these oracles. This office contributed to his revenue, the interpreters paying him £250 each.

50 Sometimes he stirred the wonder of the silly by answers to persons who had neither brought nor sent questions, and in fact did not exist. Here is a specimen :

> Who is 't, thou askst, that with Calligenia
> All secretly defiles thy nuptial bed ?
> The slave Protogenes, whom most thou trustest.
> Him thou enjoyedst : he thy wife enjoys—
> The fit return for that thine outrage done.
> And know that baleful drugs for thee are brewed,
> Lest thou or see or hear their evil deeds.
> Close by the wall, at thy bed's head, make search.
> Thy maid Calypso to their plot is privy.

The names and circumstantial details might stagger a Democritus, till a moment's thought showed him the despicable trick.

He often gave answers in Syriac or Celtic to barbarians who 51 questioned him in their own tongue, though he had difficulty in finding compatriots of theirs in the city. In these cases there was a long interval between application and response, during which the packet might be securely opened at leisure, and somebody found capable of translating the question. The following is an answer given to a Scythian :

> Morphi ebargulis for night
> Chnenchicrank shall leave the light.

Another oracle to some one who neither came nor existed 52 was in prose. 'Return the way thou camest,' it ran; 'for he that sent thee hath this day been slain by his neighbour Diocles, with aid of the robbers Magnus, Celer, and Bubalus, who are taken and in chains.'

I must give you one or two of the answers that fell to my 53 share. I asked whether Alexander was bald, and having sealed it publicly with great care, got a night oracle in reply :

> Sabardalachu malach Attis was not he.

Another time I did up the same question—What was Homer's birthplace ?—in two packets given in under different names. My servant misled him by saying, when asked what he came for, a cure for lung trouble; so the answer to one packet was :

> Cytmide and foam of steed the liniment give.

As for the other packet, he got the information that the sender was inquiring whether the land or the sea route to Italy was preferable. So he answered, without much reference to Homer :

> Fare not by sea ; land-travel meets thy need.

I laid a good many traps of this kind for him ; here is another. 54 I asked only one question, but wrote outside the packet in the usual form, So-and-so's eight Queries, giving a fictitious name and sending the eight shillings. Satisfied with the payment of the money and the inscription on the packet, he gave me eight answers to my one question. This was, When will Alexander's imposture be detected? The answers concerned nothing in heaven or earth, but were all silly and meaningless together. He afterwards found out about this, and also that I had tried to dissuade Rutilianus both from the marriage and from putting any confidence in the oracle; so he naturally conceived a violent dislike for me. When Rutilianus once put a question to him about me, the answer was:

Night-haunts and foul debauch are all his joy.

55   It is true his dislike was quite justified. On a certain occasion I was passing through Abonutichus, with a spearman and a pikeman whom my friend the governor of Cappadocia had lent me as an escort on my way to the sea. Ascertaining that I was the Lucian he knew of, he sent me a very polite and hospitable invitation. I found him with a numerous company; by good luck I had brought my escort. He gave me his hand to kiss according to his usual custom. I took hold of it as if to kiss, but instead bestowed on it a sound bite that must have come near disabling it. The company, who were already offended at my calling him Alexander instead of Prophet, were inclined to throttle and beat me for sacrilege. But he endured the pain like a man, checked their violence, and assured them that he would easily tame me, and illustrate Glycon's greatness in converting his bitterest foes to friends. He then dismissed them all, and argued the matter with me: he was perfectly aware of my advice to Rutilianus; why had I treated him so, when I might have been preferred by him to great influence in that quarter? By this time I had realized my dangerous position, and was only too glad to welcome these advances; I presently went my way in all friendship with

him. The rapid change wrought in me greatly impressed the observers.

When I intended to sail, he sent me many parting gifts, and 56 offered to find us (Xenophon and me, that is; I had sent my father and family on to Amastris) a ship and crew—which offer I accepted in all confidence. When the passage was half over, I observed the master in tears arguing with his men, which made me very uneasy. It turned out that Alexander's orders were to seize and fling us overboard; in that case his war with me would have been lightly won. But the crew were prevailed upon by the master's tears to do us no harm. 'I am sixty years old, as you can see,' he said to me; 'I have lived an honest blameless life so far, and I should not like at my time of life, with a wife and children too, to stain my hands with blood.' And with that preface he informed us what we were there for, and what Alexander had told him to do.

He landed us at Aegiali, of Homeric fame, and thence sailed 57 home. Some Bosphoran envoys happened to be passing, on their way to Bithynia with the annual tribute from their king Eupator. They listened kindly to my account of our dangerous situation, I was taken on board, and reached Amastris safely after my narrow escape. From that time it was war between Alexander and me, and I left no stone unturned to get my revenge. Even before his plot I had hated him, revolted by his abominable practices, and I now busied myself with the attempt to expose him; I found plenty of allies, especially in the circle of Timocrates the Heracleot philosopher. But Avitus, the then governor of Bithynia and Pontus, restrained me, I may almost say with prayers and entreaties. He could not possibly spoil his relations with Rutilianus, he said, by punishing the man, even if he could get clear evidence against him. Thus arrested in my course, I did not persist in what must have been, considering the disposition of the judge, a fruitless prosecution.

58 Among instances of Alexander's presumption, a high place must be given to his petition to the Emperor : the name of Abonutichus was to be changed to Ionopolis ; and a new coin was to be struck, with a representation on the obverse of Glycon, and, on the reverse, Alexander bearing the garlands proper to his paternal grandfather Asclepius, and the famous scimetar of his maternal ancestor Perseus.

59 He had stated in an oracle that he was destined to live to a hundred and fifty, and then die by a thunderbolt ; he had in fact, before he reached seventy, an end very sad for a son of Podalirius, his leg mortifying from foot to groin and being eaten of worms ; it then proved that he was bald, as he was forced by pain to let the doctors make cooling applications to his head, which they could not do without removing his wig.

60 So ended Alexander's heroics ; such was the catastrophe of his tragedy ; one would like to find a special providence in it, though doubtless chance must have the credit. The funeral celebration was to be worthy of his life, taking the form of a con-test—for possession of the oracle. The most prominent of the impostors his accomplices referred it to Rutilianus's arbitration which of them should be selected to succeed to the prophetic office and wear the hierophantic oracular garland. Among these was numbered the grey-haired physician Paetus, dis-honouring equally his grey hairs and his profession. But Steward-of-the-Games Rutilianus sent them about their busi-ness ungarlanded, and continued the defunct in possession of his holy office.

61 My object, dear friend, in making this small selection from a great mass of material has been twofold. First, I was willing to oblige a friend and comrade who is for me the pattern of wisdom, sincerity, good humour, justice, tranquillity, and geni-ality. But secondly I was still more concerned (a preference

which you will be very far from resenting) to strike a blow for
Epicurus, that great man whose holiness and divinity of nature
were *not* shams, who alone had and imparted true insight into
the good, and who brought deliverance to all that consorted
with him. Yet I think casual readers too may find my essay
not unserviceable, since it is not only destructive, but, for men
of sense, constructive also.   H.

OF PANTOMIME [1]

Lycinus. Crato

Ly. Here are heavy charges, Crato ; I suppose you have been
getting up this subject for some time. You are not content
with attacking the whole pantomimic art, practical and theo-
retic ; we too, the pleased spectators thereof, come in for our
share : we have been lavishing our admiration, it seems, on
effeminate triflers. And now let me show you how completely
you have been mistaken ; you will find that the art you have
been maligning is the greatest boon of our existence. There is
some excuse for your strictures : how should you know any
better, confirmed ascetic that you are, believing that virtue
consists in being uncomfortable ?

Cr. Now, my dear sir, can any one who calls himself a man, 2
and an educated man, and in some sort a student of philosophy,

---

[1] 'Pantomime' has been chosen as the most natural translation of ὄρχησις,
which in this dialogue has reference for the most part to the ballet-dance r
(*pantomimus*) of imperial times. On the other hand, Lycinus, in order to
establish the antiquity and the universality of an art that for all practical
purposes dates only from the Augustan era, and (despite the Greek artists)
is Roman in origin, avails himself of the wider meaning of ὄρχησις to give
us the historic and prehistoric associations of *dance* in Greece and elsewhere ;
and in such passages it seemed advisable to sacrifice consistency, and to
translate ὄρχησις dance.

—can such a one leave those higher pursuits, leave communing with the sages of old, to sit still and listen to the sound of a flute, and watch the antics of an effeminate creature got up in soft raiment to sing lascivious songs and mimic the passions of pre-historic strumpets, of Rhodopes and Phaedras and Parthenopes, to the accompaniment of twanging string and shrilling pipe and clattering heel ? It is too absurd : these are not amusements for a gentleman ; not amusements for Lycinus. When I first heard of your spending your time in this way, I was divided betwixt shame and indignation, to think that you could so far forget Plato and Chrysippus and Aristotle, as to sit thus having your ears tickled with a feather. If you want amusements, are there not a thousand things *worth* seeing and hearing ? Can you not hear classical music performed at the great festivals ? Are there not lofty tragedy and brilliant comedy,—things that 3 have been deemed worthy of state recognition ? My friend, you have a long reckoning to settle with men of learning, if you would not be repudiated altogether, and expelled from the con-gregation of the wise. I think your best course will be a point-blank denial : declare flatly that you never did anything of the kind. Anyhow, you must watch your conduct for the future : we do not want to find that our Lycinus has changed his sex, and become a Bacchante or a Lydian damsel. That would be as much to our discredit as to yours : for ours should be Odysseus's part,—to tear you from the lotus, and bring you back to your accustomed pursuits ; to save you from the clutches of these stage Sirens before it is too late. The Sirens, after all, did but plot against men's ears ; it needed but a little wax, and a man might sail past them uninjured : but yours is a captivity of ear and eye, of body and soul.

4 *Ly.* Goodness gracious ! All the Cynic in you is loose, and snarls at me. At the same time, I think your Lotus-and-Siren simile is rather off the point : you see, the people who

ate the Lotus and listened to the Sirens paid for the gratification of ear and palate with their lives : whereas I not only have
a great deal more enjoyment than they had, but am all the better
for it.   I have experienced no oblivion of my domestic affairs,
nor blindness to my own interests ; in fact—if I may venture to
say so—you will find my penetration and practical wisdom considerably increased by my theatrical experiences.   Homer has
it exactly : the spectator

> Returns a gladder and a wiser man.

Cr. Dear, dear ! Yours is a sad case, Lycinus. You are
not even ashamed ; you seem quite pleased with yourself.
That is the worst of it : there seems no hope of your recovery, while you can actually commend the mire in which you
wallow.

Ly. Now, Crato,—you talk of pantomimes and theatres,— 5
have you seen these performances yourself, that you are so hard
on them ? or do you decide that they are ' foul mire ' without
personal experience ?   If you have seen them, you are just as
bad as I am ; and if not, are you justified in censuring them ?
does it not savour of over-confidence, to condemn what you
know nothing about ?

Cr. Truly that would be the climax : that I should show my
long beard and white hairs amid that throng of women and
lunatics ; and clap and yell in unseemly rapture over the vile
contortions of an abandoned buffoon.

Ly. I can make allowance for you.   But wait till I have prevailed on you to give it a fair trial, to accept the judgement of
your own eyes : after that you will never be happy till you have
secured the best seat in the theatre, where you may hear every
syllable, mark every gesture.

Cr. While this beard is yet unplucked, these limbs un-
shaven, God forbid that I should ever find happiness in

such things. As it is, my poor friend, I see that *you* are wholly possessed.

6   *Ly.* Now suppose you were to abstain from further abuse, and hear what I have to say of the merits of Pantomime ; of the manner in which it combines profit with amusement ; instructing, informing, perfecting the intelligence of the beholder ; training his eyes to lovely sights, filling his ears with noble sounds, revealing a beauty in which body and soul alike have their share. For that music and dancing are employed to produce these results is no disparagement of the art ; it is rather a recommendation.

  Cr. I have not much time for listening to a madman's discourse in praise of his own madness. However—if you must deluge me with nonsense—I am prepared to do you that friendly office. My ears are at your service : they need no wax to render them deaf to foolishness. Henceforth I will be silent : speak on ;—no one is listening.

7   *Ly.* Thank you, Crato ; just what I wanted. As to ' foolishness,' that remains to be seen. Now, to begin with, you seem to be quite ignorant of the antiquity of the pantomimic art. It is not a new thing ; it does not date from to-day or yesterday ; not, that is to say, from our grandfathers' times, nor from *their* grandfathers' times. The best antiquarians, let me tell you, trace dancing back to the creation of the universe ; it is coeval with that Eros who was the beginning of all things. In the dance of the heavenly bodies, in the complex involutions whereby the planets are brought into harmonious intercourse with the fixed stars, you have an example of that art in its infancy, which, by gradual development, by continual improvements and additions, seems at length to have reached its climax in the subtle harmonious versatility of modern Pantomime.

8   The first step, we learn, was taken by Rhea, who was so

pleased with the art that she introduced it among the Corybantes in Phrygia and the Curetes in Crete. She was richly
rewarded : for by their dancing they saved her child Zeus,
who owes it to them (nor can he with decency deny it) that he
escaped the paternal teeth. The dancing was performed in full
armour ; sword clashed against shield, and inspired heels beat
martial time upon the ground. The art was presently taken
up by the leading men in Crete, who by dint of practice became
admirable dancers ; and this applies not only to private persons,
but to men of the first eminence, and of royal blood. Thus
Homer, when he calls Meriones a dancer, is not disparaging
him, but paying him a compliment : his dancing fame, it seems,
had spread not only throughout the Greek world, but even
into the camp of his enemies, the Trojans, who would observe,
no doubt, on the field of battle that agility and grace of movement which he had acquired as a dancer. The passage runs as
follows :

> Meriones, great dancer though thou be,
> My spear had stopped thy dancings,—

it did not, however, do so ; his practice in that art enabling
him, apparently, to evade without difficulty any spears that
might be hurled at him.

I could mention a number of other heroes who went through 9
a similar course of training, and made a serious study of dancing :
but I will confine myself to the case of Neoptolemus, the son of
Achilles, and a most eminent dancer. He it was who invented
that beautiful dance called after him the Pyrrhic ; a circumstance which may be supposed to have afforded more gratification to his father than his comeliness, or his prowess in other
respects. Thus Troy, impregnable till then, falls a victim to
the dancer's skill, and is levelled with the dust.

The Lacedaemonians, who are reputed the bravest of the 10
Greeks, ever since they learnt from Castor and Pollux the

Caryatic (a form of dance which is taught in the Lacedaemonian town of Caryae), will do nothing without the accompaniment of the Muses : on the field of battle their feet keep time to the flute's measured notes, and those notes are the signal for their onset. Music and rhythm ever led them on to victory. To this day you may see their young men dividing their attention between dance and drill ; when wrestling and boxing are over, their exercise concludes with the dance. A flute-player sits in their midst, beating time with his foot, while they file past and perform their various movements in rhythmic sequence, the military evolutions being followed by dances, such as Dionysus

11 and Aphrodite love. Hence the song they sing is an invitation to Aphrodite and the Loves to join in their dance and revel ; while the other (I should have said that they have two songs) contains instructions to the dancers : ' Forward, lads : foot it

12 lightly : reel it bravely ' (i.e. dance actively). It is the same with the chain dance, which is performed by men and girls together, dancing alternately, so as to suggest the alternating beads of a necklace. A youth leads off the dance : his active steps are such as will hereafter be of use to him on the field of battle : a maiden follows, with the modest movements that befit her sex ; manly vigour, maidenly reserve,—these are the beads of the necklace. Similarly, their Gymnopaedia is but another form of dance.

13 You have read your Homer ; so that I need say nothing of the Shield of Achilles, with its choral dance, modelled on that which Daedalus designed for Ariadne ; nor of the two dancers (' tumblers,' he calls them) there represented as leading the dance ; nor again of the ' whirling dance of youth,' so beautifully wrought thereon by Hephaestus. As to the Phaeacians, living as they did in the lap of luxury, nothing is more natural than that *they* should have rejoiced in the dance. Odysseus, we find, is particularly struck with this : he gazes with admira-

tion on the ' twinkling of their feet.' In Thessaly, again, 14
dancing was such a prominent feature, that their rulers and
generals were called ' Dancers-in-chief,' as may be seen from
the inscriptions on the statues of their great men : ' Elected
Prime Dancer,' we read ; and again : ' This statue was erected
at the public expense to commemorate Ilation's well-danced
victory.'

I need hardly observe that among the ancient mysteries not 15
one is to be found that does not include dancing. Orpheus
and Musaeus, the best dancers of their time, were the founders
of these rites ; and their ordinances show the value they attached
to rhythm and dance as elements in religion. To illustrate this
point would be to make the ceremonial known to the uninitiated :
but so much is matter of common knowledge, that persons who
divulge the mysteries are popularly spoken of as ' dancing them
out.' In Delos, not even sacrifice could be offered without 16
dance and musical accompaniment. Choirs of boys gathered
and performed their dance to the sound of flute and lyre, and
the best of them were chosen to act characters ; the songs
written for these occasions were known as chorales ; and the
ancient lyric poetry abounded in such compositions.

But I need not confine myself to the Greeks. The Indians, 17
when they rise to offer their morning salutation to the Sun, do
not consider it enough to kiss their hands after the Greek fashion ;
turning to the East, they silently greet the God with movements
that are designed to represent his own course through the
heavens ; and with this substitute for our prayers and sacrifices
and choral celebrations they seek his favour at the beginning
of every day and at its close. The Ethiopians go further, 18
and dance even while they fight ; the shaft an Ethiopian
draws from that arrow-crown that serves him in place of a
quiver will never be discharged before he has intimidated his
enemy with the threatening gestures of the war-dance.

19   Having dealt with India and Ethiopia, let us now consider the neighbouring country of Egypt. If I am not mistaken, the Egyptian Proteus of ancient legend is no other than a dancer, whose mimetic skill enables him to adapt himself to every character : in the activity of his movements, he is liquid as water, rapid as fire ; he is the raging lion, the savage panther, the trembling bough ; he is what he will. The legend takes these data, and gives them a supernatural turn,—for mimicry substituting metamorphosis. Our modern pantomimes have the same gift, and Proteus himself sometimes appears as the subject of their rapid transformations. And it may be conjectured that in that versatile lady Empusa we have but another artist of the same kind, mythologically treated.

20   Our attention is next claimed by the Roman dance of the Salii, a priesthood drawn from the noblest families ; the dance is performed in honour of Mars, the most warlike of the Gods,

21 and is of a particularly solemn and sacred character. According to a Bithynian legend, which agrees well with this Italian institution, Priapus, a war-like divinity (probably one of the Titans, or of the Idaean Dactyls, whose profession it was to teach the use of arms), was entrusted by Hera with the care of her son Ares, who even in childhood was remarkable for his courage and ferocity. Priapus would not put weapons into his hands till he had turned him out a perfect dancer ; and he was

22 rewarded by Hera with a tenth part of all Ares's spoils. As to the rites of Dionysus, you know, without my telling you, that they consisted in dancing from beginning to end. Of the three main types of dance, the cordax, the sicinnis, and the emmelia, each was the invention and bore the name of one of the Satyrs, his followers. Assisted by this art, and accompanied by these revellers, he conquered Tyrrhenians, Indians, Lydians, dancing those warlike tribes into submission.

23   Then beware, my enlightened friend, of the guilt of sacrilege.

Will you attack the holy mystic art in which so many Gods delight; by which their worshippers do them honour; which affords so much pleasure, so much useful instruction ? To return once more to the poets : when I think of your affection for Homer and Hesiod, I am amazed to find you disputing the pre-eminence they assign to the dance. Homer, in enumerating all that is sweetest and best, mentions sleep, love, song, and dance; but of these dance alone is 'faultless.' He testifies, moreover, to the 'sweetness' of song : now our art includes 'sweet song' as well as the 'faultless dance' which you take upon you to censure. Again, in another passage we read :

> To one the God hath given warlike deeds :
> But to another dance and lovely song.

And lovely indeed is the song that accompanies the dance; it is the Gods' best gift. Homer seems to divide all things under the two heads of war and peace; and among the things of peace he singles out these two as the best counterpart to the things of war. Hesiod, not speaking from hearsay, but coming 24 fresh from the sight of the Muses' morning dance, has this high tribute to them in the beginning of his poem :

> Their dainty feet round the dark waters dance,

about the altar of Zeus.—My dear sir, your onslaught upon the dance is little short of blasphemy.

Socrates—that wisest of men, if we may accept the judge- 25 ment of the Pythian oracle—not only approved of dancing, but made a careful study of it ; and, in his zeal for grace and elegance, for harmonious movement and carriage of the body, thought it no shame, reverend sage that he was, to rank this among the most important branches of learning. And well might he have an enthusiasm for dancing, who scrupled not to study the humblest arts; who frequented the schools of the flute-girls, and could stoop to learn wisdom from the mouth of an Aspasia. Yet in his days the art was in its infancy, its beauties undeveloped. Had Socrates seen the artists who have made modern Pantomime what it is, he would assuredly have given it his exclusive attention, and assigned it the first place in the education of youth.

26 I think you forget, when you advocate the claims of tragedy and comedy, that each of them has its own peculiar form of dance; tragedy its emmelia, comedy its cordax, supplemented occasionally by the sicinnis. You began by asserting the superiority of tragedy, of comedy, and of the periodic performances on flute and lyre, which you pronounce to be respectable, because they are included in public competitions. Let us take each of these and compare its merits with those of dancing. The flute and the lyre, to be sure, we might leave out of the discussion, as these have their part to play in the dance.

27 In forming our estimate of tragedy, let us first consider its externals—the hideous, appalling spectacle that the actor presents. His high boots raise him up out of all proportion; his head is hidden under an enormous mask; his huge mouth gapes upon the audience as if he would swallow them; to say nothing of the chest-pads and stomach-pads with which he contrives to give himself an artificial corpulence, lest his deficiency in this respect should emphasize his disproportionate height. And in the middle of it all is the actor, shouting away, now high, now low,—*chanting* his iambics as often as not; could anything be more revolting than this sing-song recitation of tragic woes? The actor is a mouthpiece: that is his sole responsibility;—the poet has seen to the rest, ages since. From an Andromache or a Hecuba, one can endure recitative: but when Heracles himself comes upon the stage, and so far forgets himself, and the respect due to the lion-skin and club that he carries, as to deliver a solo, no reasonable person can deny that

28 such a performance is in execrable taste. Then again, your

objection to dancing—that men act women's parts—is equally applicable to tragedy and comedy, in which indeed there are more women than men.

By comedy, the absurdity of the masks—of a Davus, for **29** instance, or a Tibius, or a cook—is actually claimed as one of its attractions.   On the other hand, I need not tell you how decent, how seemly, is the dancer's attire ; any one who is not blind can see that for himself. His very mask is elegant, and well adapted to his part ; there is no gaping here ; the lips are closed, for the dancer has plenty of other voices at his service. In old days, dancer and singer were one : but the violent exer- **30** cise caused shortness of breath ; the song suffered for it, and it was found advisable to have the singing done independently.

As to the subjects treated, they are the same for both, Panto- **31** mime differing from tragedy only in the infinite variety of its plots, and in the superior ingenuity and learning displayed in them. Dancing may not be included in our public competi- **32** tions ; but the reason is that the stewards regard it as a matter too high and solemn to be subjected to criticism. I forbear to add that in one Italian city—the greatest of the Chalcidian name—a special lustre has been added to the public games by the introduction of a dancing competition.

And now, before I proceed further, I wish to offer an explana- **33** tion of the many omissions I have made, which might otherwise be attributed to ignorance. I am well aware that the subject has already been dealt with by a number of writers, who have chiefly occupied themselves with a description of the various forms of dance, and a catalogue of their names, their characters, and their inventors ; and this they regard as a proof of erudi- tion. Such work I leave to the ambition of dullards and pedants, as foreign to my own purpose. I would have you observe, and **34** bear in mind, that I do not propose to make a complete history of the art of dancing ; nor is it my object to enumerate the

names of dances, except so far as I have already done, in
handling a few of the principal types : on the contrary, I am
chiefly concerned with pointing out the profit and pleasure to
be derived from modern Pantomime, which did not begin to
take its present admirable form in ancient days, but only in the
time of Augustus, or thereabouts. In those earlier times we
have but the beginnings of the art ; the tree is taking root ;
the flower and the fruit have reached their perfection only in
our own day, and it is with these that I have to do. The tongs-
dance, the crane-dance, and others I pass over because they are
alien to my subject ; similarly, if I have said nothing of the
Phrygian dance,—that riotous convivial fling, which was performed by energetic yokels to the piping of a flute-girl, and
which still prevails in country districts,—I have omitted it not
from ignorance, but because it has no connexion with the
Pantomime of to-day. I have the authority of Plato, in his
Laws, for approving some forms of dance and rejecting others ;
he there examines the dance from the two points of view of
pleasure and utility, banishes those forms that are unseemly,
and selects others for his recommendation.

35   Of dancing then, in the strict sense of the word, I have said
enough. To enlarge further upon its history would be pedantic.
And now I come to the pantomime. What must be his qualifications ? what his previous training ? what his studies ?
what his subsidiary accomplishments ? You will find that his
is no easy profession, nor lightly to be undertaken ; requiring
as it does the highest standard of culture in all its branches, and
involving a knowledge not of music only, but of rhythm and
metre, and above all of your beloved philosophy, both natural
and moral, the subtleties of dialectic alone being rejected as
serving no useful purpose. Rhetoric, too, in so far as that art is
concerned with the exposition of human character and human
passions, claims a share of its attention. Nor can it dispense

with the painter's and the sculptor's arts; in its close observance of the harmonious proportions that these teach, it is the equal of an Apelles or a Phidias. But above all Mnemosyne, 36 and her daughter Polyhymnia, must be propitiated by an art that would remember all things. Like Calchas in Homer, the pantomime must know all 'that is, that was, that shall be'; nothing must escape his ever ready memory. Faithfully to represent his subject, adequately to express his own conceptions, to make plain all that might be obscure;—these are the first essentials for the pantomime, to whom no higher compliment could be paid than Thucydides's tribute to Pericles, who, he says, 'could not only conceive a wise policy, but render it intelligible to his hearers'; the intelligibility, in the present case, depending on clearness of gesticulation.

For his materials, he must draw continually, as I have said, 37 upon his unfailing memory of ancient story; and memory must be backed by taste and judgement. He must know the history of the world, from the time when it first emerged from Chaos down to the days of Egyptian Cleopatra. These limitations we will concede to the pantomime's wide field of knowledge; but within them he must be familiar with every detail:—the mutilation of Uranus, the origin of Aphrodite, the battle of Titans, the birth of Zeus, Rhea's deception, her substitution of a stone for her child, the binding of Cronus, the partition of the world between the three brothers. Again, the revolt of the 38 Giants, Prometheus's theft of fire, his creation of mankind, and the punishment that followed; the might of Eros and of Anteros, the wanderings of the island Delos, the travail of Leto, the Python's destruction, the evil design of Tityus, the flight of eagles, whereby the earth's centre was discovered. He 39 must know of Deucalion, in whose days the whole world suffered shipwreck, of that single chest wherein were preserved the remnants of the human race, of the new generation born of stones; of the rending of Iacchus, the guile of Hera, the fiery death of Semele, the double birth of Dionysus; of Athene and Hephaestus and Erichthonius, of the strife for the possession of Athens, of Halirrhothius and that first trial on the 40 Areopagus, and all the legendary lore of Attica. Above all, the wanderings of Demeter, the finding of Persephone, the hospitality of Celeus; Triptolemus's plough, Icarius's vineyard, and the sad end of Erigone; the tale of Boreas and Orithyia, of Theseus, and of Aegeus; of Medea in Greece, and of her flight thereafter into Persia, and of Erechtheus's daughters and Pandion's, and all that they did and suffered in Thrace. Acamas, and Phyllis, and that first rape of Helen, and the expedition of Castor and Pollux against Athens, and the fate of Hippolytus, and the return of the Heraclids,—all these may fairly be included in the Athenian mythology, from the vast bulk of which I select only these few examples.

41 Then in Megara we have Nisus, his daughter Scylla, and his purple lock; the invasion of Minos, and his ingratitude towards his benefactress. Then we come to Cithaeron, and the story of the Thebans, and of the race of Labdacus; the settlement of Cadmus on the spot where the cow rested, the dragon's teeth from which the Thebans sprang up, the transformation of Cadmus into a serpent, the building of the walls of Thebes to the sound of Amphion's lyre, the subsequent madness of the builder, the boast of Niobe his wife, her silent grief; Pentheus, Actaeon, Oedipus, Heracles; his labours and slaughter of his children.

42 Corinth, again, abounds in legends: of Glauce and of Creon; in earlier days, of Bellerophon and Stheneboea, and of the strife between Posidon and the Sun; and, later, of the frenzy of Athamas, of Nephele's children and their flight through the air on the ram's back, and of the deification of Ino and Melicertes.

Next comes the story of Pelops's line, of all that befell in 43
Mycenae, and before Mycenae was; of Inachus and Io and
Argus her guardian; of Atreus and Thyestes and Aërope, of
the golden ram and the marriage of Pelopeia, the murder of
Agamemnon and the punishment of Clytemnestra; and before
their days, the expedition of the Seven against Thebes, the
reception of the fugitives Tydeus and Polynices by their father-
in-law Adrastus; the oracle that foretold their fate, the unburied
slain, the death of Antigone, and that of Menoeceus.

Nor is any story more essential to the pantomime's purpose 44
than that of Hypsipyle and Archemorus in Nemea; and, in
older days, the imprisonment of Danae, the begetting of Perseus,
his enterprise against the Gorgons; and connected therewith
is the Ethiopian narrative of Cassiopea, and Cepheus, and
Andromeda, all of whom the belief of later generations has
placed among the stars. To these must be added the ancient
legend of Aegyptus and Danaus, and of that guilty wedding-
night.

Lacedaemon, too, supplies him with many similar subjects: 45
Hyacinth, and his rival lovers, Zephyr and Apollo, and the
quoit that slew him, the flower that sprang up from his blood,
and the inscription of woe thereon; the raising of Tyndareus
from the dead, and the consequent wrath of Zeus against
Asclepius; again, the reception of Paris by Menelaus, and the
rape of Helen, the sequel to his award of the golden apple.
For the Spartan mythology must be held to include that of 46
Troy, in all its abundance and variety. Of all who fell at Troy,
not one but supplies a subject for the stage; and all—from the
rape of Helen to the return of the Greeks—must ever be borne
in mind: the wanderings of Aeneas, the love of Dido; and side
by side with this the story of Orestes, and his daring deeds in
Scythia. And there are earlier episodes which will not be out
of place; they are all connected with the tale of Troy: such

are the seclusion of Achilles in Scyrus, the madness of Odysseus,
the solitude of Philoctetes, with the whole story of Odysseus's
wanderings, of Circe and Telegonus, of Aeolus, controller of the
winds, down to the vengeance wreaked upon the suitors of
Penelope ; and, earlier, Odysseus's plot against Palamedes, the
resentment of Nauplius, the frenzy of the one Ajax, the destruction of the other on the rocks.

47   Elis, too, affords many subjects for the intending pantomime :
Oenomaus, Myrtilus, Cronus, Zeus, and that first Olympian
48 contest.   Arcadia, no less rich in legendary lore, gives him the
flight of Daphne, the transformation of Callisto into a bear,
the drunken riot of the Centaurs, the birth of Pan, the love of
Alpheus, and his submarine wanderings.

49   Extending our view, we find that Crete, too, may be laid
under contribution : Europa's bull, Pasiphae's, the Labyrinth,
Ariadne, Phaedra, Androgeos ; Daedalus and Icarus ; Glaucus,
and the prophecy of Polyides ; and Talos, the island's brazen
sentinel.

50   It is the same with Aetolia : there you will find Althaea,
Meleager, Atalanta, and the fatal brand ; the strife of Achelous
with Heracles, the birth of the Sirens, the origin of the Echi-
nades, those islands on which Alcmaeon dwelt after his frenzy
was past ; and, following these, the story of Nessus, and of
Deianira's jealousy, which brought Heracles to the pyre upon
51 Oeta.   Thrace, too, has much that is indispensable to the
pantomime : of the head of murdered Orpheus, that sang
while it floated down the stream upon his lyre ; of Haemus and
of Rhodope ; and of the chastisement of Lycurgus.

52   Thessalian story, richer still, tells of Pelias and Jason ; of
Alcestis ; and of the Argo with her talking keel and her crew
53 of fifty youths ; of what befell them in Lemnos ; of Aeetes,
Medea's dream, the rending of Absyrtus, the eventful flight
from Colchis ; and, in later days, of Protesilaus and Laodamia.

Cross once more to Asia, and Samos awaits you, with the fall 54
of Polycrates, and his daughter's flight into Persia; and the
ancient story of Tantalus's folly, and of the feast that he gave
the Gods; of butchered Pelops, and his ivory shoulder.

In Italy, we have the Eridanus, Phaethon, and his poplar- 55
sisters, who wept tears of amber for his loss.

The pantomime must be familiar, too, with the story of the 56
Hesperides, and the dragon that guarded the golden fruit;
with burdened Atlas, and Geryon, and the driving of the oxen
from Erythea; and every tale of metamorphosis, of women 57
turned into trees or birds or beasts, or (like Caeneus and Tiresias)
into men. From Phoenicia he must learn of Myrrha and Adonis, 58
who divides Assyria betwixt grief and joy; and in more modern
times of all that Antipater [1] and Seleucus suffered for the love
of Stratonice.

The Egyptian mythology is another matter: it cannot be 59
omitted, but on account of its mysterious character it calls for
a more symbolical exposition;—the legend of Epaphus, for
instance, and that of Osiris, and the conversion of the Gods
into animals; and, in particular, their love adventures, including those of Zeus himself, with his various transformations.

Hades still remains to be added, with all its tragic tale of 60
guilt and the punishment of guilt, and the loyal friendship
that brought Theseus thither with Pirithous. In a word, all 61
that Homer and Hesiod and our best poets, especially the
tragedians, have sung,—all must be known to the pantomime.
From the vast, nay infinite, mass of mythology, I have made
this trifling selection of the more prominent legends; leaving
the rest for poets to celebrate, for pantomimes to exhibit, and
for your imagination to supply from the hints already given;
and all this the artist must have stored up in his memory, ready
to be produced when occasion demands.

[1] Not Antipater, but Antiochus, is meant.

62 Since it is his profession to imitate, and to show forth his subject by means of gesticulation, he, like the orators, must acquire lucidity; every scene must be intelligible without the aid of an interpreter; to borrow the expression of the Pythian oracle,

> Dumb though he be, and speechless, he is heard

63 by the spectator. According to the story, this was precisely the experience of the Cynic Demetrius. He had inveighed against Pantomime in just your own terms. The pantomime, he said, was a mere appendage to flute and pipe and beating feet; he added nothing to the action; his gesticulations were aimless nonsense; there was no meaning in them; people were hoodwinked by the silken robes and handsome mask, by the fluting and piping and the fine voices, which served to set off what in itself was nothing. The leading pantomime of the day—this was in Nero's reign—was apparently a man of no mean intelligence; unsurpassed, in fact, in wideness of range and in grace of execution. Nothing, I think, could be more reasonable than the request he made of Demetrius, which was, to reserve his decision till he had witnessed his performance, which he undertook to go through without the assistance of flute or song. He was as good as his word. The time-beaters, the flutes, even the chorus, were ordered to preserve a strict silence; and the pantomime, left to his own resources, represented the loves of Ares and Aphrodite, the tell-tale Sun, the craft of Hephaestus, his capture of the two lovers in the net, the surrounding Gods, each in his turn, the blushes of Aphrodite, the embarrassment of Ares, his entreaties,—in fact the whole story. Demetrius was ravished at the spectacle; nor could there be higher praise than that with which he rewarded the performer. ' Man,' he shrieked at the top of his voice, ' this is not seeing, but hearing and seeing, both : 'tis as if your hands were tongues ! '

And before we leave Nero's times, I must tell you of the high 64
tribute paid to the art by a foreigner of the royal family of
Pontus, who was visiting the Emperor on business, and had
been among the spectators of this same pantomime. So convincing were the artist's gestures, as to render the subject
intelligible even to one who (being half a Greek) could not
follow the vocal accompaniment. When he was about to return
to his country, Nero, in taking leave of him, bade him choose
what present he would have, assuring him that his request
should not be refused. 'Give me,' said the Pontian, 'your
great pantomime; no gift could delight me more.' 'And of
what use can he be to you in Pontus?' asked the Emperor.
'I have foreign neighbours, who do not speak our language;
and it is not easy to procure interpreters. Your pantomime
could discharge that office perfectly, as often as required, by
means of his gesticulations.' So profoundly had he been impressed with the extraordinary clearness of pantomimic representation.

The pantomime is above all things an actor : that is his first 65
aim, in the pursuit of which (as I have observed) he resembles
the orator, and especially the composer of 'declamations,' whose
success, as the pantomime knows, depends like his own upon
verisimilitude, upon the adaptation of language to character :
prince or tyrannicide, pauper or farmer, each must be shown
with the peculiarities that belong to him. I must give you the 66
comment of another foreigner on this subject. Seeing five
masks laid ready—that being the number of parts in the piece—
and only one pantomime, he asked who were going to play the
other parts. He was informed that the whole piece would be
performed by a single actor. 'Your humble servant, sir,' cries
our foreigner to the artist; 'I observe that you have but one
body : it had escaped me, that you possessed several souls.'

The term ' pantomime,' which was introduced by the Italian 67

Greeks, is an apt one, and scarcely exaggerates the artist's versatility. ' Oh boy,' cries the poet, in a beautiful passage,

> As that sea-beast, whose hue
> With each new rock doth suffer change,
> So let thy mind free range
> Through ev'ry land, shaping herself anew.

Most necessary advice, this, for the pantomime, whose task it is to identify himself with his subject, and make himself part and parcel of the scene that he enacts. It is his profession to show forth human character and passion in all their variety ; to depict love and anger, frenzy and grief, each in its due measure. Wondrous art !—on the same day, he is mad Athamas and shrinking Ino ; he is Atreus, and again he is Thyestes, and next Aegisthus or Aërope ; all one man's work.

68   Other entertainments of eye or ear are but manifestations of a single art : 'tis flute or lyre or song ; 'tis moving tragedy or laughable comedy. The pantomime is all-embracing in the variety of his equipment : flute and pipe, beating foot and
69 clashing cymbal, melodious recitative, choral harmony. Other arts call out only one half of a man's powers—the bodily or the mental : the pantomime combines the two. His performance is as much an intellectual as a physical exercise : there is mean-ing in his movements ; every gesture has its significance ; and therein lies his chief excellence. The enlightened Lesbonax of Mytilene called pantomimes ' manual philosophers,' and used to frequent the theatre, in the conviction that he came out of it a better man than he went in. And Timocrates, his teacher, after accidentally witnessing a pantomimic performance, ex-claimed : ' How much have I lost by my scrupulous devotion to
70 philosophy ! ' I know not what truth there may be in Plato's analysis of the soul into the three elements of spirit, appetite, and reason : but each of the three is admirably illustrated by the pantomime ; he shows us the angry man, he shows us the

lover, and he shows us every passion under the control of reason; this last—like touch among the senses—is all-pervading. Again, in his care for beauty and grace of movement, have we not an illustration of the Aristotelian principle, which makes beauty a third part of Good? Nay, I once heard some one hazard a remark, to the effect that the philosophy of Pantomime went still further, and that in the *silence* of the characters a Pythagorean doctrine was shadowed forth.

All professions hold out some object, either of utility or of 71 pleasure: Pantomime is the only one that secures both these objects; now the utility that is combined with pleasure is doubled in value. Who would choose to look on at a couple of young fellows spilling their blood in a boxing-match, or wrestling in the dust, when he may see the same subject represented by the pantomime, with the additional advantages of safety and elegance, and with far greater pleasure to the spectator? The vigorous movements of the pantomime—turn and twist, bend and spring—afford at once a gratifying spectacle to the beholder and a wholesome training to the performer; I maintain that no gymnastic exercise is its equal for beauty and for the uniform development of the physical powers,—of agility, suppleness, and elasticity, as of solid strength.

Consider then the universality of this art: it sharpens the 72 wits, it exercises the body, it delights the spectator, it instructs him in the history of bygone days, while eye and ear are held beneath the spell of flute and cymbal and of graceful dance. Would you revel in sweet song? Nowhere can you procure that enjoyment in greater variety and perfection. Would you listen to the clear melody of flute and pipe? Again the pantomime supplies you. I say nothing of the excellent moral influence of public opinion, as exercised in the theatre, where you will find the evil-doer greeted with execration, and his victim with sympathetic tears. The pantomime's most admirable 73 quality I have yet to mention,—his combination of strength and suppleness of limb; it is as if brawny Heracles and soft Aphrodite were presented to us in one and the same person.

74 I now propose to sketch out the mental and physical qualifications necessary for a first-rate pantomime. Most of the former, indeed, I have already mentioned: he must have memory, sensibility, shrewdness, rapidity of conception, tact, and judgement; further, he must be a critic of poetry and song, capable

75 of discerning good music and rejecting bad. For his body, I think I may take the Canon of Polyclitus as my model. He must be perfectly proportioned: neither immoderately tall nor dwarfishly short; not too fleshy (a most unpromising quality

76 in one of his profession) nor cadaverously thin. Let me quote you certain comments of the people of Antioch, who have a happy knack in expressing their views on such subjects. They are a most intelligent people, and devoted to Pantomime; each individual is all eyes and ears for the performance; not a word, not a gesture escapes them. Well, when a small man came on in the character of Hector, they cried out with one voice: ' Here is Astyanax; and where is Hector ? ' On another occasion, an exceedingly tall man was taking the part of Capaneus scaling the walls of Thebes; ' Step over ' suggested the audience; ' you need no ladder.' The well-meant activity of a fat and heavy dancer was met with earnest entreaties to ' spare the platform '; while a thin performer was recommended to ' take care of his health.' I mention these criticisms, not on account of their humorous character, but as an illustration of the profound interest that whole cities have sometimes taken in Pantomime, and of their ability to discern its merits and demerits.

77 Another essential for the pantomime is ease of movement. His frame must be at once supple and well-knit, to meet the

78 opposite requirements of agility and firmness. That he is no

stranger to the science of the boxing- and the wrestling-ring, that he has his share of the athletic accomplishments of Hermes and Pollux and Heracles, you may convince yourself by observing his renderings of those subjects. The eyes, according to Herodotus, are more credible witnesses than the ears ; though the pantomime, by the way, appeals to both kinds of evidence.

Such is the potency of his art, that the amorous spectator is 79 cured of his infirmity by perceiving the evil effects of passion, and he who enters the theatre under a load of sorrow departs from it with a serene countenance, as though he had drunk of that draught of forgetfulness

That lulls all pain and wrath.

How natural is his treatment of his subjects, how intelligible to every one of his audience, may be judged from the emotion of the house whenever anything is represented that calls for sorrow or compassion. The Bacchic form of Pantomime, which is particularly popular in Ionia and Pontus, in spite of its being confined to satyric subjects has taken such possession of those peoples, that, when the Pantomime season comes round in each city, they leave all else and sit for whole days watching Titans and Corybantes, Satyrs and neat-herds. Men of the highest rank and position are not ashamed to take part in these performances : indeed, they pride themselves more on their pantomimic skill than on birth and ancestry and public services.

Now that we know what are the qualities that a good panto- 80 mime ought to possess, let us next consider the faults to which he is liable. Deficiencies of person I have already handled ; and the following I think is a fair statement of their mental imperfections. Pantomimes cannot all be artists ; there are plenty of ignorant performers, who bungle their work terribly. Some cannot adapt themselves to their music ; they are literally ‘ out of tune ’; rhythm says one thing, their feet another

Others are free from this fault, but jumble up their chronology. I remember the case of a man who was giving the birth of Zeus, and Cronus eating his own children : seduced by the similarity of subject, he ran off into the tale of Atreus and Thyestes. In another case, Semele was just being struck by the lightning, when she was transformed into Creüsa, who was not even born at that time. Still, it seems to me that we have no right to visit the sins of the artist upon the art : let us recognize him for the blunderer that he is, and do justice to the accuracy and skill of competent performers.

81 The fact is, the pantomime must be completely armed at every point. His work must be one harmonious whole, perfect in balance and proportion, self-consistent, proof against the most minute criticism ; there must be no flaws, everything must be of the best ; brilliant conception, profound learning, above all human sympathy. When every one of the spectators identifies himself with the scene enacted, when each sees in the pantomime as in a mirror the reflection of his own conduct and feelings, then, and not till then, is his success complete. But let him reach that point, and the enthusiasm of the spectators becomes uncontrollable, every man pouring out his whole soul in admiration of the portraiture that reveals him to himself. Such a spectacle is no less than a fulfilment of the oracular injunction KNOW THYSELF ; men depart from it with increased knowledge ; they have learnt something that is to be sought after, something that should be eschewed.

82 But in Pantomime, as in rhetoric, there can be (to use a popular phrase) too much of a good thing ; a man may exceed the proper bounds of imitation ; what should be great may become monstrous, softness may be exaggerated into effeminacy,

83 and the courage of a man into the ferocity of a beast. I remember seeing this exemplified in the case of an actor of repute. In most respects a capable, nay, an admirable performer, some

strange fatality ran him a-ground upon this reef of over-en-
thusiasm. He was acting the madness of Ajax, just after he
has been worsted by Odysseus ; and so lost control of himself,
that one might have been excused for thinking his madness
was something more than feigned. He tore the clothes from
the back of one of the iron-shod time-beaters, snatched a flute
from the player's hands, and brought it down in such trenchant
sort upon the head of Odysseus, who was standing by enjoying
his triumph, that, had not his cap held good, and borne the
weight of the blow, poor Odysseus must have fallen a victim
to histrionic frenzy. The whole house ran mad for company,
leaping, yelling, tearing their clothes. For the illiterate riff-
raff, who knew not good from bad, and had no idea of decency,
regarded it as a supreme piece of acting; and the more intelligent part of the audience, realizing how things stood, concealed
their disgust, and instead of reproaching the actor's folly by
silence, smothered it under their plaudits ; they saw only too
clearly that it was not Ajax but the pantomime who was mad.
Nor was our spirited friend content till he had distinguished
himself yet further : descending from the stage, he seated himself in the senatorial benches between two consulars, who
trembled lest he should take one of them for a ram and apply
the lash. The spectators were divided between wonder and
amusement ; and some there were who suspected that his ultra-
realism had culminated in reality. However, it seems that 84
when he came to his senses again he bitterly repented of this
exploit, and was quite ill from grief, regarding his conduct as
that of a veritable madman, as is clear from his own words.
For when his partisans begged him to repeat the performance,
he recommended another actor for the part of Ajax, saying that
' it was enough for him to have been mad once.' His mortification was increased by the success of his rival, who, though a
similar part had been written for him, played it with admirable

judgement and discretion, and was complimented on his observance of decorum, and of the proper bounds of his art.

85 I hope, my dear Crato, that this cursory description of the Pantomime may mitigate your wrath against its devoted admirer. If you can bring yourself to bear me company to the theatre, you will be captivated; you will run Pantomime-mad. I shall have no occasion to exclaim, with Circe,

> Strange, that my drugs have wrought no change in thee!

The change will come; but will not involve an ass's head, nor a pig's heart, but only an improved understanding. In your delight at the potion, you will drain it off, and leave not a drop for any one else. Homer says, of the golden wand of Hermes, that with it he

> charms the eyes of men,
> When so he will, and rouses them that sleep.

So it is with Pantomime. It charms the eyes—to wakefulness; and quickens the mental faculties at every turn.

Cr. Enough, Lycinus: behold your convert! My eyes and ears are opened. When next you go to the theatre, remember to take a seat for me next your own. I too would issue from those doors a wiser man.   F.

LEXIPHANES

Lycinus. Lexiphanes. Sopolis

Ly. What, our exquisite with his essay?

Lex. Ah, Lycinus, 'tis but a fledgeling of mine; 'tis all incondite.

Ly. O ho, conduits—that is your subject, is it?

Lex. You mistake me; I said nothing of conduits; you are behind the times; incondite—'tis the word we use now when a thing lacks the finishing touches. But you are the deaf adder that stoppeth her ears.

Ly. I beg your pardon, my dear fellow; but *conduit, incondite*, you know. Well now, what is the idea of your piece?

Lex. A symposium, a modest challenge to the son of Ariston.

Ly. There are a good many sons of Aristons; but, from the symposium, I presume you mean Plato.

Lex. You take me; what I said could fit no other.

Ly. Well, come, read me a little of it; do not send me away thirsty; I see there is nectar in store.

Lex. Ironist, avaunt! And now open your ears to my charming; adder me no adders.

Ly. Go ahead; I am no Adam, nor Eve either.

Lex. Have an eye to my conduct of the discourse, whether it be fair in commencement, fair in speech, fair in diction, fair in omenclature.

Ly. Oh, we know what to expect from Lexiphanes. But come, begin.

Lex. *'Then to dinner,' quoth Callicles, ' then to our post-prandial 2 deambulation in the Lyceum; but now 'tis time for our parasolar unction, ere we bask and bathe and take our nuncheon; go we our way. Now, boy, strigil and mat, towels and soap; transport me them bathwards, and see to the bath-penny; you will find it a-ground by the chest. And thou, Lexiphanes, comest thou, or tarriest here?' "Tis a thousand years,' quoth I, ' till I bathe; for I am in no comfort, with sore posteriors from my mule-saddle. Trod the mule-man as on eggs, yet kept his beast a-moving. And when I got to the farm, still no peace for the wicked. I found the hinds shrilling the harvest-song, and there were persons burying my father, I think it was. I just gave them a hand with the grave and things, and then I left them; it was so cold, and I had prickly heat; one does, you know, in a hard frost. So I went round the plough-lands; and there I found garlic growing, delved radishes, culled chervil and all herbs, bought parched barley, and (for not yet had the meadows reached the redolency that tempts the ten toes)—so to mule-back again; whence this tender-*

ness behind. And now I walk with pain, and the sweat runs down; my bones languish, and yearn for the longest of water-swims; 'tis ever my joy to wash me after toil.

3   '*I will speed back to my boy; 'tis like he waits for me at the pease-puddingry, or the curiosity shop; yet stay; his instructions were to meet me at the frippery. Ah, hither comes he in the nick of time: ay, and has purchased a beesting-pudding and girdle-cakes and leeks, sausages and steak, dewlap and tripe and collops.—Good, Atticion, you have made most of my journey no thoroughfare.*' '*Why, sir, I have been looking round the corner for you till I squint. Where dined you yesterday? with Onomacritus?*' '*God bless me, no. I was off to the country; hey presto! and there we were. You know how I dote on the country. I suppose you all thought I was making the glasses ring. Now go in, and spice all these things, and scour the kneading-trough, ready to shred the lettuces. I shall be off for a dry rub.*'

4   '*We are with you,*' *cried Philinus,* '*Onomarchus, Hellanicus, and I; the dial's mid point is in shadow; beware, or we shall bathe in the Carimants' water, huddled and pushed by the vulgar herd.*' *Then said Hellanicus:* '*Ah, and my eyes are disordered; my pupils are turbid, I wink and blink, the tears come unbidden, my eyes crave the ophthalmic leech's healing drug, mortar-brayed and infused, that they may blush and blear no more; nor moistly peer.*'

5   *In such wise conversing, all our company departed. Arrived at the gymnasium, we stripped; the finger-wrench, the garotte, the standing-grip, each had its votaries; one oiled and suppled his joints; another punched the bladder; a third heaved and swung the dumb-bells. Then, when we had rubbed ourselves, and ridden pick-a-back, and had our sport of the gymnasium, we took our plunge, Philinus and I, in the warm basin, and departed. But the rest dipped frigid heads, soused in, and swam subaqueous, a wonder to behold. Then back we came, and one here, one there, did this and that. Shod, with toothed comb I combed me. For I had had a short crop, not to convict-measure, but saucer-wise,*

depilation having set in on crown and chin-tip. One chewed lupines, another cleared his fasting throat, a third took fish soup on radish-wafer sippets ; this ate olives, that supped down barley.

When it was dinner-time, we took it reclining, both chairs and 6 couches standing ready. A joint-stock meal it was, and the contributions many and various. Pigs' pettitoes, ribs of beef, paunch and pregnant womb of sow, fried liver lobe, garlic paste, sauce piquante, mayonnaise, and so on ; pastry, ramequins, and honeycakes. In the aquatic line, much of the cartilaginous, of the testaceous much ; many a salt slice, basket-hawked, eels of Copae, fowls of the barn-door, a cock past crowing-days, and fish to keep him company ; add to these a sheep roast whole, and ox's rump of toothless eld. The loaves were firsts, no common stuff, and therewithal remainders from the new moon ; vegetables both radical and excrescent. For the wine, 'twas of no standing, but came from the skin ; its sweetness was gone, but its roughness remained.

On the dolphin-foot table stood divers store of cups ; the eye- 7 shutter, the ladle, slender-handled, genuine Mentor ; crane-neck and gurgling bombyl ; and many an earth-born child of Thericlean furnace, the wide-mouthed, the kindly-lipped ; Phocaean, Cnidian work, but all light as air, and thin as eggshell ; bowls and pannikins and posied cups ; oh, 'twas a well-stocked sideboard.

But the kettle boiled over, and sent the ashes flying about our 8 heads. It was bumpers and no heeltaps, and we were full to the throat. Then to the nard ; and enter to us guitar and light fantastic toe. Thereafter, one shinned up the ladder, on postprandial japery intent, another beat the devil's tattoo, a third writhed cachinnatory.

At this moment broke in upon us from the bath, all uninvited, 9 Megalonymus the attorney, Chaereas the goldsmith, striped back and all, and the bruiser Eudemus. I asked them what they were about to come so late. Quoth Chaereas : ' I was working a locket and ear-rings and bangles for my daughter; that is why I come after the fair.' ' I was otherwise engaged,' said Megalonymus ;

' know you not that it was a lawless day and a dumb? So, as it was linguistice, there was truce to my calendarial clockings and plea-mensurations. But hearing the governor was giving a warm reception, I took my shiniest clothes, fresh from the tailor, and my unpatched shoes, and showed myself out.

10 'The first I met were a torch-bearer, a hierophant, and others of the initiated, haling Dinias before the judge, and protesting that he had called them by their names, though he well knew that, from the time of their sanctification, they were nameless, and no more to be named but by hallowed names; so then he appealed to me.' 'Dinias?' I put in; 'Who is Dinias?' 'Oh, he's a dance-for-your-supper carry-your-luggage rattle-your-patter gaming-house sort of man; eschews the barber, and takes care of his poor chest and toes.' 'Well,' said I, 'paid he the penalty in some wise, or showed a clean pair of heels?' 'Our delicate goer is now fast bound. The governor, regardless of his retiring disposition, slipped him on a pair of bracelets and a necklace, and brought him acquainted with stocks and boot. The poor worm quaked for fear, and could not contain himself, and offered money, if so he might save his soul alive.'

11 'As for me,' said Eudemus, 'I was sent for in the gloaming by Damasias, the athlete many-victoried of yore, now pithless from age; you know him in bronze in the market. He was busy with roast and boiled. He was this day to exdomesticate his daughter, and was decking her out for her husband, when a baleful incident occurred, which cleft the feast in twain. For Dion his son, on grievance unknown, if it were not rather the hostility of Heaven, hanged himself; and be sure he was a dead man, had I not been there, and dislocated and loosed him from his implication. Long time I squatted a-knee, pricking and rocking, and sounding him, to see whether his throat was still whole. What profited most was compressure of the extremities with both my hands.'

12 'What, Dion the effeminate, the libertine, the debauchee, the mastich-chewer, the too susceptible to amorous sights?' 'Yes;

the lecher and whore-master. Well, Damasias fell down and wor-shipped the Goddess (they have an Artemis by Scopas in the middle of the court), he and his old white-headed wife, and implored her compassion. The Goddess straightway nodded assent, and he was well; and now he is their Theodorus, or indeed their manifest Artemidorus. So they made offerings to her, among them darts and bows and arrows; for these are acceptable in her sight; bow-woman she, far-dartress, telepolemic.'

'Let us drink, then,' said Megalonymus; 'here have I brought 13 you a flagon of antiquated wine, with cream cheese and windfall olives—I keep them under seal, and the seals are worm-eaten—and others brine-steeped, and these fictile cups, thin-edged, firm-based, that we might drink therefrom, and a pasty of tripe rolled like a top-knot.—Now, you sir, pour me in some more water; if my head begins to ache, I shall be sending for your master to talk to you.—You know, gentlemen, what megrims I get, and what a numskull mine is. After drinking, we will chirp a little as is our wont; 'tis not amiss to prate in one's cups.'

'So be it,' quoth I; 'we are the very pink and perfection of 14 the true Attic.' 'Done with you!' says Callicles, 'frequent quizzings are a whetstone of conversation.' 'For my part,' cries Eudemus, '—it grows chill—I like my liquor stronger, and more of it; I am deathly cold; if I could get some warmth into me, I had rather listen to these light-fingered gentry of flute and lyre.' 'What is this you say, Eudemus?' says I; 15 'You would exact mutation from us? are we so hard-mouthed, so untongued? For my tongue, 'tis garriturient. I was just getting under way, and making ready to hail you with a fine old Attic shower. 'Tis as if a three-master were sailing before the breeze, with stay-sails wind-bellied, scudding along wave-skimming, and you should throw out two-tongued anchorage and iron stoppers and ship-fetters, and block her foaming course, in envy of her fair-windedness.' 'Why then, if you will, splash and dash and crash through the waves; and I upsoaring, and drinking the while, will watch like Homer's Zeus from some bald-crowned hill or from Heaven-top, while you and your ship are swept along with the wind behind you.'

16   *Ly.* Thanks, Lexiphanes; enough of drink and reading. I assure you I am full beyond my capacity as it is; if I do not succeed in quickly unloading my stomach of what you have put into it, there is not a doubt I shall go raving mad under the intoxication of your exuberant verbosity. At first I was inclined to be amused; but there is such a lot of it, and all just alike; I pity you now, poor misguided one, trapped in your endless maze, sick unto death, a prey to melancholia.

17   Where in the world can you have raked up all this rubbish from? How long has it taken you? Or what sort of a hive could ever keep together such a swarm of lop-sided monstrosities? Of some you are the proud creator, the rest you have dug up from dark lurking-places, till 'tis

> Curse on you, piling woe on mortal woe!

How have you gathered all the minor sewers into one *cloaca maxima*, and discharged the whole upon my innocent head! Have you never a friend or relation or well-wisher? Did you never meet a plain-dealer to give you a dose of candour? That would have cured you. You are dropsical, man; you are like to burst with it; and you take it for muscular healthy stoutness; you are congratulated only by the fools who do not see what is the matter; the instructed cannot help being sorry for you.

18   But here in good time comes Sopolis; we will put you in the good doctor's hands, tell him all about it, and see if anything can be done for you. He is a clever man; he has taken many a helpless semi-lunatic like you in hand and dosed him into sanity.—Good day, Sopolis. Lexiphanes here is a friend of mine, you know. Now I want you to undertake his case; he is afflicted with a delirious affection of the vocal organs, and I fear a complete breakdown. Pray take measures to cure him.

Lex. Heal him, not me, Sopolis; he is manifestly moon- 19
struck; persons duly pia-matered he accounts beside their five
wits; he might come from Samos and call Mnesarchus father;
for he enjoins silence and linguinanity. But by the unabashed
Athene, by Heracles the beast-killer, no jot or tittle of notice
shall he have from me. 'Tis my foreboding that I fall not in
with him again. For his censures, I void my rheum upon them.

Sop. What is the matter with him, Lycinus ? 20

Ly. Why, *this* is the matter; don't you hear ? He leaves us his
contemporaries, and goes a thousand years off to talk to us, which
he does by aid of these tongue-gymnastics and extraordinary
compounds—prides himself upon it, too, as if it were a great thing
to disguise yourself, and mutilate the conversational currency.

Sop. Well, to be sure, this is a serious case; we must do all
we can for him. Providentially, here is an emetic I had just
mixed for a bilious patient; here, Lexiphanes, drink it off; the
other man can wait; let us purge you of this vocal derange-
ment, and get you a clean bill of health. Come along, down
with it; you will feel much easier.

Lex. I know not what you would be at, you and Lycinus,
with your drenches; I fear me you are more like to end than
mend my speech.

Ly. Drink, quick; it will make a man of you in thought and
word.

Lex. Well, if I must. Lord, what is this ? How it rumbles !
I must have swallowed a ventriloquist.

Sop. Now, let it come. Look, look ! Here comes *in sooth,* 21
anon follows, close upon them *quoth he, withal, sirrah, I trow,*
and a general sprinkling of *sundry.* But try again; tickle your
throat; that will help. *Hard by* has not come up yet, nor
a-weary, nor *rehearse,* nor *quandary.* Oh, there are lots of
them lurking yet, a whole stomachful. It would be well to
get rid of some of them by purging; there should be an

impressive explosion when *orotundity* makes its windy exit. However, he is pretty well cleaned out, except for what may be left in the lower bowels. Lycinus, I shall now leave him in your charge; teach him better ways, and tell him what are the right words to use.

22 *Ly.* I will, Sopolis; and thank you for clearing the way. Now, Lexiphanes, listen to me. If you want sincere commendations upon your style, and success with popular audiences, give a wide berth to that sort of stuff. Make a beginning with the great poets, read them with some one to help you, then go on to the orators, and when you have assimilated their vocabulary, proceed in due time to Thucydides and Plato, not forgetting a thorough course also of pleasant Comedy and grave Tragedy. When you have culled the best that all these can show, you may reckon that you have a style. You have not realized it, but at present you are like the toymen's dolls, all gaudy colouring outside, and inside, fragile clay.

23 If you will take this advice, put up for a little while with being called uneducated, and not be ashamed to mend your ways, you may face an audience without a tremor; you will not then be a laughing-stock any more; the cultivated will no longer exercise their irony upon you and nickname you the Hellene and the Attic just because you are less intelligible than many barbarians. But above all things, do bear in mind not to ape the worst tricks of the last generation's professors; you are always nibbling at their wares; put your foot upon them once for all, and take the ancients for your model. And no dallying with unsubstantial flowers of speech; accustom yourself, like the athletes, to solid food. And let your devotions be paid to the Graces and to Lucidity, whom you have so neglected.

24 Further, put a stopper on bombast and grandiloquence and mannerism; be neither supercilious nor overbearing; cease to

carp at other people's performances and to count their loss your gain. And then, perhaps the greatest of all your errors is this : instead of arranging your matter first, and then elaborating the diction, you find some out-of-the-way word, or are captivated by one of your own invention, and try to build up your meaning round it ; if you cannot get it in somehow or other, though it may have nothing to do with the matter, you are inconsolable ; do you remember the *mobled queen* you let off the other day ? It was quite off the point, and you did not know what it meant yourself ; however, its oddness tickled the ears of the ignorant many ; as for the cultivated, they were equally amused at you and at your admirers.

Again, could anything be more ludicrous than for one who claims to be a purist, drawing from the undefiled fountain of antiquity, to mix in (though indeed that reverses the proportion) expressions that would be impossible to the merest schoolboy ? I felt as if I should like the earth to swallow me up, when I heard you talk of a man's *chemise*, and use *valet* of a woman ; who does not know that a man wears a shirt, and that a valet is male ? But you abound in far more flagrant blunders than these : I have *chidden*, not *chode* you ; we do not *write* a friend, we *write to* him ; we say *'onest*, not *honest* ; these usages of yours cannot claim even alien rights among us. Moreover, we do not like even poetry to read like the dictionary. But the sort of poetry to which your prose corresponds would be Dosiadas's *Altar*, Lycophron's *Alexandra*, or any more pestilent pedantry that may happen to exist. If you take the pains to unlearn all this, you will have done the best you can for yourself. If you let yourself be seduced by your sweet baits again, I have at least put in my word of warning, and you will have only yourself to blame when you find yourself on the downward path.

H. & F.

ALPHABETICAL TABLE OF CONTENTS

(Roman numerals indicate the volume, and Arabic the page.)

In this table all the titles are given in the English list. The other lists are added for those to whom the Greek or Latin names are familiar; but they do not contain the titles that are practically identical with the English ones.

ENGLISH TITLES

LATIN TITLES NOT READILY TO BE FOUND
IN THE ENGLISH LIST

GREEK TITLES NOT READILY TO BE FOUND
IN THE ENGLISH LIST

OXFORD

PRINTED AT THE CLARENDON PRESS

BY HORACE HART, M.A.

PRINTER TO THE UNIVERSITY